Great Wedding Tips from the Experts

Great
Wedding Tips
from the Experts

WHAT EVERY BRIDE CAN LEARN FROM
THE MOST SUCCESSFUL WEDDING PLANNERS

Robbi G.W. Ernst III

foreword by Cele Goldsmith Lalli

LOWELL HOUSE

LOS ANGELES

NTC/Contemporary Publishing Group

Library of Congress Cataloging-in-Publication Data

Ernst, Robbi G.W.
    Great wedding tips from the experts : what every bride can learn from the most successful wedding planners / Robbi G.W. Ernst, III ; foreword by Cele Goldsmith Lalli.
        p. cm.
    Includes index.
    ISBN 0-7373-0112-0 (pbk.)
    1. Weddings—Planning.   I. Title.

HQ745 .E76 2000
395.2'2—dc21

00-056431

Published by Lowell House
A division of NTC/Contemporary Publishing Group, Inc.
4255 West Touhy Avenue, Lincolnwood, Illinois 60712-1975 U.S.A.

Managing Director and Publisher: Jack Artenstein
Executive Editor: Peter L. Hoffman
Director of Publishing Services: Rena Copperman
Managing Editor: Jama Carter
Project Editor: Maria Magallanes

Interior design by Laurie Young
Interior illustrations by Ilene Robinette

Printed in the United States of America

International Standard Book Number: 0-7373-0112-0

4567890 DOC DOC 01987654

To Olga/Ella (Mrs. Bertram D. Wolfe), who has always believed in me. She will always be my one true intellectual and spiritual mentor, my inspiration, my love [1897–2000].

Contents ❧

Foreword ❧

I HAD SIX MONTHS TO PLAN OUR WEDDING IN 1964, AND IT WAS NOT difficult. I lived in Manhattan and my fiancé lived in a nearby suburb. We selected a small hotel near my office in New York. The food and beverage manager had done many parties for the company that employed me (*Modern Bride* magazine), so we knew the quality of the food and service. We trusted this professional to recommend a florist in the neighborhood as well as a band. I selected a well-known photography studio. The officiant was a priest who was also a personal friend. He got permission for us to be married at a church a mere one block from the hotel. I addressed the invitations in the best penmanship I could muster. My family and friends drove from my hometown in eastern Pennsylvania; other family flew in from the Midwest. A few college friends drove in from nearby states. All were accommodated at the hotel. My fiancé's family and friends and our mutual friends, too, lived within driving distance, and a parking garage was conveniently located. The rehearsal dinner was at the hotel. The wedding was at 11 A.M., followed by a seated luncheon. Hot and cold hors d'oeuvres and champagne were served during the brief receiving line (my only attendant was a matron of honor). The menu was shrimp cocktail, salad, beef filet, vegetables, and sherbet with the wedding cake. It was a lovely celebration and the best wedding I'd ever attended!

Fast forward to 1995. My daughter becomes engaged and asks how long it will take to plan an evening, black-tie wedding. My response: "Twelve months minimum." She and her fiancé allowed fourteen. The logistics of pulling this together were monumental. *Now*, having been editor in chief of *Modern Bride* magazine for many years, I knew what to do—but finding the time to interview the multiple vendors, check references, read contracts, organize lists, arrange transportation from the hotel to the church three miles away, mail save-the-date letters, and provide activities for the guests who would be traveling from throughout the United States and London was more than my daughter and I could handle with our full-time professional commitments. So I did what I had advised others to do in a similar situation: hire a wedding consultant. What a relief! She pulled a team of professionals together that worked as a unit. The results were so satisfying and the camaraderie among the team and with us so strong that everyone who worked on the wedding will always be warmly remembered as good friends.

I have known Robbi Ernst III since the late 1970s, shortly after he began June Wedding, Inc.® From the moment I spoke with him and learned of his philosophy of serving clients for their special events and particularly for weddings, I knew he was the consummate professional. With four postgraduate degrees, he is thoroughly versed in history, manners, and mores. He is also facile with today's computer capabilities. Plus, he is gregarious and thoughtful and devoted to teaching students how to become the high-caliber wedding consultant he is. Above all else, Robbi is committed to making the wedding planning as well as the wedding day itself a couple's happiest time of life.

In this book he accomplishes that. Planning as perfect a wedding as possible is complicated, often confusing, and very time consuming. There is so much to choose from and much to be wary of in terms of reliability of services. Legalities today are extremely important. No detail can be overlooked. Careful organization and follow-through are mandatory. If you can hire a wedding consultant to assist you with this, it will make things a lot easier. But you need to know how to find the best one for you. Robbi tells you how to do that. He also tells you exactly how to plan your own wedding like a pro. His instructions for setting up all the necessary data and records via your computer make this book different from any other wedding planning book. His honest, straight-talking style is also unique.

For engaged couples who want to leave nothing to chance (and I can't imagine any who do), this book is absolutely essential. Until now only Robbi's clients were fortunate to have him by their side. But now every bride who reads this book will have Robbi's thoroughly experienced hand on her shoulder.

—CELE GOLDSMITH LALLI
Former editor in chief, *Modern Bride*

Acknowledgments ❧

MY LOVE TO TOM, BARBARA, DEEDY, JEFFREY, MARK, AND THE LATE GREG BAIZE, who invited me into their family when I was sixteen and without a home. To Stephanie Dahl, who wrote the first article on wedding consultants to appear in a major bridal magazine, which featured me and the incomparable New York City society wedding consultant, Marcy Blum. To Cele Goldsmith Lalli, who in 1998 retired after thirty-three years with *Modern Bride* magazine (seventeen years as executive editor and sixteen years as editor in chief) and who led the parade to enlighten and educate consumers and the wedding industry, and to her husband, Mike.

To Millie Martini Bratten, editor in chief of *Bride's* magazine, who in steering the helm has seen to it that *Bride's* has promoted knowledge and sophistication in the contemporary bride. To Diane Forden, editor in chief of *Bridal Guide*.

To Madeline Barillo, who first began quoting and featuring members of June Wedding, Inc.® more than twelve years ago because she believed in our credibility and integrity. To Patricia Bellew Gray, who went to San Francisco and covered one of my weddings, putting it on the front page of the June 26, 1987 issue of *The Wall Street Journal*.

To Edward and Loretta Coufal and their children, who have remained valued friends.

To Pat Bruneau, JWIC; Denice D'Andrea; Ami Davenport; the Reverend Robert Dittler, OSB; Lily Dong; Dolores Enos, JWIC; Jim Eagan; Gloria Gasser; the Reverend Ed Holt; Vernon Jacobs; Johanna Kaestner; Domonie Mattson; Christine Morrissey; Annena Sorenson, JWIC; Laurence Whiting; and Betty Downey Wise, JWIC, who each had the tenacity to read parts or all of this manuscript in its rawest of forms and give me much-needed direction.

I am especially grateful to Suzanne Princiotta, JWIC, who provided the forms contained in this book.

To the men and women who believed enough in my experience and knowledge to take the June Wedding, Inc.® Wedding/Event Consultant Training and Certification courses via home study as well as through Norwalk Community Technical College in Connecticut and the College of San Mateo in California. You will recognize them in your area; they use the initials *JWIC* proudly after their names.

To the members of JWI who have remained loyal and faithful to JWI.

To my brides and grooms: I hope your marriages are as happy as your wedding day was.

To Bud Sperry of Lowell House, who asked me to write this book in the first place and who has endured reading the manuscript, giving direction all along the line, and after whom I labeled my computer manuscript files the "budbook."

To Aaron Henry, who so carefully read, edited, and shaped the final manuscript.

To Maria Magallanes, managing editor, and to L. Hudson Perigo, editor, at Lowell House.

To Joe McMullen and Max Wells, who provided spiritual nourishment during the long months of writing. To Alex Rivas, Perry Aubuchon, and Ruda Lenska, who have remained friends and who wouldn't even think of letting me take myself too seriously.

And finally, to Ella (Mrs. Bertram D. Wolfe), who always believed in me and to whom this book is dedicated.

Great Wedding Tips from the Experts

Congratulations! ≈

YOU'RE GETTING MARRIED! CONGRATULATIONS FROM US, *GREAT WEDDING Tips from the Experts*, to you, the bride and groom. Whether it's your first marriage or whether you are marrying again, whether you are on a restricted or a lavish budget, the advice of the professionals in this book has a threefold task: to familiarize you with the various parts of a wedding, show you how to proceed in planning one, and explain the best method of hiring the right team. All the experts quoted or listed in the Resources section of this book are respected members of June Wedding, Inc.® (JWI), An Association for Event Professionals. As such, they have the credentials required of their individual professions, business licenses, or at least registration of their DBA (Doing Business As), and appropriate liability insurance and health permits for those in the food industry. Moreover, they have a proven track record working as *team players*, a phrase you will encounter often in the chapters ahead. A team player, as you know, is a person who demonstrates talent individually and with other creative people to work steadfastly toward a common objective. *Great Wedding Tips from the Experts* teaches you how to put together a team of vendors—your team!—people whose concern is to work for you and with you and who have a vision of the entire wedding beyond their own role. Learning how to successfully put your team together is probably one of the most important tips offered by this book. This issue is so important, we have spelled out the key team players in each chapter.

As wedding professionals, our sole goal is to produce the weddings that brides and grooms have dreamed about. In the long months of planning, often as many as thirty different professionals work on a wedding. As many as twenty-five will come together to present their services on the actual wedding day. A wedding, filled with all its emotion and personal significance to the bride and groom, is no small task to orchestrate.

When I was approached by Lowell House to write this book, my first response was, "Aren't there enough wedding books? Even with my more than twenty years' experience in the industry and more than fifteen years' teaching and training wedding consultants, what more is there to be said?" Then I reflected on the reasons I embarked on this career.

As an event planner in San Francisco, I constantly saw vendors who simply arrived at the weddings, did their jobs, and went home. They had minimal contact with the bride and groom (many after the initial interview only met personally with the couple on the wedding day). More often than not, there was no contact or interaction with other participating vendors. In addition, many didn't have proper licenses and insurance, or health permits if they were in the food industry. Some, and even one is too many, didn't have contracts. They didn't attend workshops and conferences to learn new ideas as well as the latest trends in weddings. There were no inquiries about who else was being hired and, subsequently, no *involvement* in the entire wedding. Happily, this is beginning to change, though as an industry we still have a long way to go.

Great Wedding Tips from the Experts organizes the major aspects of a wedding and gives you the information you need to make informed decisions when interviewing vendors. We explain the jargon, or terminology, that our industry uses, and we give you guidelines to help streamline your process of searching for the right vendors in each field so you are not running around in circles, interviewing people who should have been eliminated from the onset. Within each chapter you will find valuable tips that will explain how the wedding industry works, along with points you can, and often should, consider when planning your own wedding.

While professionals are involved in dozens of weddings a year, we recognize that your wedding is a once-in-a-lifetime occurrence. The modern bride and groom are older and nearly always have begun their professional careers. *Bride's* editor in chief, Millie Martini Bratten, has emphasized the importance of "older" marrying couples, dedicating an entire issue to "Getting Married 20, 30, 40" (June/July 1999). It follows then that time for you is not expendable. Each hour spent planning your wedding should be productive. It's one of the most important days in your life, and you want to be assured that everyone involved is taking it as seriously as you are.

Have you noticed that everyone you talk to—friends, relatives, even strangers—has ideas and suggestions? It won't take long after you announce your engagement for your mailbox and e-mail to be flooded with brochures, coupons, and "specials" from wedding and event vendors you have never heard of—you never knew there were so many people interested in *your* wedding! While you'll be reading numerous bridal magazines, wedding books, and wedding planners, I want to point out that *Great Wedding Tips from the Experts* is different.

Most of all, this book is written by the wedding consultant who "pioneered the contemporary profession of wedding consultation" (those are author Stephanie Dahl's words, not mine). I founded June Wedding, Inc.® in San Francisco in 1979, when wedding consultation was still new to the West Coast. Even in the East, the profession was perceived in a negative way or as too costly. Many parents planning their daughters' weddings in those days didn't feel they got the full value of their money when hiring a wedding consultant, and often they didn't.

After the cultural revolution of the sixties and seventies, when weddings took place on beaches and out in fields with flowered wreaths adorning the heads of brides, came a generation who moved hotels, town halls, restaurants, churches, synagogues, and temples back into the forefront as the sites for weddings. Wedding venues have become more varied in recent times. Today, popular sites have broadened to include bed-and-breakfasts, art or science museums, yachts, and country clubs.

Cakes used to be white, white, white, with tacky tiers atop ugly plastic columns, belonging more in a doll's kitchen set than in the spotlight wedding cakes deservedly attract at a reception. Today's wedding cakes are veritable creations of art, even acting as centerpieces on tables. The Southern tradition of having a groom's cake has not only gone North, it has traveled to the West and East Coasts.

Moreover, studio photographers epitomizing the traditional portraiture style were eventually joined by future photojournalists, and then these were joined by professionals who mix various styles. Modern technology has made even the medium-format camera easier to use, and more often than not, this camera has replaced the 35mm. Finally, digital imaging cameras and processing are now readily available.

Previously, wedding flowers were inevitably provided by the local florist. For the most part, wedding arrangements were merely clones; now there are floral designers not only in retail floral shops but also working as independents, out of their homes or in studios. Their creativity, along with the accessibility of exotic and rare flowers, produces unusually beautiful and one-of-a-kind creations.

For their part, musicians are no longer employees of a place of worship who double as performers for a wedding and reception. Brides and grooms are now interested in a sophisticated mixture of music styles in an effort to make the ceremony and reception more enjoyable for their guests.

The most important renaissance in the wedding industry has been the move from "dabblers"—well-intentioned people who simply enjoy helping brides plan their weddings—to wedding consultants—serious entrepreneurs who have developed their talents and created professional businesses.

In the past, "dabblers" were sweet (sometimes not so sweet) and talented (sometimes not so talented) ladies who enjoyed doing crafts, making favors, addressing envelopes, and providing moral support to the nervous bride on her wedding day. They sold cake tops, garters, imprinted napkins, and matchboxes to subsidize their meager incomes. You often heard them proclaim: "I enjoyed planning *my wedding* so much, and it was so organized, I decided to start doing others!"

Today, it is not enough to *enjoy* having planned one's own wedding. Today's consultants are men and women trained in the administrative and legal affairs of their industry, taking on the role as the team leader of the more than twenty-five vendors that a bride and groom will hire to provide services on the wedding day.

Since 1979, JWI has been involved with more than 760 weddings with budgets ranging from $2,000 to $450,000. In the mid-1980s, JWI began training and educating wedding consultants throughout the world. Today, JWI wedding consultants help brides and grooms develop realistic budgets and guide them to stay within those budgets. By referring vendors who are professionals, providing regularly updated computerized readouts and monthly planning schedules, maintaining contact with the wedding attendants in the months of planning, tracking the budgets and disbursements, and sending wedding day schedules to the vendors, to the wedding attendants, and to all sets of parents two weeks before the wedding, JWI consultants orchestrate the entire wedding, including the wedding day itself.

From the beginning, JWI has taken the bride and groom seriously and thus become a pioneer in training and educating the industry. In seminars, conferences, and courses in college programs, JWI has worked to unite a diverse group of independent consultants into wedding professionals.

Since 1985, June Wedding, Inc.®, An Association for Event Professionals, has conducted hundreds of seminars, workshops, and conferences. Plus, as an association for professionals, JWI annually monitors the professional status of its members. In the past, there did not exist the high standards present in today's wedding industry. JWI wedding professionals have done a lot to increase integrity and credibility within the industry. We are at the forefront creating uniformity and consistency among our peers throughout the world. Pay careful attention when you read tips from JWI members in each chapter. These, along with other information in this book, will demonstrate how we think and work as professionals.

In the past, magazines were little more than bridal gown catalogs. Now every issue contains articles on hiring professional vendors, the value of a wedding consultant, and the importance of having contracts. *Modern Bride* magazine—under the direction of the now retired editor in chief, Cele Goldsmith Lalli, and the former executive editor, Mary Ann Cavlin—and *Bride's*, helmed by editor in chief Millie Martini Bratten, have been the leaders in introducing educational articles about the wedding industry. Other publications, such as *Bridal Guide*, Peter Grimes's *Vows: A Bridal & Wedding Business Journal*, and books such as Cele Goldsmith Lalli and

Stephanie H. Dahl's *Modern Bride Complete Wedding Planner* and Madeline Barillo's *The Wedding Sourcebook Planner*, have covered not only traditional views of weddings but also contemporary trends as well as discussed how to hire appropriate vendors for the wedding day.

Great Wedding Tips from the Experts, for its part, is for everyone having a wedding, small or grand, whether on a restricted or lavish budget. After reading this book, you will have the necessary tools to plan your wedding and you will know how to compare "apples to apples" when interviewing vendors. In each chapter, you will be given all the information you need, and you will find tips and advice about specific types of vendors. Our goal is to help you avoid any snares, traps, or mishaps.

There should be no doubt who the most important people are in this event. They're not the wedding consultant, the florist, the family, or the photographer. The most important people involved in a wedding are *you*, the couple getting married. The responsibility of the vendor is to listen to you and to work with you to help you create your dream wedding, no matter what amount of money you are spending.

Today, brides and grooms, rather than their parents, are the people most involved in the wedding planning process. Make certain that during the months of planning, the two of you take time out for romance and fun. There is absolutely no reason that you should not be enjoying this planning time.

There will be times when you or your parents become tense and frustrated. You will occasionally find it difficult to communicate your ideas; money will become a stress factor; the amount of work will become overwhelming. You may even become angry with various vendors or even with your wedding consultant. If you are taking the normal fourteen months to plan your wedding, there will be times you simply get bored with the task. These are the times you especially need to step back and take a breather.

Go out to dinner or the theater. Sign up for dance lessons. Take a time-out and spend some nonplanning time with each other. At some point you will simply have to trust that all your efforts will come to fruition. And they will!

Read on, and again we congratulate you on this important rite of passage you are about to undertake. Most of all, we wish you many years of happiness and the love that your wedding day signifies.

CHAPTER 1

Can We Talk Money?

✌ The Wedding Budget

WELL, YOU'VE GOT YOUR RING, AND YOU ARE OFFICIALLY ENGAGED. YOU ARE as excited as you can possibly be. You have met your one true love and decided to spend the rest of your lives together. All you need to do now is plan the wedding that symbolizes and celebrates this decision.

For years, wedding magazines and books failed to write about the realities of planning a wedding except to list the expenses traditionally incurred by the bride's and groom's families. There were few articles about actual dollars, though. The authors felt that talking about money would detract from a woman's dreamy fantasies about her wedding.

That has changed. Contemporary wedding periodicals and books are more realistic and thus provide a greater service to the consumer in that they *are* mentioning actual costs; however, costs they mention may be misleading. That's because mostly they average the cost of a potluck wedding in a town with a population of a mere 5,000 with the cost of a wedding in a major city like San Francisco, Chicago, or New York. For example, in 1999, magazines stated that the average wedding in the United States costs about $17,500 for 125 to 150 people. Actually, the amount is more like between $25,000 to $35,000, and in most larger cities that is on the low side.

Do the average bride and groom really know what producing a wedding costs? Can they even guess what individual vendors charge for their services? Are they aware how incidental costs can add up? Our experience in producing weddings across the country is that people are unenlightened when it comes to budgeting a wedding realistically. Cele Goldsmith Lalli and Stephanie H. Dahl, authors of *Modern Bride Complete Wedding Planner*, say that even "the incidental costs (travel to visit parents during the engagement and wedding, adding to one's wardrobe, trips to the beauty parlor, or even eating out because you're too tired to cook) can add up fast, even if planned for."

So, let's talk about money, because that should be the first topic of conversation after the initial rush of the engagement. With the guidance of the experts quoted in this book, you will know from the onset how to determine costs realistically and therefore how to establish a realistic budget. We will also give you information about ways you can create an upscale wedding on a tight budget.

As we will discuss at length in chapter 2, weddings have always been about how to organize formal events and how to pay for them. Either you have enough money so expense is no concern, or you are like the average bride and must produce this very special event within a certain cost range. In the past, weddings were a means to set up housekeeping. Today, people marry after establishing a household of some kind. Even a first-time bride or groom has a home or apartment with furnishings. Frequently, couples have already combined their households. They want a wedding to be a public proclamation of their love and union; they want it to be an event that is expressive of themselves. Ideally, they want to be a good host and hostess and yet still feel like guests at their own wedding celebration.

The future bride is faced with numerous questions and considerations. Wedding gown? That's certainly important! (We don't call it a dress in the wedding trade; when you spend that kind of money, it's a gown!) Sites for the ceremony and reception? For sure! A huge cathedral, mile-long aisle; tulle, Alençon lace, silk, and satin flowing for days as you and your father walk arm in arm; your bouquet of lily of the valley, orchids, and roses cascading to the tips of your gown's hem. Flowers! Can't forget the flowers.

Still, none of these considerations, as warm and fuzzy as they make you feel, should be where you start. "Where do I start then?" you ask. Fortunately, I'm here to tell you. *You start with a consideration of finances!* Yep, sorry about that. I know it sounds mundane, but it's the only way to go. You've got to sit down and analyze your finances. Otherwise, within a month, you may be in analysis yourself! Like it or not, even if you are careful, your wedding is likely to cost you twice as much as you had originally imagined. Really, *every* major expense *always* costs more than we expect to pay. Remember your first new car? You decide on the model and style and then check out different dealers. Then eureka! You find the ideal car. It's just the right color, even the right shade. Plus, the interior is the right fabric and color: a lush gray leather. Sitting behind the steering wheel, you inhale that wonderful new smell that only a new car has. It's perfect. *It's you.* But then, as you drive it around the block of the dealer's lot, you notice that the radio doesn't really have the tone you want. And horror of horrors, there's no cassette tape or CD player. Can you live without listening to your favorite symphony orchestra playing Prokofiev—much less the latest "How to Be Aggressive in the Business World" success and motivation tape? Not to worry—stereo speakers as well as cassette and CD players can be installed. A chrome luggage rack on the trunk lid? Sure, that, too, can be added.

Whoa! Wait a minute. What are you doing? You started out wanting a good-looking, comfortable, reliable new automobile. You went shopping and found one within your budget. But then you began to add all those "extras." Suddenly, your basic automobile is fast approaching something unaffordable. Is this the dealer's fault? He is simply responding to what you're asking for and, in turn, telling you what it's going to cost. After all, *he* is not buying the car. Lesson I: It's your wedding. Lesson II: You'll have to pay for it if you want to have it.

Consideration of Finances

Writers of wedding books and articles have asked me for years, "When you talk with a bride, where do you start in helping her to plan her wedding?" I reply, "I always start with the finances." As a wedding consultant, my client's budget is of the utmost importance. After all, if I can't help her remain within her budget, how can she justify paying me a fee?

After getting sufficient information from the client, I can quickly draw up a realistic appraisal of what things "out there" are going to cost. The financially responsible person (a.k.a. the "financial minister") can then make informed decisions. To do otherwise is to get off to a bad start. Most brides and grooms shop before they think, or they shop in increments, without a view of the entire picture. However, if you start from the dream rather than the reality, it is too easy to get persuaded into buying something that is over budget. Once you have come up with a dollar amount, then an allocation of amounts, as specific as possible, needs to be drawn up for each major component of the wedding. To figure out whether you are in touch with reality or if your dream wedding is going to tip the scales right into credit card debt, follow the steps below.

Appointing a Financial Minister

More often than not today, it is the bride and groom who are financing their own wedding. Many are given a lump sum by their parents. If this is your situation, it's time to give yourselves a wake-up call. Brides: You *and* the groom need to be fiscally responsible. Grooms: Have you noticed yourself saying things like: "Whatever you want, darling"? That's not being a helpmate. If you are responsible for any part of the finances, then all the more reason to read each contract carefully and compare the cost with your realistic budget, before you and your fiancée sign on the dotted line. Don't say, "Yes, darling; whatever you want," unless you really mean it and can afford it. This is especially true if someone else (for example, her parents) will be paying for the wedding. You need to show your loyalty to them by being attentive and aware as you and your bride begin to prepare for married life together.

Here's the first major tip of this book: Appoint a financial minister! All sets of parents should get together with the couple and decide how the wedding will be financed. Someone needs to determine a realistic and affordable budget, how that affects the type of wedding being planned, and how the money will be made available. We call this person the financial minister because there will be times when that person has to minister to the bride and groom or, in case the bride and groom are together the financial minister, when they have to minister to each other. There will be times when the financial minister will need to say "Put this into perspective" or to affirm "No, that's not in the budget!" Since the financial minister is in charge of the purse strings, he or she, along with the bride and groom, should be signing the contracts.

Creating Wedding Budget Spreadsheets

Overall Wedding Budget

When beginning to plan a wedding, sit down with your fiancé and talk about the wedding you want, the wedding of your dreams, the wedding that will relate to your friends and relatives, to who you are and what you are becoming. After deciding on some general parameters, you will want to have a system that will help you best determine and track costs. This is our second major tip: Create a spreadsheet. Go to your computer software, open the file you have named "Wedding Day" (how to set up your computer files will be explained in chapter 2), create a subdirectory, and put in a spreadsheet. Entitle this spreadsheet "Overall Wedding Budget." You'll create rows for the following:

- A list of categories pertaining to a wedding (wedding consultant, ceremony and reception sites, florist, photographer, cake, and other vendors). This is your first column. It should be labeled "Vendor Type."
- Label the second column "Dream Wedding"; it will contain the amounts you think you will be spending on each category.
- Label a third column "Realistic Budget." Here you will list costs quoted by various vendors. Once you have all their quotes, you can add up this column for an idea of what your wedding will actually cost. You will then have your realistic budget for the entire wedding. Does it match the budget you began with, before you did any research—the sum total of the dream wedding column? Remember, you are giving a party for 50, 100, 150, or 200 people. Unless you have already given parties of that size, you may not know what things cost.

- Entitle your fourth column "Actual Costs" (the amounts for this column will be taken directly from your contracts).
- Finally, label your fifth column "Source of Money."

Wedding Budget According to Vendor Type

Separate spreadsheets entitled "Wedding Budget According to Vendor Type" will assist you in keeping track of the individual costs quoted by vendors you will be interviewing in each category (caterer, florist, photographer, etc.). In each chapter devoted to vendors, I stress the importance of narrowing down your lists to three in each category. I will say more about this in the next chapter; for now, I want to teach you an easy way to track some of the costs you will encounter in each category so you can prioritize the various components of your wedding.

Create five columns for each spreadsheet. Label the first column "Company," the second "Dream Wedding," the third "Realistic Budget," the fourth "Actual Costs," and the fifth "Source of Money." Above the company column, create a box, and in this box type "Vendor Type."

In the company column, create rows for three different companies; simply number these 1, 2, and 3. For each company, leave space to indicate the company name, contact person, phone and fax numbers, and e-mail address. As you determine who you will be interviewing, fill out this information. Go ahead and attempt to determine what amount you *think* vendors will quote according to their reputation or brochures. As you interview vendors, they will be able to give you a general idea of realistic costs for your dream wedding. Put these figures into the column labeled "Realistic Budget." Once you have contracted the vendor for each type, you can fill in the actual costs column.

Overall Wedding Budget*

Vendor Type	Dream Wedding	Realistic Budget	Actual Costs	Source of Money

*Source: Suzanne Princiotta, JWIC

WEDDING BUDGET ACCORDING TO VENDOR TYPE*

Company	Dream Wedding	Realistic Budget	Actual Costs	Source of Money
1. Company name Contact person Phone Fax E-mail				
2. Company name Contact person Phone Fax E-mail				
3. Company name Contact person Phone Fax E-mail				
4. Company name Contact person Phone Fax E-mail				

*Source: Suzanne Princiotta, JWIC

Determining Realistic Costs

To arrive at an idea of what vendors (photographer, caterer, florist, videographer, etc.) really do cost, first prepare lists of reputable vendors in the geographical area where the wedding will be held (we will give you more specific information about this process in later chapters). Start by asking friends who have recently been married. Also ask friends or associates who may have hired vendors for corporate or other social events. Or make an appointment with your local wedding consultant. Then get on the telephone and call these vendors. Let them know who you are, when your wedding is taking place, and who referred you. Ask them for the following to be sent by mail or fax: a price list, a copy of their brochure, and any other promotional materials. Find out how long they have been in business. Ask for a copy of their business license and a certificate of proof of insurance. While you have them on the phone, request a list of businesses they work with regularly. You can also get much of this information when you talk to vendors at trade shows or view their Web sites.

Recognize that vendors may charge similar fees. For instance, professional photographers are going to offer similar packages; the same is true of videographers and limousine providers. However, caterers and florists may vary considerably in costs, and this has more to do with the quality of their service and what you desire for your wedding than it does with the product itself.

If a vendor is not willing to give you information over the phone or send you material, think twice about scheduling an appointment. In fairness to the vendor, most wedding professionals have small, privately owned businesses and they prefer to meet the bride and groom in person so they can show them their products or services firsthand.

Take all the information you have gathered, look at the costs (even if these are ranges), and then put these amounts into your realistic budget column. When you add this column, that is, all the vendors' costs, you will have a realistic idea of how much it will cost to produce your dream wedding. By knowing the real costs of each category, you have greater flexibility. You can prioritize your desires and are in a better position to make decisions about how you want to spend your money.

Once you have arrived at a realistic budget, stick to it! Dee Merz, JWIC, owner of Everlasting Memories in California's wine country (Penngrove), urges her clients: "Do keep in mind that unexpected costs can crop up, especially if you make any last-minute changes. But, most importantly, be realistic about what you can afford."

After you have pared down the guest list and aligned your dream wedding with your budget by prioritizing your vendors' services, you will be able to arrive at some "actual costs." These will be the amounts you actually contract for with each vendor. Enter the contracted amounts into the fourth column of your overall wedding budget spreadsheet.

QUESTIONS TO ASK YOURSELVES WHEN DETERMINING YOUR BUDGET ☙

- What degree of formality do we want for our wedding?

- How much can we afford to spend?

- What does each major vendor in our area charge?

- What are our priorities (food, decorations, the ceremony, etc.)?

- What are our potential incidental costs (makeup appointments, long-distance calls, maintenance of our wardrobe)?

- Who signs the contracts?

- How do we keep track of our expenses (people we owe money to)?

- What do we do if a friend wants to offer his or her services?

- Who is responsible for paying for the different components of the wedding?

Where's the Money Going to Come From?

Are the bride and groom paying for the entire wedding? Will either set of parents be assisting or contributing? What about friends and relatives? Does a favorite uncle or grandparent want to give a gift of money? Obviously one should not solicit such offers, but certain friends or relatives may eagerly volunteer to contribute to some feature of the wedding or other. (What's the difference if someone buys a piece of Waterford stemware or contributes to the cost of a bouquet? Especially if the stemware isn't needed.) For the "financially impaired" bride, maybe the bridal attendant would prefer to pay for her own bouquet instead of buying an unneeded gift. When there is little disposable or discretionary income, creative measures are called for. If you are one of the lucky brides receiving an infusion of funds, then indicate the amounts and sources of that income in the fifth column of your overall wedding budget and wedding budget according to vendor type spreadsheets.

Contracts: Get Everything in Writing

While we will discuss contracts in chapter 2, and again in the relevant chapters on vendors, we do want to give some tips here. Once you have reviewed each vendor's proposal, call the vendor you think is right for your wedding. Have her draw up a contract and send it to you. Take several days to study the contract. Get any changes in writing. If necessary, have the proposal and contract rewritten. You'll also want to have your financial minister read the final contract carefully before signing it. Be sure to initial any changes that are handwritten. If a vendor does not have a contract, at least *get all your agreements in writing;* you may have to draft this document yourself. Send the document to the vendor to sign, date, and note the amount contracted. If the vendor isn't able or willing to do this, don't even think of hiring this person to provide products or services for your wedding.

Since we are discussing contracts, the bride and groom and/or parents should decide who is going to sign them. This decision should be handled up front, before any plans are formalized. As individuals forming a union, you and your fiancé must each take responsibility. While one often hears that 50 percent of marriages end in divorce, one seldom hears the obverse: that 50 percent of weddings last a lifetime. We are presuming that yours is going to be among the 50 percent that last, so we encourage you to act as a team from the onset.

In the summer of 1997, a groom in Kansas called off the wedding one month before the wedding date. When he asked for the return of the engagement ring, saying it was a family heirloom, the bride refused, hop-

ing to be able to sell it and use the money toward recovering some of her losses. *She* had signed all the contracts. The groom, however, wasn't the understanding type and sued in court for the return of the ring. He won the lawsuit (the judge ruled that an engagement ring is an "anticipated gift"; it does not become an actual gift until the legal ceremony has been performed and the couple have exchanged their vows). Before the end of that summer, nine states recognized and upheld this decree as a binding precedent in their own states. If a wedding is canceled shortly before the wedding day, you may not only expect to lose money placed as deposits or payments, but you may also have to pay the balances of all contracts. (Some sites and vendors will relax the rules if they are able to book the day of the wedding with another bride.) It is for this reason that I urge the bride and groom to both be responsible for all contracts. This is not an issue that should be skirted.

Figure out your budget and *stay within it.* This means *figure out a budget for the wedding of your dreams,* and then figure out the wedding *according to a realistic budget.* A lot of money is going to be spent on your wedding day; make sure you are getting the true value of your money. But, most of all, don't go into debt over this day marking the start of your lives as husband and wife.

Tracking Your Disbursements

Create a disbursements spreadsheet for deposits paid to vendors, and take note when additional payments are due. This is not as difficult as it sounds. Simply open a subfile in your computer, under your wedding budget file, and name it "Disbursements for Contracted Vendors" (see page 23). Make a table with five columns.

- Label the first "Date" (for payments made and still outstanding).
- Label the second column "Vendor" (these will be companies you have actually contracted).
- Label the third "Amount" (this column will contain the amount of deposits and those amounts still outstanding).
- Your fourth column will be labeled "Method of Payment" (to record whether or not you paid by cash, check, or credit card and which credit card was used).
- As you sign contracts, you will note that you have made a deposit to each vendor contracted. (Note: Unless you have put down a deposit and signed a contract, you might not necessarily have a contract.)

DISBURSEMENTS FOR CONTRACTED VENDORS*

Date	Vendor	Amount	Method of Payment	Security Deposit/ Requirements

Go through all your contracts and put this information on your disbursements sheet, in order, according to the dates paid and when future payments are owed. Your fifth column will be used to record any security deposits that are returnable if certain requirements are met (for example, a security deposit on the site). After the wedding, you can easily go through this column and call those vendors who have not returned your money. Isn't that a nice tip?

Your disbursements sheet will allow you to see at a glance when, to whom, and what amount you paid or owe a particular vendor. There will be no excuse for not making payments on time. Nothing will cause greater unhappiness and destroy a relationship with a vendor than not paying in a timely fashion. Remember, treat your wedding not only as a "creative" event with lots of imagination and personalization but also as a business venture—an investment. Certainly you wouldn't like it if the tables were turned and they owed *you* money! Also, don't wait until the wedding day to be writing out checks; take care of this in advance. Simply date the checks the day of the event and consider it money already spent.

One last important point on finances: The financially responsible person (the financial minister) should create a time line for money going out. Again, creativity is called for. Some vendors require substantial deposits (as much as 50 percent). Will the vendor take a lesser deposit at the time of signing the contract with increased payments as time goes by? After all, why can't you be collecting interest on your money instead of the vendor using it to coordinate his cash flow? Moreover, you should be putting money aside, earmarked for the wedding, in a special account so it is collecting interest. When you have final payments due just days before or on the day of the wedding itself, you will not only have the money to pay the bills, but you also may have collected considerable interest. Let your money work for you!

Remember, just because you have the credit cards doesn't mean you can pay the bills that are going to be stacking up; make sure you are not spending money you don't have. We strongly recommend setting up a special wedding account or at least a plan to transfer money at appropriate times.

Whose Checkbook/Charge Card to Get Out and When

There are traditional as well as more contemporary guidelines for determining whose checkbook or charge card to get out when payment is due. When using plastic money, whether yours, his, or your parents', be careful! Again, make certain you have the money to pay the cards off. Some charge cards have a recourse policy if a company doesn't deliver what was contracted. Always inquire with the credit card company you are using. Call the 800 number on the back of your credit card, talk with the customer service department, and ask what their policy is. Many vendors will require that final payments be made in the form of a cashier's check, money order, or advance payment. However you decide to pay your debts, don't forget to record the method of payment in the fifth column of your disbursements sheet.

CONTRACTS ❧

- Decide who is going to sign all contracts, sales receipts, or letters of agreement. That person will be known as the financial minister. Both the bride and groom, if together they are the financial minister, should sign all contracts. If the bride's parents are the financial minister, the bride and groom should still sign in conjunction with them.

- Get *everything* in writing, and *everything* spelled out in the contract.

- Compare all costs stated in your contract with your realistic budget on your overall wedding budget spreadsheet.

Determining Priorities

As you determine actual costs, see if it is necessary to "rob Peter to pay Paul"; think not only money but also style. For example, for an informal wedding, a nice business suit can be worn instead of a tuxedo, or a lovely evening dress instead of a gown. To decide where you want to spend your money, list in order of preference the components of your wedding. For instance, if food and beverage is at the top of your list (you can depend on the catering bill being your largest expense), you will want to first do a reality check. Many people say that the mood or style of the wedding is determined by the gown. Gown designers will hate me for this, but I disagree. I think the actual wedding and the reception are your primary concerns. Usually, catering (as much as 54 percent of your budget) and decorations (as much as 20 to 30 percent) are your biggest expenses. If these are your priorities, then start with them as you begin to map your wedding journey. After all, the length of time for the event, not the length of your gown, will determine most of your other expenses, and this is true whether the bride and groom are wearing a simple dress and suit or a designer gown and tails!

If you find prioritizing difficult, check out *The Wedding Sourcebook* by Madeline Barillo. She has an excellent priority checklist she calls "Getting Started: An Expectations Worksheet."

Finally, be aware that there are going to be unexpected costs, that no matter how well you plan or how much wedding savvy you have, you simply can't know everything. Just try to be as alert as possible to even minor changes. Recognize, too, that last-minute changes or additions can incur phenomenal late costs.

One of the ways I help couples prioritize the different types of wedding services is I have them do an imagery exercise during the first consultation. I ask them to close their eyes and relax. Then I ask them to place themselves at their wedding day. They'll take a minute or two and then open their eyes. Next I have them describe what they saw, heard, and smelled. What they tell me first is usually the most important item to them. We then work on the rest of what they experienced. After we have determined the services and prioritized them, we adjust the budget accordingly. A couple's budget should reflect their priorities, based on their anticipation of the event.

—PAT BRUNEAU, JWIC, L'AFFAIRE DU TEMPS (MILPITAS, CALIFORNIA)

Ask a Friend or Hire a Professional?

All too often, we professionals hear: "I have a friend who is a really good baker. She offered to bake my wedding cake. *For free!*" Whether it's a near and dear uncle who "takes good pictures" or a cousin who sews fantastically, is it wise to entrust your wedding day to friends? Do you want to take the chance that if something goes wrong, it could mean the end of a friendship? I always tell brides and grooms that when it comes to determining their vendors, they should rely on professionals. Have a friend assist in some way; for example, let him or her sing a solo at the ceremony, but don't make him or her the primary musician. If your friend becomes ill at the last minute or otherwise can't sing your favorite song, then you still will have professionals providing music. If you must have a friend take on some major responsibility, at the very least before the event, let this friend know in a letter how much you appreciate his services, but that if something goes wrong, the most important thing is that you remain friends. Better still, given the serious planning needed for a successful event, ask your friend if he would mind having a contract with you. If your friend doesn't take your wedding as seriously as a vendor you are hiring, think twice about having him assume a role in your wedding. As Suzanne Princiotta, JWIC, owner of A Formal Engagement (Novato, California), says, "Let your friends be guests at your wedding and enjoy it with you."

 For a recent wedding that I coordinated, the couple *insisted* that their friend, who lives on the East Coast, play the guitar for their ceremony. "It will save us time, money, and we know he's good," was their reply after I warned them that this wasn't such a good idea. The situation made me nervous, so I contacted a violinist I've used in the past and asked if he could reserve that date for me, *just in case*. As fate would have it, three days before the wedding, the guitarist friend called to say that he would not be able to come to California for the wedding. The couple was furious and now are on nonspeaking terms with him. As they turned to me with a "What do we do now?" look, instead of saying I told you so, I told them not to worry, I already had another musician lined up. As a matter of fact, they were going to pay for the guitarist friend's flight, which would have cost them $410, whereas the violinist only cost $350, so in the end they saved money by hiring a professional!

—SUZANNE PRINCIOTTA, JWIC, A FORMAL ENGAGEMENT (NOVATO, CALIFORNIA)

Modern Bride has published an excellent set of guidelines for the modern bride and groom. It not only gives the traditional answer to the question "Who pays for what?" but also a wonderful alternative dubbed "Bucking the Trends." As I have said elsewhere, creative times call for creative measures. Etiquette exists to help us, not hassle us. A wedding is a new and unknown financial situation for most people, so give the contemporary trends some consideration.

Traditional Manner in Which Costs Are Divided*

Bride's Responsibility

- Wedding ring for the groom
- Wedding gift for the groom
- The wedding consultant (may be shared by groom or paid by the bride's family)
- Gifts for bridal attendants
- Your physical exam and blood test
- Your personal stationery and thank-you notes
- Guest book

Groom's Responsibility

- Marriage license
- Bride's engagement and wedding rings (guidelines say it should cost a certain amount)
- Special gift for the bride
- Rental of your formal wear

*Reprinted with permission from *Modern Bride*

- Your blood test and physical exam
- Gifts for your attendants
- The bride's bouquet and going away corsage (although flowers are usually paid for in one lump sum)
- Boutonnieres for yourself and your attendants
- Corsages for both mothers and grandmothers
- Lodging for male attendants
- Officiant's fee
- Bachelor party (optional)
- The honeymoon
- Ketubbah

The Bride's Family
- Engagement and wedding pictures (including videographer)
- The wedding consultant
- Engagement party
- Wedding invitations, announcements, and mailing costs
- Ceremony fees: rental of synagogue or chapel; aisle carpets, chuppah, or other decorating items
- Bride's gown and accessories
- Entire reception: rental (rental of hall), caterer, food (including wedding cake), tipping, taxes, and decorations
- Music (ceremony and reception)
- Flowers (ceremony and reception)
- Bridal attendants' dresses
- The bridal attendants' luncheon
- Father's boutonniere
- Transportation for bridal party to ceremony and reception
- Rehearsal dinner (optional)

The Groom's Family

- Wedding clothes for themselves
- Wedding gift for newlyweds
- Shipment of wedding gifts to the couple's new home after they return from honeymoon
- The rehearsal dinner (optional) or any other expense they determine would be helpful

The Bridal Party

- Bridal shower
- Their wedding attire
- Any traveling expenses they incur
- Joint gift to the bride
- Individual wedding gift for the newlyweds
- The bachelorette party

The Ushers

- Rental of formal wear
- Joint gift for groom
- Individual gift for the newlyweds
- The bachelor party

The Guests

- Their own traveling expenses
- Wedding gift for the newlyweds

Bucking the Trends*

Modern Bride makes the following sensible suggestions on how the wedding expenses can be divided in a more contemporary manner:

The Groom's Family

- All beverages
- Limousines
- Music for the reception
- Photography and/or videography

The Bride and/or Groom

- Bride's clothes and trousseau
- Wedding flowers
- Bridal attendants' get-together
- Invitations, announcements, and personal stationery

The Bride's Family

- Ceremony site and music
- Reception site and food
- Wedding cake

*Reprinted with permission from *Modern Bride*

CHAPTER 2

Getting Organized with a Plan of Attack

❧ Hiring the Right Team

LET ME SAY FROM THE BEGINNING THAT TO PRODUCE A SUCCESSFUL WEDDING means you have to be superorganized, compile many lists, and interview professionals who are as varied in personality as they are in the product or service they provide. While attempting to discern whether or not vendors will work well together, you are going to need some basic tools that are imperative for keeping organized. Order is what makes the difference between the mad bride, the bride who is going mad, and the one who's ready to face the music and prepare.

The Guest List

It's obvious that the bride and groom and the two sets of families are going to have people that they really want to be present at the wedding. Thankfully, the days are gone when parents insisted that distant second and third cousins, nieces and nephews, or business associates absolutely "must be on the guest list." Keep in mind that the number of guests is going to affect expenses and make constraints on the sites for the ceremony and reception. Most important, a wedding is a special moment of intimacy, shared with people who are truly near and dear to the bride and groom.

At the onset, you, your groom, and the sets of parents must sit down and have a frank conversation about the size of the wedding. This need not be threatening. Just deal with the facts. How many people can you really afford to entertain? How many guests will your sites comfortably accommodate?

After you have determined a firm count, or number of guests that you want to invite, you and your fiancé should each compile your own individual list. Happily, a computer makes this easier today. Not only is sorting according to alphabet and zip code or adding a name a piece of cake, but it's also very easy to press that delete button for those you decide not to invite.

The JWI system for cutting down lists, outlined below, is simple, and though I can't guarantee it will work for you, it is the most objective method I have yet found.

- There are certainly relatives and friends who you are sure you want to invite and who will no doubt attend. Each of you is to make your own lists of these people.
- Combine and input these lists into your computer organizer. To facilitate cross-referencing, put a number beside each entry. Label the list simply "Guest List," or "Guest and Response List." Proper

titles (Dr., Mrs., etc.) and complete addresses and phone numbers should be typed in. In a field of the organizer, input "A list" for each name.

- Have each parent, you, and your groom complete a second list. This list should have a field that designates these as your "B list." There should not be any duplication of names from the A list.

- Sort and print both lists. Each of you takes a copy of the lists and reviews them. Make notations that indicate anyone who should be moved from the B list and placed onto the A list. If necessary, have an informal gathering to go over the lists together and reach agreement. Make final decisions and then input these changes into the organizer. By simply typing "A list" into the sort field, your organizer will automatically move those names to your primary guest list. Congratulations, you have completed your first cut!

- Add up the total on your A list and decide if this number is within your budget. Pass the lists around one more time to determine if there are any changes. This time, determine those people who you know won't be able to attend but who you still want to inform about the wedding. Write "Announcements" beside their names. Additional names can be added at this time. On this printout, you will each want to check accuracy for use of complete names and titles, spelling, phone numbers, and addresses.

- Input the word *Announcements* into your sort field; do another printout. You should have three complete lists: your primary, or A list, the people who are actually going to receive invitations; your secondary, or B list, those who still have a chance to be invited if a name is deleted from the A list; and finally, your Announcements list, those who won't be invited but who will receive announcements.

If you are really ambitious, and desire to maximize use of your A list, turn it into a response spreadsheet. You will need such a response spreadsheet to really be organized. It should contain columns labeled "RSVP" (so you can simply write yes or no to indicate if a guest is attending), "Entrée" (to indicate the person's choice of dinner item), "Gift" (to write in a brief description of the gift and date it was received), and finally, "Thank-You" (to write in the date when you send the thank-you note).

Use of the nine-numbered zip codes, along with up-to-date area codes for phone numbers, is especially important in a day when mail delivery takes so long and area codes change so frequently. The last four numbers of the zip code indicate the exact neighborhood of the addressee and, believe it or not, the full code does speed up delivery since postal computers and personnel read and sort according to these numbers.

Now that you have conquered the first obstacle, which very well may take months, set a cutoff date for sending the invitations, and mark your calendar. Also on a calendar reserved only for "wedding things"—essentially, a "to-do" calendar—indicate a cutoff date for when you can properly send invitations to those on your B list. On the same calendar, highlight your RSVP date.

 Never send an invitation less than three weeks before the event—your friend or relative may be insulted.

—CELE GOLDSMITH LALLI AND STEPHANIE H. DAHL,
AUTHORS OF MODERN BRIDE COMPLETE WEDDING PLANNER

Get Ready for Your First Power Play (A Message for the Groom)

Did I say that the bride and groom are the most important people at the wedding? Did you hear me say that this is the *couple's* day? Please forgive me. I forgot about the guest list! Today, most young couples may work together, sharing responsibilities, total costs—and also decision making. However, it's been my experience that creating the wedding guest list can strain even the noblest efforts toward equality.

A wedding truly is the bride's *and* groom's day—but in that order. For as strongly as we want the groom to be involved in the wedding planning, even this book is addressed primarily to the bride. If your bride's parents are paying for the wedding, they have the right to ultimately determine how the guest slots are doled out. And even if you and your bride are sharing the costs equally, time-honored tradition maintains that she should be allotted the greater number of guests.

So how do you make your needs known? Start by discussing the number of your own friends you think can and should attend your wedding. You don't want to waste your bargaining chips, so *don't* include close friends of your family. (They will be "must invites" on your parents' list.) And *do* divide your own list into "A" and "B" categories. This allows you some flexibility, and shows your willingness to cooperate with your bride as she tries to negotiate these same waters with her parents.

Setting the Date

Selecting a date may be more difficult than you imagined. Narrow your choices by finding out the high season for weddings in your area.

As you can see by the bar graph in this chapter, the summer months are no longer the only ones for weddings. With more couples being in the work force, availability of vacation time is now spread out over twelve months instead of three. So, check with your respective employers and find out the best time for you to be off work.

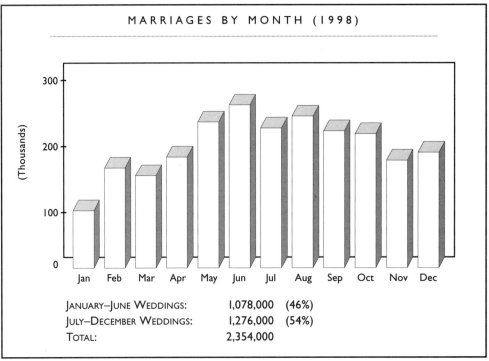

MARRIAGES BY MONTH (1998)

(Thousands)

JANUARY–JUNE WEDDINGS:	1,078,000 (46%)
JULY–DECEMBER WEDDINGS:	1,276,000 (54%)
TOTAL:	2,354,000

*Reprinted with permission from *June Wedding, Inc.® Wedding Consultant Training and Certification Manual,* page 17.

Another reason for weddings taking place year-round today is the greater availability of fast and easy travel and lower fares in off-seasons, resulting in greater creativity in selecting honeymoon sites and dates. Windows of opportunity for travel have also broadened to the point that more and more guests travel from out of state to attend a wedding.

There is another important consideration you don't see discussed often in wedding planning books, but it must be given attention, and since we are the professionals, we do not skirt issues. While it is true that some brides do not give their menstrual cycle a second thought, there are those who want to look and feel their best on the wedding day and honeymoon. All the months of planning and dieting need not be jeopardized because you didn't take into consideration the timing of a natural bodily function.

A wedding day is a day of high drama and theater with a great deal of public attention focused on two people—more the bride than the groom. When selecting a date, the bride and groom (or the bride and her mother) should frankly discuss the bride's menstrual cycle. You want to be at your peak spiritually, mentally, and physically. So pay attention to your body chemistry and do not neglect this very personal matter, which will strongly affect your nerves and your body.

—GLORIA GASSER, FLORAL IMAGES (LAS VEGAS, NEVADA)

The Ceremony and Reception Sites

Once a date and an alternative date are determined, and as the guest lists are being compiled, the next thing for the bride and groom to do is make decisions about the ceremony and reception sites. Many wedding consultants believe that the style of the gown should be kept in mind when selecting a site. Our experts disagree. The site itself should be a place that has significance for the bride and groom. It should be a place that speaks romance and love. If a couple is religious, that certainly will be a major influence on selecting the site for the ceremony. The desired style and mood will also influence the decision on the site. Obviously, the site must be appropriate for the number of guests. Simply because of availability, selecting ceremony and reception sites has priority over other decisions.

Formal weddings are increasing annually. The term *marrying again* refers to second- and third-time marriages (or more). "Marrying again" brides and grooms are having lavish and large weddings, inviting their business associates and people with whom they mingle daily. Add to that the relatives traveling from out of town and "marrying again" weddings are often quite large. Taken together, all the "first-time married," along with the "second- or third- or even fourth-time married," have decreased the availability of sites appropriate for ceremonies and receptions. At the same time, religions have become more conservative and restrictive, limiting the use of their facilities, parish, or synagogue and further affecting the availability of sites.

A tip from the experts who deal with this issue on a daily basis: If you have a site in mind that the two of you simply cannot live without, and your preferred date is available at that site, book it—even if your wedding date is a year or more away. You will have to put down a deposit to reserve it, but if you survive the engagement to make it to the wedding day, then you will be married in the setting that means the most to you and it will have been worth the wait.

If you do not have a specific site in mind, at least decide on the type and style of setting you want. You may want to contact a wedding consultant solely for site referrals. Or contact the conventions and visitors bureau where your wedding is to take place to inquire about reception sites in the area. An excellent regional book that provides detailed descriptions of sites as well as their costs is *By Recommendation Only: Party and Wedding Resource Guide for the Greater San Francisco Bay Area*, by Johanna Kaestner and Tosca J. Clark. Use such resources to help you narrow your choices to a half dozen. Call to see if they are available for your date, and ask the site manager to pencil you in until you can get there for an appointment. Make an appointment within a few days. If you find something you really like, have your checkbook in hand and sign a contract to reserve it.

Your Plan of Attack

In this chapter, we are going to give you some overall guidelines for hiring vendors, inform you about the importance of contracts and getting everything in writing, and tell you how to proceed step by step in putting your ideas and the information that you gather down on paper so that from day one you will have a plan of attack. We will provide formulas guaranteed to relieve most of your stress while preparing for this very important day in the lives of you and your groom.

At first glance, planning a wedding seems an insurmountable task. One simply does not know where to begin. Often parents, other close relatives, and even the best of friends live in different states. Fortunately, personal computers, the Internet, and e-mail have not only brought us closer together, but they have also done so in a very economical manner. Previously, days went by before we got answers to letters or even phone calls, and the expense of the latter is often prohibitive simply because of the volume of phone calls required in planning a wedding. Now one can send an e-mail asking an important question and get a response within seconds. Moreover, instead of getting into the car and going from shop to shop to learn about a product or service, you can search the Web and at least get an introduction to wedding vendors. Some Web sites are quite sophisticated, providing pictures and even videos of a site or choice of wedding cakes or flower arrangements. Prices and rates, terms for contracting services, and e-mail addresses to make further inquiries are all available on the Internet. You may even find out if your desired wedding site is available for your date.

Creating Your Tools:
Resource and Wedding Day Binders

You will need the following tools to begin your plan of attack:

- three-hole paper puncher
- three-ringed 4-inch binder
- three-ringed 2-inch binder

Label the larger binder "Resource" and the smaller "Wedding Day." Each binder needs twenty-five to thirty-five tab insert dividers, the same number of plastic sheets to hold business cards, and about a dozen plastic pocket inserts to hold pictures, brochures, and the like. One sheet that holds several business cards will probably suffice per tab. The resource binder will contain printouts of your computer files, handwritten, "hen-scratched" notes, information from business cards that you will have transferred to your computer files, brochures, flyers, discount coupons, and all sorts of information that you will begin collecting as religiously and steadfastly as any top administrative secretary. No matter how small and intimate your wedding, you will want to be organized from day one! Another final and primary tool will be your computer, with software capable of creating tables and charts or spreadsheets.

At first these files will be extensive. By the end of the second or third month of planning, you will have narrowed your files considerably, but do not throw any of your notes away. Do a complete printout of every note, comment, or feeling, and store these in your file cabinet. You want to keep these printouts, just in case you may need to refer to the information at some later date.

Assembling Your Binders

You can assemble your binders according to the tabs listed below. The wedding day binder differs from the resource binder in that it will have a components or vendors list at the beginning, your wedding day schedule file, your wedding party information, and tabs for each vendor you actually contract.

Resource

- Wedding consultants
- Wedding attendants
- Ceremony sites
- Reception sites
- Cakes
- Caterers
- Favors
- Florists (with a subfile, Lighting/decoration)
- Gown (with subfiles: Gown preservation and storage, Attendants' dresses, Mothers' dresses)
- Music (with subfiles: Ceremony, Reception)
- Officiants
- Parties, showers, rehearsal dinner
- Photographers
- Stationery/invitations
- Transportation
- Videographers
- Miscellaneous
- Budget/finances

- A guest list/response spreadsheet
- B guest list
- Announcements list

Wedding Day
- Vendors
- Wedding day schedule
- Wedding attendants
- Ceremony site
- Reception site
- Cake
- Caterer
- Favors
- Florist (with a subfile, Lighting/decoration, if needed)
- Gown (with subfiles: Gown preservation and storage, Attendants' dresses, Mothers' dresses)
- Music (with subfiles: Ceremony, Reception)
- Officiant
- Parties, showers, rehearsal dinner
- Photographer
- Stationery/invitations
- Transportation
- Videographer
- Miscellaneous
- Budget/finances
- Wedding consultant
- A guest list/response spreadsheet
- B guest list
- Announcements list

You will notice that for the most part these files are created in alphabetical order according to service or product. The reason is that when you start planning your wedding, you will not know which vendors will actually be contracted to provide the services or products for your wedding. Additionally, you will have updated printouts of your A guest list/response spreadsheet, B guest list, and announcements list. In setting up the actual resource binder, you want to do so in exactly the same manner. Putting the divider tabs in alphabetical order will allow for easier access.

Did you notice that we changed the order somewhat for the wedding day binder? We have put the wedding consultant file near the back (because this file is going to be extensive), and we have added both a vendors and a wedding day schedule file in the front (I will say more about these two files later). Putting the budget/finances file at the back of the binder is wise for reasons of confidentiality.

> **TOOLS FOR YOUR PLAN OF ATTACK** ✄
>
> - three-hole paper puncher
> - 4-inch binder (resource binder)
> - 2-inch binder (wedding day binder)
> - stapler
> - Scotch tape
> - two sets of tabs (you will need 25 to 35 for each binder)
> - 70 to 80 plastic pages for business cards
> - organizer and spreadsheet software

Your mission in the twelve- to nine-month countdown preceding the wedding is to gather lists and information on sites and on vendors you will potentially interview. All of this information will go into the resource binder. Later in this chapter, you will learn ways to narrow down the lists; additionally, in each individual chapter, you will learn to further fine-tune your lists and thus be able to home in on those vendors you are actually going to contract.

Now that we have our computer set up and our resource and wedding day binders sitting empty except for their tab dividers and plastic sheets for business cards and plastic pocket inserts, we need to start finding vendors to interview. As with sites, there are some priorities here. If you have your heart set on a specific photographer or florist or other vendor, and if the date is open for this vendor, put a deposit down and reserve her, even if you are planning your wedding a year in advance. This is especially important regarding photographers, who *do* book as much as a year ahead. If you do not have specific vendors in mind, then you've got to begin the long process of determining who is going to compose the right team for your wedding.

Your Software Organizer

In your computer, create a wedding directory. Under the wedding directory, you want to create a file and label it "Resource." In this file, create subdirectories labeled with each category of vendors needed for a wedding (see pages 43 to 44). These are vendors you potentially will interview. Create a second file (not a subfile) in the wedding directory, and label that "Wedding Day." Create subfiles exactly as listed in your resource file. In the wedding day file, you will be inputting information from vendors that you actually contract.

Assembling the Right Team

Some general questions apply to all vendors. The first thing you need to know is whether or not you are dealing with professionals. A restricted budget and family intimacy may require you to rely on a creative sister-in-law to decorate your sites or a talented aunt to bake your wedding cake; however, we urge you to seriously consider hiring professionals to provide your services or products. This advice is not to be taken lightly. While it may be quaint and special for a friend or family member to offer a labor of love as a gift, going this route can cause last-minute havoc, not to mention disappointment.

Business licenses, appropriate insurance, contracts, health permits (if the vendor is a food provider, inclusive of your wedding cake), years in business, number of weddings worked on, and ability to work well with other professionals should be at the top of your lists when gathering information about vendors.

 I would not hire any vendor who shares commissions or requires referral fees in order to refer me.

—LYN SNYDER, JWIC, GREEN ROSE, LLC (DALLAS, TEXAS)

Referral Fees and Commissions

You want to know from the start if the vendors whose names you are gathering receive or give referral fees or commissions. You are spending thousands of dollars on your wedding, so you want to know—indeed, you have a right to know—where your money is going. For example, if a band costs $2,000 and pays a referral fee to whoever referred them, that band is giving as much as $200 to $400 to someone else just to get the gig. That means you are not getting the full value of your money. Or it means the band is going to have to raise its rates to earn the income they deserve. Moreover, if something goes wrong and the performance isn't as it should be, or if the band fails to show up, you may have to involve two parties (the band *and* the person who referred the band) to get your full refund. Do you really want to deal with that sort of hassle in the weeks/months after your wedding, as you begin setting up your new home? Keep it simple; don't hire vendors who trade referral fees.

 June Wedding, Inc.® takes a strong position on the kickback issue; they advise members to never take vendor referral fees.

—Alan and Denise Fields, authors of
Bridal Bargains: Secrets to Throwing a Fantastic Wedding on a Realistic Budget

---

Professional Associations

Obtaining copies of vendors' licenses and health permits and a certificate of proof of insurance may not be enough. Most companies retain membership in professional associations and organizations, but claims to membership or certification by professional associations should be checked and verified by you.

Some vendors do initially get appropriate licenses or certification training, then fail to maintain their membership or even their legal status. Professional associations and organizations are sometimes held hostage by these unethical people. We know of no other association, besides JWI, that requires its members to submit copies of their licenses, proof of insurance, and health permits (if applicable). We attempt to monitor the quality of our membership with this procedure; even that doesn't always protect us.

Sometimes after a year or so, a vendor may decide that she can save money by not paying membership dues, while continuing to use the logo and credentials of the association illegally. Just before going to press with this book, I received a letter from an unhappy bride in Sacramento, California. A vendor in her area who had provided inadequate service had given the bride a brochure containing our logo and attestation that she was a member of JWI. In truth, the vendor had only been a member for one year, and that was in 1992! Don't accept the vendor's word about having the proper and appropriate credentials; ask for an updated copy of the certificate showing professional standing or membership. Besides JWI, two respected wedding associations are Richard Markel's Association for Wedding Professionals International (Sacramento, California) and Doris Nixon's National Bridal Service (Richmond, Virginia).

 June Wedding is probably the best-run professional organization [of associations]. . . . Director Robbi Ernst teaches ongoing training courses for both new and experienced wedding planners.

—ALAN AND DENISE FIELDS, AUTHORS OF
BRIDAL BARGAINS: SECRETS TO THROWING A FANTASTIC WEDDING ON A REALISTIC BUDGET

Narrowing Down Your List of Quality Vendors

We will give more information about wedding sites in chapter 6, but for now, let's work with the presumption that you've already selected your site. Ask the ceremony or reception site manager for a list of preferred or required vendors, if available. Many sites require that you use someone from their list so as to protect the beauty and integrity of their space. If they do have such a list, ask that it be mailed or faxed to you along with the packet of other information they usually send out. If not, ask if there are particular vendors they enjoy working with regularly. A wedding consultant is a good source, too, for reliable referrals. Or ask friends who have recently married if they would recommend any of the vendors they worked with.

Also, go to the Internet and do a search for wedding-related vendors where your wedding will be held. You should be able to get names and addresses and possibly some ideas of rates and prices, and view pictures of products and services. After studying relevant Web pages, e-mail the vendors with your list of questions not already answered on their Web sites. And, as you talk with wedding professionals, ask them for names in *other* categories. Bridal trade shows are an additional place to get leads.

As you collect vendor information, input your data in the corresponding computer files. For each vendor, type in the name of the business, the contact person (*always* get the name of a contact person), the address, phone, fax, e-mail, etc. Be sure to leave enough space so you can write notes—for example, answers to questions you've posed. Do printouts of this information on a regular basis, and add the pages following the appropriate tab in your resource binder.

 Good bridal shows can be like a seminar to gather information and meet all sorts of credible vendors.

—DOLORES ENOS, JWIC, WEDDING CONSULTANT (LARKSPUR, CALIFORNIA)

First Conversations with Vendors

Your next step is to begin calling the vendors. Prepare for the telephone call by having a list of written questions at your fingertips. Note that the sample questions provided in this book are from wedding experts, so they are phrased using the terminology that makes sense within the industry. Also, the questions are more direct and thus elicit more specific responses than those someone not familiar with the profession might ask.

As you begin to do your telephone interviewing, stay in one category (for example, catering) until you have exhausted your list rather than going from category to category. This will keep you in the frame of mind to learn the most about each profession. It also keeps you comparing "apples to apples" so that if one vendor's quote is considerably higher than another, you will be able to determine the reason. This method will enhance your "comparative shopping."

First Impressions Are Telling

Pay attention to the manner in which the vendor talks with you on the telephone. Indeed, note whether or not a live person answers, or if day after day you get an answering service or machine. After introducing yourself and informing the vendor of your wedding date (find out if she is available that day), ask if this is a convenient time to talk. If not, set up a time to call back when you can get her full attention. Let her know who referred you, explain that you want to get as much information as possible so you can decide whether it is worthwhile for you to make an appointment, and tell her that you appreciate her taking the time to answer your questions. If you know how much of your budget is allocated for her vendor category, let her know that amount up front. Ask if she can work within your budget, and if so, what services/products can she provide? Also ask about any "plans" or "packages" she has available as well as à la carte pricing.

Be attentive to the conversation. It should be congenial. Note, too, the vendor's interest level. Does she carry on a conversation, or just answer your questions? Does she talk to you about *your* wedding? Does she ask about other components of the event? Does she have suggestions as to how she can make your budget work?

While talking to the vendor, ask if she has a Web site. Jot down this information with the other notes you have been taking. Ask for references, but remember that no smart businessperson is going to give you an unhappy bride as a reference. Also ask for references of other professionals. For example, what florists, caterers, videographers, etc., does she work with regularly?

Finally, let the vendor know if you think there is a possibility of working together and ask how much lead time she needs to book an appointment so you don't lose out on the possibility of hiring her. Don't be anxious if the vendor gives you a hard sell about how fast she books weddings. Of course, some vendors use this method as an "arm twister" to try to get you to book early with them. However, if you are getting married during the busy wedding season, you can be sure she is on the level.

After the conversation, input your notes in the appropriate spots in your computer files. Be sure to add fields for the names of vendors recommended by the person you spoke with. You should make it a point to contact them; this is especially true if you hear a vendor's name repeated often. After you have exhausted your lists in one category, go through it carefully; try to narrow down your choice to three or four names.

Now go to your wedding budget according to vendor type spreadsheet and type in the information about the companies to be interviewed. Then and only then should you begin telephoning to schedule on-site appointments. Most vendors prefer that you come to their place of business. This makes sense, because they work out of their shop, salon, or home, and it's best for you to see as much as you can of their operation. You have the opportunity to form an opinion of how they run their office.

All of this work has probably taken you three or four weeks, possibly longer. A professional wedding consultant can provide you the same information—actually more accurate information and more reliable referrals. If you're already worn out, you may want to start your resource binder by collecting information on wedding consultants.

Common Points on All Vendor Contracts

While we will talk specifically in each chapter about contracts as they pertain to each vendor, here are some tips regarding what all vendors' contracts should include.

- Exactly what services are going to be provided should be spelled out.
- The date and site of your wedding should be listed.
- Names of primary people (vocalist or band leader, photographer) should be written into the contract.
- Total, exact payments, as well as dates when they are due, should be indicated.
- If there is a security deposit (money that will be returned to you at a later date), that should be noted.
- If it is important or necessary that the vendor communicate with another vendor, have this stated.
- What is the policy for a "no show" or inability to provide the services/products? Will a comparable substitute be provided? As a wedding consultant, I am very direct with the vendor. I ask, "What happens if you die before my client's wedding? Who will be present to provide your services or products?" Such questions make vendors nervous. Sometimes they reply, "Well, if I'm dead, I won't have to worry about that, will I?" If you get such a reply, think twice about hiring that vendor!
- If the wedding is canceled by the bride or groom, are any payments refundable?

- Get everything in writing (proposals as well as contracts).

- Get a copy of the business license or at least a DBA (Doing Business As, or fictitious name registration), a certificate of proof of insurance, and if the vendor is providing food service, a copy of the health permit.

- Make certain the vendor is approved to work at the site. Some site-specific religious or ethnic restrictions may apply to vendors; approval of those not on the restricted list must be stated.

- Specify total costs and how payments are to be made.

- Does the vendor offer a variety of services? It is not generally to a client's benefit for a business to provide many services. Optimally, it should offer a specialized service.

Other Important Vendor Information

Change-of-Name Kits

Though some grooms have been known to take the bride's surname as his last name, traditionally, it is the bride who takes the groom's surname for her own.

Changing your name is a bureaucratic process. Thankfully, someone has come along to make this process easier. Katharine Weissmann, owner of the Official New Bride Name Change Kit (Carlsbad, California), offers a packet that shows step by step what needs to be done if you (or your groom) are going to take the other's surname. Weissmann will even process the papers for you.

Wedding Insurance

Be prepared to take out a rider on your homeowners' or renters' insurance to secure the site for your ceremony and reception. This is a common practice, especially for museums, Victorian mansions, and bed-and-breakfasts. Don't worry. The cost of the rider is minimal, usually about $25 or $50, since it is only in effect the day of your wedding and the premium has already been paid. "But what about my wedding; can that be insured?" you ask. Yes, you can take out insurance on your wedding. Besides the rider most sites will require you to take out on your policy or their policy protecting them against any damages or lawsuits, additional coverage is available through a company called Weddingsurance (1-800-ENGAGED).

If you're planning a wedding in the Northeast or Midwest in February, or in Oklahoma during the late summer, or anywhere in California, anytime, think of protecting yourself against snowstorms, hurricanes, tornadoes, and even earthquakes. Most natural catastrophes are covered by Weddingsurance, provided by Fireman's Fund Insurance Company. Whether it's a nonrefundable deposit, a photographer's film that gets lost in the mail on its way to the lab, or a wedding cake that topples to the floor, you are covered. Coverage can cost from a low of $95 to the standard premium of $129.

If you have gotten through this chapter and still want to have a wedding, read on. Rest assured, we don't want to put a damper on your wedding plans. We just want you to approach them as wedding professionals do—from a business as well as a creative standpoint. We want the beginning of your wedding planning to be the beginning of a shared life together, and your wedding day to be a day that is memorable each day of your life.

CHAPTER 3

Hiring Your Team Leader

❧ The Professional Wedding Consultant

DO YOU FIND EVEN THINKING ABOUT, MUCH LESS PLANNING, YOUR WEDDING to be overwhelming? There are important reasons to at least consider hiring a wedding consultant to assist you in planning your wedding.

You seek the services of a health care provider to make sure you're healthy, don't you? You go to a lawyer to get legal advice; some people even have an attorney on retainer. Planning a formal event can be stressful! Your wedding is an important moment in your life. Indeed, it's one of life's rites of passage. That's true whether it's an intimate wedding of 20 to 30 people or a big production of 500. You may very well want or need the expertise of a professional consultant to be your team leader, to help you orchestrate the months of planning and direct the cast and crew on the wedding day itself. As you see your bank account dwindle, juggle schedules and appointments, attempt to come up with ideas to make your wedding *unique*, try to differentiate one photographer from another, figure out which vendors work well together, or worry about contracts you will be signing, I promise you are going to feel the stress at times.

To determine if you could benefit from the services of a professional wedding consultant, sit down with your groom and your parents and figure out if you have the wherewithal not only to hire competent vendors but also ones who will work together well. Do you know how to arrange a schedule so that all your vendors, wedding party, and parents know what to do when as well as where? Are you adept at figuring out what your wedding will actually cost, and then the means to track your disbursements? Do you know what information should be in each contract you'll be signing? Even if you have an administrative staff at your disposal, you still are going to have to oversee and manage many things. Will that leave you time for the creative, *fun* things you will want to do to make your wedding truly memorable? From the moment of your engagement, you are going to be one very busy person. Learn early to economize your time.

After discussing the need for professional advice, you will want to discuss with your groom and parents whether you can afford a wedding consultant. Or put another way: Can you afford *not* to hire an expert to be in charge of one of the most important events in your life? "I've planned plenty of great parties without a consultant!" you say emphatically, "so why hire a consultant now?" Because this is a wedding, a formal occasion marking an event of great importance, and you have only one time to get it right.

The best way to answer the question "Is a wedding consultant affordable?" is to find out what wedding consultants do and what they charge. Only then can you make an informed decision. The answer may surprise you, but be wary: There are some wedding consultants out there who are not competent. Did I say that? You bet I did. Below are some guidelines to help you discern the difference between a wedding consultant who is competent and one who isn't.

Brides need to prioritize the segments of their wedding. They should consider the items they want to include in their wedding and prioritize those items according to their desires. This prioritization may of course change as the bride and groom go about creating their day.

—PAT BRUNEAU, JWIC, L'AFFAIRE DU TEMPS (MILPITAS, CALIFORNIA)

Finding a Competent Professional Wedding Consultant

I don't use the term *professional* lightly. There are many incompetent wedding consultants who, after planning their own wedding ("It just went perfectly! It was so beautiful, so romantic. I really loved planning it!" can often be heard in their refrains), decide to have business cards printed and then to "hang out their shingle." Without any thought of getting professional help (of an educational, not psychiatric, nature), these people—we call them "dabblers"—simply appropriate the title of "professional."

Other dabblers have taken cursory correspondence courses. Check into the association or organization that has supposedly trained a consultant. While you probably will not find one association bad-mouthing another, any training organization should be able to tell you how their program differs from others. Notoriety (not just in the media, although this is very important) is not enough. How long have they been teaching? Are their courses taught in a college or secondary school? If the association claims to be "approved" by a state governing agency, ask for the name and phone number of the agency so you can determine their current standing and what such "approval" means. We know of one person who claims her certification program is "approved" by the state regulatory board of secondary schools; however, she often will let a year or so lapse and not pay the annual fee required of the state in order to keep her "approval" in effect. A simple phone call to the state board will give you the facts. An additional tip: Find out if the association head has ever been a wedding consultant, or better still, if she continues to work as one. Someone needs to be out in the field, in the trenches as it were, to keep her skills fine-tuned.

To assist you in finding a trained and experienced consultant, ask the site manager and other vendors which wedding consultants they work well with. Besides the site manager, the caterer, videographer, and photographer are good references since they actually work with the wedding consultant on the wedding day.

Call the wedding consultant on the telephone before going to interview him personally; when calling, note how the phone is answered. Is it a business or private line? Do you hear dogs barking uncontrollably in the background? Is the person congenial and friendly? Does he seem to know his business? Ask what his training or education has been. What are some prominent sites and vendors he has worked with in your area? In other words, you want references (not just of brides but of professionals he works with *regularly*). How long has he been in business? This is really a more important question than how many weddings he has worked on, though that is important as well. Some wedding consultants contract only weddings that require extensive work and constant personal attention. Ask, too, what professional associations he holds membership in. Don't be content to take his word. Call the corporate headquarters of the association to inquire whether his membership is current and in good standing. As we said earlier, many former members of associations still use association logos though they haven't paid dues or attended any meetings. Finally, you want to know how and how much he charges.

By being attentive to this information, you will quickly be able to narrow the list of wedding consultants you want to interview. Keep in mind that the consultant will likely want to know information about you and your wedding plans before setting an appointment. With an honest and straightforward exchange of information on the telephone, both you and the consultant can approach your wedding planning in a professional manner, and both of you will know that your time—and money—is being well spent.

If the consultant is congenial and answers your questions appropriately, ask him to mail you his company's brochure and other business materials. Then take the list of references, including the name of the professional association that trained him and that he says he belongs to, and call to check him out.

 Every bride wants her dream wedding interpreted into reality. It is my job to organize, orchestrate, listen, and then listen some more, so that I understand her dream fully. This is the primary role of the wedding consultant, who is responsible for not only understanding what you want and what your budget is, it is also her job to communicate that understanding to your vendors. The wedding consultant is your primary team player.

—PACKY BOUKIS, JWIC, ONLY YOU (BROADVIEW HEIGHTS, OHIO)

How Wedding Consultants Work

Unless you are referred by someone, be wary if a wedding consultant offers you a complimentary, or free consultation. This freebie may be just a hook to get you in the door. A genuinely professional wedding consultant isn't going to talk with you for free, unless it is simply an introductory meeting. An introductory meeting is exactly what it implies. It's a short meeting to give you and the consultant an opportunity to determine if you are fit for each other. It's also an opportunity for the consultant to show you a portfolio, which should feature a wide variety of weddings (hotel ballroom affairs, tented events, cocktail and dinner parties, religious and secular settings, formal and casual celebrations). The consultant may even display magazine articles in which she has been quoted or featured; these are an indication of her capabilities—though not always—as well as how she is perceived in the industry. I say "not always" because I often see lengthy articles about a wedding consultant who has long since gone out of business or who no longer is a full-time consultant.

You will want to know if the person you are interviewing is computer-literate—if she has e-mail and if indeed she has a computer. A wedding consultant simply cannot do the work that needs to be done without one.

At this point, let me say something about part-time vs. full-time wedding consultants. While it is more advantageous to hire a career and seasoned wedding consultant, one who works at it full-time, it's also a fact that our profession is new and up-and-coming. There aren't many of us who have been around for twenty years or so. (Annena Sorenson, JWIC, of Tie The Knot, in Sunnyvale, California; JoAnn Gregoli of Elegant Occasions, in Denville, New Jersey, and New York City; and Pat Bruneau, JWIC, of L'Affaire Du Temps, in Milpitas, California, are three professionals who have been around for more than a decade.)

We decided to offer a wedding consultant course because many of our community education students are attracted to entrepreneurial classes. A major reason we offer presenter Robbi Ernst's quality course is because of his training background, his real-life experience, and his professionalism in marketing.

—MICHAEL HABEEB, DIRECTOR, CORPORATE AND COMMUNITY EDUCATION,
COLLEGE OF SAN MATEO (CALIFORNIA)

If possible, I advise hiring a wedding consultant who works full-time. The reality is that most of your other vendors will have regular business hours; it should be the same with your wedding consultant since she will need to be interacting with these vendors.

Many of the newer wedding consultants are different from those of the past. They don't just order invitations, tie rice into tulle to be used as favors, and then show up for your wedding. Some of these novices are indeed formally trained and educated, graduates of the JWI home study course or the JWI programs at Norwalk Community Technical College (Connecticut) on the East Coast or the College of San Mateo (California) on the West Coast.

Additionally, many of these newer consultants have experience in wedding-related businesses such as catering or event planning. Dee Merz, JWIC, owner of Everlasting Memories (Penngrove, California), is a good example. She began her career in catering, starting and running two successful delicatessens. She compiled personnel manuals and recipes and trained and managed staff. After several years of planning and coordinating fund-raising events and community festivals and fairs, she took the internationally known and respected JWI home study course and started her wedding consultant company. Consultants such as Merz bring a wealth of knowledge and experience to the industry. Finding out about previous experience and training may assuage your doubts when someone tells you she has only been a wedding consultant for a short time.

As with other vendors, the professional wedding consultant approaches weddings from two standpoints: the business, or administrative, and the creative. As an administrator, she is the detail person, creating files, keeping them updated and organized, giving your contracts careful scrutiny before you sign them, putting all communications in writing, tracking your finances, and keeping all the participants on schedule on your wedding day.

As an artist, the wedding consultant is helpful in creating the overall ambience of the wedding; she knows who the most creative vendors are and will match you with them according to your desires and budget. After attending one of your gown fittings to make sure that a photograph is taken of you in your gown, she will have the picture sent to the florist so that your bouquet is designed for you *and* your gown and isn't just another bridal bouquet. And she'll be concerned that the men wear formal dress socks if they are wearing tuxedos.

 The schedule I create with the bride and her vendors is my biggest asset on the wedding day. I always want the bride and groom to really enjoy their day, and I do not want them to feel rushed. This can be accomplished if we stay on schedule from the very beginning. Once you get behind schedule, there is constant pressure to catch up.

—HELEN LOUIE, JWIC, HLOUIEWEDDNGS@AOL.COM (ON-LINE WEDDING COORDINATING SERVICE) AND MOTHER OF THE BRIDE CONSULTANCY FIRM (SACRAMENTO, CALIFORNIA)

When interviewing a wedding consultant, be sure to ask about his proficiency in these two areas: Do his files show an orderliness? Does his portfolio show a flair for creativity? After establishing his credentials, your next concern is how he works and whether he can be hired for an individual meeting or for several meetings, for the full production or for the wedding day only.

Initial Consultation

An initial consultation appointment will most benefit the recently engaged bride who is just beginning to think about her wedding and doesn't know where to start. A competent wedding consultant can sit down with you and show you how to put yourself on a monthly planning schedule as well as how to create a wedding day schedule, point out concerns about contracts before you sign them, and refer competent vendors. In this meeting, the consultant can educate you about what services and products really do cost and guide you in creating a sensible budget. She can offer suggestions on how to save money and how to create a payment schedule, thus enabling you to track your disbursements.

In the initial consultation, then, you are hiring the consultant for an extensive show-and-tell session. But, more than that, the consultant will actually teach you what you need to do if you don't continue to use her services.

"Why would a consultant do that?" you ask dubiously. "Why would she give away trade secrets?" If you're on a restricted budget, a professional wedding consultant knows you aren't going to hire her to orchestrate and direct the full production. So, why not work with you for a couple of hours and get paid for it? (Yes, she will charge you for this initial consultation.) In addition, she is creating "good press" for herself. After all, if you get the full value of your three hours with a wedding consultant, aren't you going to tell others? By the way, don't think you are paying only for those three hours; your wedding consultant will have spent at least that much time preparing for your appointment before you arrive.

Before your meeting, the consultant is going to give your wedding a lot of thought, based on what you communicated to her over the phone, and make some phone calls. A consultant can help you find three or four vendors in each category, so when you go to interview them, you're not wasting your time setting up and keeping appointments with people who don't fit with your personality, style, and budget or who aren't on your site's preferred vendors list. In fact, if the wedding consultant has done her homework well, the most perfect vendor for you is probably going to be at the top of her list. You will need to interview competing vendors only if you aren't completely satisfied. The wedding consultant will of course refer more than one so that she isn't putting herself in the position of being an agent and allying herself too closely with one vendor. Do insist that the consultant explain how she works in relation to the vendors. You need to be confident that the referrals given to you by your wedding consultant are legitimately established businesspeople.

If you find the consultant has given you your money's worth in this one appointment, you may decide later that you want to go in for another individual consultation or hire her for the preparation planning or even the full production of your wedding.

"But I've already decided on the site for the ceremony and the reception and have a preferred vendors list. That should make everything else pretty easy," you say. Let's see, what else is there to do? You still have to prepare guest lists, decide on stationery and invitations, address and mail them, determine menus, make gown alteration appointments, get proposals, study contracts, start a budget, keep a budget, track a budget, create files that are orderly and organized, write instructions for the parents and attendants, and more. Even though you may be well on your way, you still could benefit from an appointment for an individual consultation with a professional, just to fine-tune everything you've done.

QUESTIONS FOR THE WEDDING CONSULTANT

- How long have you been in business?

- What professional organizations/associations do you belong to? (Confirm with the association that membership is current and in good standing.)

- Are you certified, and if so, by whom? (Check out the certifying association; what are their requirements for certification?)

- How do you charge? Do you receive commissions/referral fees? Do you charge a flat fee? A percentage of the wedding costs? How is the percentage determined?

- How many meetings will you have with us? How many meetings with us *and* our vendors?

- Will you provide us regularly with printed updates on the planning of our wedding? Is your office computerized?

- Who is your "backup" if you become ill or otherwise unable to complete the work?

- Will you be there throughout the rehearsal and wedding day? Is this included in the fee?

- How will you be attired at the wedding?

- Will you be able to work within our budget?

- Can you be hired for an initial or individual consultation?

- Can you be hired for the wedding day only?

- Do you have a business license, DBA registration, and liability insurance? (The latter is required if the wedding consultant sees clients in his own home or in a retail space.)

- What are the names of other professionals you work with on a regular basis?

- Will you put the other vendors we hire in contact with one another long in advance of the wedding?

- Are costs such as postage/telephone/other such expenses included in your fee?

- How many weddings do you book in a year, in a month, on a weekend?

- Will you direct the rehearsal unless the officiant/minister prefers to do so?

- How do you deal with last-minute changes and emergencies?

Event production is an art and a profession requiring creativity and ongoing research. Finding new resources, along with reevaluating existing resources and vendors, is a primary focus. New trends, great quality, creative presentations of food and decor, the best vendors, and those vendors who have gotten too big to provide the attention that a wedding deserves need to be updated constantly.

—Annena Sorenson, JWIC, Tie The Knot (Sunnyvale, California)

Individual Consultation

You may find that you want to be in complete control of your wedding, that you have the time and you enjoy making these plans. No problem. Besides getting vendor referrals, you can set up an individual appointment with a professional wedding consultant to discuss your overall planning, go over your budget, help you create a wedding day schedule, or review the contracts you are signing, in addition to any other specific matter. Most professional wedding consultants will allow you the opportunity to come in for one or two meetings (that is, contract by the hour or by the meeting) where they'll simply serve as a troubleshooter or problem solver and give you guidance in a particular area.

Preparation Planning

Wedding consultants can be hired for preparation planning, where they will book a specific number of meetings with you and/or your vendors. In addition to the initial or individual consultation, you are contracting for full administrative and creative services. The vendor will set up and organize your wedding day binder, providing you with a duplicate complete with updates during the months of planning. She will also receive copies of all of your contracts and become the liaison between you and the vendors. If there are minor changes to your plans, you will be able to simply telephone your consultant and let him communicate the information to your vendors, wedding party, and/or family. (Any major changes should be discussed and arranged directly by you and the relevant vendor.) If you are lucky enough to have a creative and artful consultant as well as an efficient one, he will also be valuable in helping you design your wedding. Otherwise, he will be able to set you up with vendors who have the necessary creative abilities.

 The importance of having someone in charge on the wedding day cannot be overlooked—having a wedding consultant not only checking that all vendors have arrived on time but also making sure they arrive in proper order. It's the domino effect. If the florist is supposed to decorate the cake and the cake hasn't arrived yet, she may simply leave the flowers in a bucket of water. This presents a couple of problems. The pastry chef may not be able to find the flowers that are left behind for the cake, and he may not be adept in decorating with fresh flowers.

—LORA WARD, JWIC, A DAY TO REMEMBER (SACRAMENTO, CALIFORNIA)

When scheduling initial appointments with recommended vendors, your consultant will fax that person the necessary details (names and addresses of all parties concerned, location of the site, wedding date, and other important information) so you are not bothered with filling in a vendor's interview sheet during the initial meeting. As your personal administrative assistant, the consultant takes notes at meetings and sends "wrap up," or summarizing letters to the vendor interviewed. One of his most important roles is to communicate your desires and needs, as well as your budget, to your vendors when appointments are set up. Invaluable time is saved when the vendor has a grasp on your needs, desires, and budget before the meeting.

 I always call the vendors who have been hired. Those I've never worked with I schedule a visit to meet. It's important to get to know them and how they work as a vendor and also to let them know how I work on that important day.

—PATTY ANDERSEN, 24 KARAT GOLD (BURBANK, CALIFORNIA)

Additionally, in the preparation planning stage, the consultant will create the wedding day schedule and floor plan and send these to your wedding party, all sets of parents, and all vendors two to three weeks before the wedding. He will track your disbursements and regulate your budget and actual costs.

If you are having a small wedding (less than fifty people), let's say you've hired most of the vendors, along with the wedding consultant for preparation planning. You can always decide at a later date to engage the full production services of the consultant. You may very well want the reassurance and added sense of security knowing that someone is completely in charge.

 If I haven't worked with a selected vendor before, I introduce myself and explain how I work and what role I play. I then make a request for a contract and get input for the wedding day schedule. It's important that we all work as a team. That benefits everyone.

—MARIE HOUSON, JWIC, CREATIVE OCCASIONS (NOVATO, CALIFORNIA)

Full Production

Wedding consultants are able to be contracted for your entire event. Normally, they will determine a specific number of meetings with you and your vendors (nine to twelve meetings is average), and they will be contracted either for a specific fee or on a percentage basis. Some who charge a flat fee may be able to tell you what that fee will be after your initial consultation. Others, whether they charge a flat fee or work on a percentage basis, will be able to tell you what they charge once you have contracted all your vendors. After you sign your consultant's contract, you will be put on a monthly planning schedule so you see things being accomplished in an orderly fashion and your stress level is always in check! The full-service wedding consultant will get copies of all of your contracts and set up the wedding day binder for you—in other words, the consultant becomes the liaison between you and your vendors. You will regularly be provided with complete and updated readouts on your wedding, to have at your fingertips. (A note of warning: Only you, your future husband, or the financial minister should sign contracts, and checks should be written directly to the vendors for their services, not to the wedding consultant.) An adept wedding consultant will constantly keep you apprised when you are making decisions that may be taking you over budget. You will be the one making the choice whether or not to exceed your original budget.

After months of planning, the full-production wedding consultant will send the wedding day schedule and reception floor plan to all your vendors, wedding party, and family two to three weeks before the wedding. And, of course, the same consultant will be with you throughout the rehearsal and the wedding day to "direct" the performers, handle any emergencies that might arise (you will probably not even know about any mishaps), and, in general, keep the day on schedule. Once again, when you contract a consultant, especially for the full production or preparation planning, hire a proven professional—one who has a track record in the business. Hire someone who has a strong and competent business ability as well as creativity and personability. This person will become your confidant, your arbitrator, your financial adviser, your designer and personal shopper, and often even your friend. I have been a wedding consultant for more than twenty years, and I still have friends who were clients as far back as seventeen years ago. It has always been special for me, as a caring and concerned professional, to have a role in this important moment.

Wedding Day Director

When hiring a wedding consultant as director of your wedding day only, recognize that this may mean different things to different people. Either the consultant is being hired to simply "hold the bride's hand" or, more often than not, she is being contracted to create a plan to be able to handle any emergency that arises.

Be wary of the consultant who will do the wedding day only, without any prior meetings with you and your groom. If you are looking for such a person, then you really aren't looking for a competent professional. A competent professional will recognize that she can't handle emergencies unless she knows what agreements and responsibilities rest on the shoulders of the vendors. She will need to meet with you at least a month prior to your wedding to get copies of your contracts; she will need to set up a file for you and have each vendor's phone numbers in case there are any questions. (Have you ever tried to get hold of a rental company on a Saturday afternoon? A tried-and-true wedding consultant will have not only the vendor's pager and cell phone numbers but also an emergency phone number.) She will also need to create a wedding day schedule and floor plan to send out to all the vendors at least two weeks before the wedding.

Be aware of the difficulty involved in hiring a wedding day director, even a competent one, at the last minute. Even if that person is able to meet with you at least twice before the wedding day, she is going to have a tremendous amount of work to accomplish in a very short period of time. "When hired for the wedding day only," says Marie Houson, JWIC, owner of Creative Occasions (Novato, California), "I will still be working a minimum of forty-five hours just to prepare adequately." And if you think hiring a wedding consultant at the last minute can save you money, think twice. A professional consultant must be adequately compensated for these rush services. Still, the benefits outweigh the costs. The time just before your wedding is when you and your groom should feel confident in the decisions you have made and actually begin to enjoy the process of getting married.

Can a Wedding Consultant Really Save You Money?

One of the most contentious discussions held whenever wedding professionals get together at our conferences or workshops is whether or not a wedding consultant can save a bride money. In my experience, I have seen literally thousands of consultants' brochures that boldly proclaim "We can save you time" and "We can save you money." The first claim is entirely accurate and, if taken with the second, both are true; but, since the claims appear broken up in the brochures, they give the wrong impression. Some wedding consultants even dare to proclaim "We can get you more for your money." This seems to indicate that the wedding consultant is going to be able to negotiate and get vendors to lower their prices. That's not the case, and a professional consultant will be up front about that.

"If a wedding consultant isn't going to get me a lower price with vendors, how can she save me money?" you ask. Here's how: If the wedding consultant has been trained properly and has longevity in the business, she will have the experience and knowledge to refer you to vendors who are in keeping with the style and budget of your wedding. She's going to know the people who have a good track record and those who don't. Moreover, and this is very important, she's going to know, from experience, those vendors who work well together *as a team*! She will have decided long ago to work only with proven professionals. By steering you in their direction, she will save you endless hours on the phone—time that would otherwise be wasted interviewing vendors who are not suitable for you and your wedding. Remember, time is money!

A wedding consultant is going to be economizing your efforts as well as your time. She is going to be making the phone calls and doing your legwork and maintaining the wedding files—while you are at your office, earning your paycheck.

As far as "getting you more for your money," don't believe it; I don't know anyone who can legitimately say that. However, a wedding consultant *can* get you the true value of your money, if that is what she means. She will know, again from experience, which vendors charge fairly for their services. With this knowledge, she will be able to provide you with suggestions on how, within your budget, you can still have your dream wedding. You may have to compromise on style, but you won't be compromising on quality. For instance, she may recommend a two-hour cocktail party reception instead of a full-course meal or dispensing with favors so you can add to your floral budget. In other words, she will be able to assist you in prioritizing products and services.

There is another way that the wedding consultant can save you money in the sense of getting the most bang for your buck. Her vendors consider her a valued patron because she sends them business and doesn't accept referral fees or commissions. They will bend over backward not just to please you but to keep her happy as well. After all, they know who is contributing to their success and prosperity. When my company had its base in San Francisco, I regularly referred Laura Little, owner of Floramor Studios, there in the city. Laura *always* provided beautiful and creative floral arrangements. When I had a client with a restricted budget, Laura would give her as full a presentation as clients with lavish budgets received. She never said no or pulled back the reins just because my client didn't have an endless supply of money.

Can a Wedding Consultant Really Save the Day?

This isn't the sort of book that will talk about disasters because, frankly, disasters only happen to other people's weddings, not a JWI member's wedding! I can only relate near disasters that would have become catastrophes except for quick and competent handling by the professionals involved. Our chief concern is solving problems in such a timely fashion that the bride, groom, and parents aren't even aware that a problem occurred.

Linda Shafer of Vows & Veils in the Vail Valley (Edwards, Colorado) relates a situation in which a reception site informed her, just days before the wedding, that the contracted on-site manager wouldn't be at the event and that, indeed, even the banquet staff would be different than those originally contracted. She arrived to find that the dance floor had been laid out in the space where the full orchestra was to set up, while a huge cake table had been set up on the dance floor, not allowing enough room for guests to dance comfortably. She immediately asked that the cake table be dismantled and set up elsewhere. After making the dance floor larger and moving chairs and tables closer together, there finally was enough space for everything. Fortunately there was beautiful weather and the guests were all outside while this transformation was taking place. The bride and groom knew nothing about the last-minute reconstruction!

How Wedding Consultants Charge

Commissions and Referral Fees

Let's consider first those wedding consultants who charge a low fee for their services but who require commissions or referral fees from their referred vendors to make up the true receipts of their income. Everything we said about vendors accepting referral fees or commissions goes double for the wedding consultant. She should know better! Unless acting as an agent, a wedding consultant who receives such income is certainly walking a legal tightrope.

A professional consultant just isn't going to be accepting "referral fees" or commissions. Today, when wedding consultants charge a flat fee or percentage for their services, there is no excuse for accepting referral fees—again, unless they are acting as agents. This should be clear in the contract. Don't hesitate to ask how a consultant charges and if she receives commissions.

Percentage Basis

Consultants differ in the way they are compensated for their services, just as they differ in the types of services they offer. In any case, just as clients need to be aware at every stage of the process what vendors have been hired, deposits made, and balances are due, they need to know the percentage rate of total wedding costs owed to the consultant. The percentage is paid only by the client, not the vendor; therefore this is not the same as receiving commissions or referral fees from the vendors.

Flat Fee

To keep it simple, most consultants charge a flat fee for their services. If you are hiring a consultant only for a three-hour initial or individual consultation, he will be able to quote you a flat fee for that meeting. Across the country, the fee for a single meeting ranges from $175 in rural areas to as

My fees are based on complete involvement in all aspects of the planning. A percentage is taken against the total costs of the vendors the bride and groom hire, regardless of whether they have been hired on our recommendation.

The percentage system works for us because of the time we devote to the client. Our clients enjoy the added benefit that we travel with them to all appointments and meetings (in addition to office time spent with them). They see the benefit of us being available for them when they need us. A client will know what the percentage is, and an estimated fee is determined on their budget and what they are planning on spending. There are no surprises with my fee, though there may be with what they end up spending on the wedding itself.

—PAT BRUNEAU, JWIC, L'AFFAIRE DU TEMPS (MILPITAS, CALIFORNIA)

much as $500 in large cities. After the initial consultation, the consultant should be able to offer you a range of what his fee will be for the full production or preparation planning. Of course, it may take a couple of weeks, while you are deciding on your vendors, before he can offer you a firm, or committed, fee. If you hire most of the vendors the wedding consultant has worked with and who he knows are credible professionals, then his workload will be lightened because he will not have to train them how to do weddings. Thus, the fee may also be decreased if less time is required. In rural areas, the preparation planning fee starts at $2,000; in metropolitan areas, the fee can start at $4,500. Add on another $1,500 in less-populated areas to $3,000 or more in larger cities, and you can have a full production wedding consultant who will be present to orchestrate and direct the rehearsal and wedding day. Obviously these fees can be much higher, depending on the size and complexity of your wedding.

An important tip so that you are not caught off guard: For preparation planning and full production services, wedding consultants contract for a specific number of meetings or consultations with you and/or your vendors, and this should be stated in your contract. Additional meetings or consultations may be cost out and billed separately. The terms *meetings* and *consultations* can be confusing. To help interpret the products or services you desire and indeed to keep you on budget, it is necessary that your consultant accompany you when you interview with some of your vendors, even if the consultant isn't necessarily contributing to the interview; these "interviews" may be considered meetings or consultations.

We have a marvelous example of this. We had a client who planned to hold her wedding at a country club. We arranged a meeting to do a walk-through with the floral designer, a meeting that did not in fact require my presence as the wedding consultant. However, the new site manager appeared and wanted to review the client's contract. Five months previously, the parents had reserved the entire site, but the site manager's worksheet showed only half the site reserved, though the room could not possibly hold the number of guests invited. Also, the client had been promised round tables, instead of the square tables normally used; the site manager simply informed us that "these would have to be rented." Finally, though having talked with the mother of the bride about the menu just two days prior and having had the menu faxed back, with each part initialed, the site manager still had it wrong on the worksheet. As it was, I was able to find out about all this while everyone was present. And, the next day, I was able to send a letter addressing every point that was discussed and decided so there would no longer be "confusion," and all of us could move on to other issues. While this meeting was not a formal consultation, it was greatly to the benefit of the client that I was present.

If a wedding consultant deems it important to attend even a short meeting with you and your vendors, and while it may count as one of your contracted meetings, trust the professional. She's only seeing that your desires are met. Your consultant is able to look at each segment and see how it fits into the entire picture. Though your consultant's fee may increase slightly, it will be worth the expense in the long run. Additional consultations, beyond those contracted, should be cost out in your contract.

The higher fees of today's wedding consultant are attributable to their level of expertise as well as to their formal training, which sometimes includes an apprenticeship. The competent wedding consultant constantly attends workshops and conferences in order to keep updated on trends, along with ways to more effectively provide services to brides.

How Wedding Consultants Differ from Site Managers or Bridal Coordinators

In a day when wedding consultancy has become a bona fide need, it seems that each business in the wedding industry is adding a "wedding consultant" to its staff. Florists, caterers, churches and synagogues, hotels, and restaurants have suddenly given one of their employees the title "wedding coordinator" or "wedding consultant." While these people may provide vendor referrals, in reality they will be concerned about the details of your wedding only as these affect their particular service or product. Don't be fooled.

Many churches, vestries, synagogues, hotels, museums, and the like have added the title "bridal coordinator" to their site manager. Some of these employees may call themselves wedding consultants; however, an on-site coordinator is exactly that, although she may take on other responsibilities. Christy Lofton, JWIC, Hyatt San Jose Airport (San Jose, California), is an on-site consultant who sometimes provides broader services. It is important to ask the site consultant about the full scope of her responsibilities. If she is willing to provide other services, then be certain to get this in writing—with or separately from your contract with the site. If she is simply going to give you a list of referrals restricted to the site and appear on the wedding day to get you down the aisle or be present to direct traffic before and during the wedding reception, you should know this.

For Destination Weddings, A Professional Wedding Consultant Is a Must

Planning exotic honeymoons is easier today with the use of the Internet and travel agents. But more than ever, couples are also planning destination weddings, in which all their guests meet them in another state or even a foreign country. The reasons are many and varied, but the primary reality is that couples want a truly unique and extended experience with their family and friends.

It is important to realize that even though you are planning a wedding in another state or country, you will still have the usual concerns and worries with additional stress of something going wrong in a different location. Aside from making travel reservations and accommodations for the group, you need to consider local legal issues. A marriage license, a decree of divorce (if applicable), a passport, or a birth certificate may be required. Experts advise that anyone planning an out-of-state or out-of-country wedding give serious consideration to hiring a local wedding consultant for direction and advice and an on-location wedding consultant at the destination, especially if you are taking a group to a foreign country.

Search the Internet to see if your desired destination has a certified wedding consultant. Myrtle Dwyer, JWIC (Half Moon Golf, Tennis & Beach Club, Jamaica), Marcia Bullock (The Jamaica Tourist Board), and Roy Anderson (Glamour Tours, Jamaica) consider this fact so important that they have had several members of their staff trained and certified by JWI so that everyone—the guests, family, and especially the bride and groom—is treated as a special guest.

When planning a destination wedding, your on-location wedding consultant is more than a travel agent; she will see that you have all the required documentation, that every detail is planned long before your arrival, and that you have competent wedding vendors with proper contracts. She can even assist you if you choose to bring in some of your own vendors (e.g., your own photographer, floral designer, videographer, etc.). She will check that each person is properly picked up at the airport and given the planned-for accommodations, and that your guests are well rested from travel before they begin the schedule of any local tours and sightseeing that she has prepared with you far in advance. She can also suggest local customs that will make your wedding truly unique, one that your friends will talk about for a very long time.

The Wedding Consultant's Contract

Most wedding consultants do not require a contract for their initial or individual consultations. Few will send a contract to a person they've not actually met.

- The contract with your wedding consultant should state how fees are charged—on a percentage basis or a flat rate—and stipulate that he does not receive commissions or referral fees in any form or fashion.

- The contract should have a place to write in the number of meetings that are going to be held with you, as well as the number of meetings the consultant will attend with you and your vendors.

- The duties of the consultant and his total costs should be clearly stated.

- Usually, wedding consultants get half their fee when the contract is signed. The reason is simple. The consultant will be working the most during the first month to six weeks he is hired; his involvement with you, while remaining constant, will taper off until the month before the wedding, when it will once again become intense. It is very likely there will not be a refundable clause. Similarly, few wedding consultants accept a "deposit"; rather, since they are actually working for you throughout, they spread out their fee over the months leading up to your wedding.

- Any and all fees that are outside the consultancy fee should be listed separately (for example, cost of invitations if ordered from the consultant, doing calligraphy, etc.).

Transfer the figures from your contract to the appropriate columns of your overall wedding day budget. In your file labeled "Wedding Day Schedule," note the times the wedding consultant "goes on duty."

CHAPTER 4

Who's Going to Do What and When?

⚶ The Wedding Day Schedule

THE WEDDING DAY SCHEDULE IS THE MOST IMPORTANT DOCUMENT (BESIDES your invitation, of course) that you will be sending out. It follows then that one of the most important things I have done for the modern-day bride and vendors is to devise a wedding day schedule *that works*. It is detailed but easy to read. At a glance, it is obvious to all where they are supposed to be and what time they are supposed to be there. From the moment the first vendor arrives on the wedding day until the last table and chair are broken down and the floors swept, the major participants know what to do and when to do it.

The wedding day schedule I've devised is a comprehensive three- to four-page document that includes the names of the wedding attendants and how they are going to enter for the processional, stand for the ceremony, and walk out behind you during your triumphant recessional. Names of the mothers, who is going to escort them down the aisle during the "Seating of the Mothers," what songs are going to be played during the ceremony, the name of the person(s) making the toasts and when this happens, and the order that the wedding dances are going to occur, should all be in this important document. After you have read this chapter—if you do not have a wedding consultant to create one for you—you are going to know how to customize your own wedding day schedule. Teaching you how to do this is perhaps one of the most important tips in *Great Wedding Tips from the Experts*. (This method for creating a wedding day schedule, by the way, is the same one we teach the wedding consultants and professionals in our JWI home study and college courses.)

As with all of your wedding planning, it is easiest to begin thinking about your wedding day schedule in segments. The schedule is going to be completed over a period of time, as much as four months; you're not going to be able to sit down and write it out in one day, or even one month. That's because until you contract your venue and vendors, you aren't going to have all of the needed information to complete the schedule. As you begin to think about the schedule for your wedding day, start with the segments for which you do have information.

Creating the Schedule

In your computer or binder, create a file or page labeled "Wedding Day Schedule." On this blank page, in the top right corner, insert the date as a "header." (When you do future printouts, you will then know the latest day the schedule was printed.) In the top left margin, type "Rehearsal." Leave the space that follows blank so you can later add the rehearsal site's name and address. Under that, type "Time," and under that, "Phone number." Next leave some blank lines under the telephone number. An important tip: Always include area codes when entering phone numbers anywhere in your wedding day binder files. Telephone companies have a way of changing area codes at the drop of a hat. Today what may be a local call, five months from now may have become a long-distance or toll call requiring the dialing of an area code. Prepare for all contingencies.

Now, in the center of your page, type "Wedding Day Schedule." This is your title. You may, if you wish, even increase the font size to make it stand out properly. There, doesn't that look fine? "But where do I go from here?" you ask. Again, start with the information that you know.

Adding in Your Venue and Vendors

In the left margin of your no-longer-blank page, create a column reserved for the time, indicating when something is to occur; the space to the immediate right of each time "slot" will be used to explain what it is that is occurring. You know, first of all, that the site at some time on your wedding day is going to be available to receive your vendors. So, on your first line, leave some blank spaces in your left-hand margin, and then type "Site Opens to Receive Vendors." You also know that there must be a natural flow to the arrival and work of vendors (makeup and hair artist show up; the site or caterer will be setting up tables and chairs; your photographer/ videographer arrives to begin photographing the wedding party while they are preparing for the wedding; the caterer sets the table linen; the floral designer arrives to decorate the ceremonial site, distribute flowers, then decorate the reception site; the pastry chef arrives to set up the cake). Pay attention to the sequence; something may have to happen before someone else can do his or her job (for example, the cake can't be set up until the linen is placed; that can't be done until the cake table is set up; the cake table can't be set up until it is delivered; it can't be delivered until the site is open; and so on).

For now, figure out the sequence of events that will be occurring on your wedding day. Make a list of these events, in sequence, to the right of the time column. The time slots can be filled in once you have your proposals and contracts in hand. Once you have your contracts you will also have the names of those who will provide their services. Add these to your schedule. For example:

3:00 P.M.   Jennifer Kalman, Licensed Makeup Artist, arrives at 1331 Burnham Avenue.

5:00 P.M.   Photographer Ami Davenport, A Day to Remember, arrives at Temple Emanuel, 2041 Arguello Drive, to photograph the bride, Anita, and her attendants.

Listing the name of the vendor along with the name of the company or service does two things: It alerts the vendor in two ways that he is to be in a certain place at a certain time, and it gives a personal reference for your attendants and other vendors. Instead of saying, "Hey, you, can you take this photograph?" the interested party can ask, "Hey, Ami, can you take this photograph?" By using names, your entire wedding day will be more personal. By listing the address, the vendor has no excuse for "getting lost."

Information from Your Contracts

Before you put copies of contracts into your wedding day binder, study each one carefully. Transfer all needed data onto your wedding day schedule. All addresses of where your vendors will be doing their work, as well as what time they will be doing it, should be on your schedule. Vendors' setup and breakdown times should be on the contract; be sure to enter this information on your schedule.

The Ceremony

Following the arrival of vendors, the next major event on your wedding day about which you have information is your ceremony. You may not know much about your ceremony; you may not even know the site, but you at least know there is going to be a ceremony and generally what it will include. Technically, a wedding ceremony is broken into the following segments: prelude, seating of the mothers, processional, ceremony, and recessional.

Prelude

The prelude is when music is provided for the entertainment of your arriving guests. It precedes the ceremony by thirty minutes. Depending on the number and type of musicians, usually an additional thirty minutes is required for setup.

Establish the hour that your ceremony is to begin and type that time in your left margin; next to it, type "Ceremony."

Above that information, type the time thirty minutes earlier and next to it "Prelude." If you desire, you can list at least the important pieces to be performed.

An important tip: If the music is "complicated," I type in the amount of time needed to complete each piece. Specifying the amount of time for each piece also allows your wedding consultant to know how long she has to get the mothers, attendants, you, and your father ready for their entrance. Here's an example from one of my weddings in 1990:

7:00   *Prelude*

"Te Deum" (3 minutes)

Bach: "Jesu Joy of Man's Desiring" (4 minutes)

Vivaldi: "Spring" from *Four Seasons* (8 minutes)

Purcell: Rondeau from *Abdelazer* (2 minutes)

Mouret: Rondeau (1 minute)

Next, back up thirty minutes (an hour before the ceremony) and again enter the time. Then, to the right, type the names of the musicians and "Musicians arrive at (address)."

Seating of the Mothers

The mothers of the bride and groom receive special seating attention. There may or may not be a pause in the music, but above all, they are seated last: first the mother of the groom, escorted by a favored relative who is in the wedding party or an usher, her husband following behind; next the official hostess of the wedding, your mother. She also is escorted by a favored relative or friend who is in the wedding party. If you or the groom have any other close, special relatives, these should be seated prior to the mothers. Seating of the mothers takes place just before the processional begins (unless yours is a Jewish ceremony, in which case the parents escort their son and daughter, the groom and bride, respectively).

Input the time (five minutes before the processional) that is appropriate. Again, to personalize your wedding day schedule, write in the mother's name and the name of the person escorting her, for example,

Mother of the Bride, Mrs. Antonio (Mary) Didone, escorted by her nephew, Mario.

Processional

The processional marks the official entrance of the wedding party and should occur at the time stated on the invitation. Though, realistically, the ceremony nearly always starts ten to fifteen minutes late, you should still put the "supposed" time on your schedule. To do otherwise might tempt you to start even later.

Type in the time to the left, and then to the right type "Processional." If you desire the attendants to make an entrance on a particular piece played for the prelude, then type in the name of that piece. After you have decided on the order your attendants are going to enter, then, in the center of the page and in that order, write their names. Having their names, instead of Bridesmaid #1, Bridesmaid #2, Bridesmaid # 3, and so on, will make for a smoother and more personal rehearsal. Obviously, the processional ends with the entrance of you and your father.

Ceremony

There is no need to put a time in your left margin for the rest of the ceremony. At this point, time is out of your control. You do, however, want to diagram across the page the manner in which your officiant, you, the groom, and the attendants are going to stand. Put the officiant's name in the center; on the next line are yours and your groom's; on the next, your honor attendant's and the best man's. Then, across the page to the left, type your attendants' names, and to the right of the groom, type his attendants' names. For example:

Rev. Heron Freed Toor

Anita   John

Rebecca   Jack

Samantha, Kimberly, Melissa   Vincent, Glenn, Scott

Obviously, for a Jewish ceremony the configuration would be different; simply create what is appropriate.

Usually, the flower girl and ring bearer will not endure the full length of the ceremony, no matter how short. But you should still put in their names so that they will know where to stand, no matter how briefly, for the ceremony. The flower girl usually stands next to the maid/matron of honor and the ring bearer next to the best man.

Recessional

Here you will note the title of the music you will be exiting to. Also, center and type the names of the wedding party, this time as couples. This list should end with the mother and father of the bride, followed by the parents of the groom.

If photographs are to be taken after the recessional, put the time, name, and company name of your photographer/videographer. Formal portraits and family postceremonial photographs should *never* take longer than thirty minutes.

If there are any special instructions, put that information here (for example, ceremony musicians leave synagogue and set up at reception; include name and address of site). Also, list any transportation that has been prearranged.

The Reception

The next major segment of time will be your reception. Your reception time, stated on your invitation or reception card, should be put in your left margin with the name and address of the site to the right. A reception usually lasts an hour if followed by lunch or dinner. It is normally during this time that the gown and makeup are refreshed; note these on the schedule.

Dinner

The time stated on your invitation is the time you put in your slot. If you opt for a "grand entrance" with special music, for example, a trumpet fanfare, write the title of the musical piece next to the time for dinner. Also, list all names according to how they are to be announced (as a help to your DJ or band leader, also write the names phonetically).

Decide on when you want the toasts to be offered and by whom. Insert that information in the correct spaces. List the cake cutting, wedding dance and/or round of dances, and the participants. Note that it isn't necessary to assign these events specific times. A dinner takes on a life of its own, and the caterer will know what to do and when to do it. But do list the order of the events in which you want them to occur.

The bouquet and garter toss are reserved until near the end of the evening since those send a signal to your guests and staff that the evening is winding down. The last items on your schedule should be instructions for the security of the gifts, for the time and means of the departure of the newlyweds, and for the caterers and musicians to break down and vacate the premises.

Do pay attention to your contracts when filling out your wedding day schedule. Give some thought to potential last-minute changes in the schedule that could greatly affect your budget. If you ask the band to stay an extra half hour, for example, it may mean an increase of expenses to each of your other vendors too.

CHAPTER 5

Let's Party

❧ The Engagement, Wedding Attendants, and Celebrations

ONCE YOUR IMPENDING WEDDING BECOMES PUBLIC KNOWLEDGE, YOU ARE going to be enveloped in party going—and deciding how important certain relationships are to you and your groom. While you will want to refer to etiquette manuals regarding who should host certain events, your decisions should ultimately be based on common sense as well as the bond you share with relatives and friends. For instance, though traditionally the engagement party is hosted by the bride's parents, this may not be possible if you're not on good terms with your parents or if they live in a different region of the country. While the rehearsal dinner is traditionally hosted by the groom's parents, financial circumstances may not make this feasible. Finally, the number of attendants chosen to assist the bride and groom in the months of planning and on the day of the wedding should not be increased in an attempt to avoid hurting someone's feelings.

Although this is a new adventure for you, and you want to make it as pleasant as possible, you are going to have to deal with very real issues that will affect your relationships for the future. I recommend that you sit down with your groom and all parents to determine what their roles will be, and then you and your groom talk directly about the people you want to be in your wedding party. Don't assume that it's all right to arbitrarily make these decisions. They should be made together.

You'll also want to avoid skirting the issue with those who may want to have a special role in your wedding. Not being clear and direct may send the wrong signals to people. Keep in mind that those people who really love you are not going to be offended if they are not selected for a specific role. They will understand that you have to make decisions that are possibly going to exclude them, and they will continue to love and support you in the months of planning.

The Engagement

Developing Your Own Traditions

The difficulty for most brides in planning a wedding is that they've never been married before! The best way to start is to figure out the degree of formality or informality in your family. Nevertheless, the choices you make over the next few months don't necessarily have to reflect your lifestyle in the past. Quite the contrary, they should reflect the style in which you and your fiancé plan to shape your lives. Moreover, you may someday have children and want to pass on some things that may very well become traditions for *them*.

I say this because I remember so vividly two of my clients, Anita and John. One day while doing a prewedding site inspection, the groom and I were standing in the courtyard while Anita went to obtain the keys to the temple of the synagogue. I asked John what he foresaw for the future, after the wedding. He replied, "We want to have children. I already have daughters, but Anita and I want to have our own children so that we can pass on our values and traditions." He was quite serious. In the quiet moment that followed, I was reminded why I had become a wedding consultant. I have always wanted to be part of people's lives at important moments. It wasn't just a business for me. And what more important moment than a wedding?

Today, while I write, Anita and John are the proud parents of twin girls! Someday, they will indeed be able to pass on their values and traditions to their daughters. Such passing on of tradition in a couple about to be married begins with the engagement party.

The Engagement Party

Engagement parties do not have to be highly structured, formal events. Dozens of people do not have to be invited, nor lots of money spent. While some engagement parties are catered, many are more informal, such as a picnic or a potluck event at the bride's home. The engagement party may consist only of the bride and groom, their parents, and the grandparents in each family, siblings, and any other close relatives or friends. At the very least, the engagement party may be the first opportunity for the sets of parents to visit and get to know one another. While it isn't the time to necessarily discuss planning the wedding, it should provide the opportunity for bonds to begin being established.

It's not necessary that the parents be the ones to put on the engagement party, nor is it mandatory that the engagement announcement be a surprise (though it should definitely not be a surprise to the sets of parents).

Invitations may be sent out, though they are not invitations to an "engagement party." If you want to give people a hint of what is to be announced, the invitation should read: "You are invited for [dinner, cocktails, a barbecue, etc.] in honor of Carmen and Jon." While the norm is that the father of the bride makes the announcement at the party, it may be the mother or a sibling or even a best friend. It is also not required that the bride's parents host the engagement party. Very near and dear friends may offer to do this for the couple. In today's world, when so many people do not live in the area where they grew up, most couples have what is called an "extended family." Indeed, for some, the extended family has replaced blood ties.

Sometimes parents or couples use the engagement party as an opportunity to court their professional colleagues or repay social obligations. This is not the place or the time. The guests invited to an engagement party should be very close to both the bride and groom as well as close to the parents.

The engagement party should occur within a reasonable time after the couple becomes engaged. After all, while an engagement party isn't mandatory or necessary, you certainly don't want to be walking around for months saying you are engaged, and then suddenly have a party to announce it. Cele Goldsmith Lalli and Stephanie H. Dahl, authors of *Modern Bride Complete Wedding Planner*, put the average length of an engagement at fourteen months. Such a length of time is often needed to secure the necessary site for the ceremony and reception as well as vendors that do the best work. Besides the fact that so many different vendors and people have to be brought together to make the wedding happen, the right gown has to be found, ordered, and then altered (alterations alone could take as long as two to three months). Before you begin worrying about things that have to be done, first give some thought to each other and the people you most care about.

Newly engaged couples should, together, tell their parents. While the groom doesn't have to ask the father for permission to marry his daughter, doing so can express a nice sentiment. If it's not possible to inform the parents in person, then a phone call or a letter is appropriate. (Don't even think about sending an e-mail to your parents announcing your engagement!)

If either or both bride and groom have children, the engaged couple should sit down and talk with them about this being a new adventure for all of you. Unless you have only recently met each other and decided suddenly to get married, the children are already going to know that your relationship is taking on new and deeper dimensions. If either of you senses the least bit of anxiety or discomfort from the children, take time to communicate with them. More importantly, take time to listen. Your new relationship and marriage are going to call for adjustments from everyone.

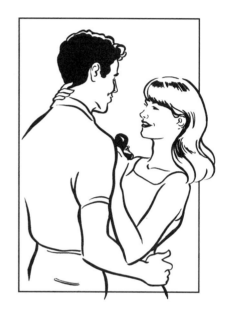

Once the parents and children have been informed, then and only then do you make the information public. After the engagement is announced, "it is customary for the groom's mother, or father, to call the bride's mother, or father, and to welcome the new daughter into the family," say Lalli and Dahl. It is also a tradition, especially in smaller towns, once the immediate family and best friends on both sides have been informed, to send a written statement and/or black-and-white photograph to the newspaper where the couple as well as the families live. Call the newspapers that apply and ask them for specific instructions. Do not write your name on the back of the picture; most newspapers scan pictures, and handwriting may bleed through. If you have mailing stickers, attach one of these to the back of the picture. Although you do *not* want your address published in the newspaper, you may want the photo returned, so include your address. (Also include a note asking the newspaper not to publish your address but to simply use it to return your photo.)

Though some people may give you an engagement gift, this is not to be expected. If people who are invited to an engagement party do bring gifts, these should be opened in private. Receiving gifts places you on your next road to proper etiquette: getting into the habit of sending thank-you notes. A thank-you note should also be sent to the person(s) who hosted the engagement party, even if the parents were the hosts.

Selecting Those Who Are Going to Stand Up for You

Planning a wedding often requires that some decisions have to be made in a relatively short period of time. One of these is selecting your attendants. While you can certainly have as many attendants as you desire, you want to be careful; after all, you don't want more people under the chuppah or at the altar than are seated behind you.

Take into consideration the potential size of the ceremonial site and be aware of limitations on how many people it can comfortably accommodate. That should be a relatively easy question to answer. However, selecting the right people to stand there with you may require the skills and expertise of a high-wire trapeze artist. While you and your groom are giving thought to the people you want to invite to take on the role of attendants, make a list of these people and discuss them with each other. Remember, this is an event for both of you. Relationships are very important, and the one between you and your fiancé is now the most important. While a sibling should be considered to be an attendant, if you are not on good terms, this might not be a good idea; however, it could possibly offer an opportunity to put past feuds behind you.

Take into consideration the situations of friends. Some may not be able to afford the financial commitment (usually attendants pay for their own attire, travel, and other expenses); possibly they have already been attendants in numerous weddings and simply want a breather from the responsibilities. Let such friends do something else in the wedding, or let them just have the pleasure of being guests.

The best man and the maid/matron of honor should be decided on first. These roles have seen dramatic changes in recent times. For example, it is perfectly all right to have a woman as the groom's honor attendant and a man to stand to the side of the bride as her honor attendant. Once the best man and maid/matron of honor have been selected, the other attendants should be chosen. While you might be tempted to think about your photographs and how they will look with different-sized people, this really should not be a consideration. You determine who is going to be in your wedding according to the degree of love between you. Though it might not be wise to select a friend who is pregnant and due at the time of your wedding, again, selection of attendants is based on relationship. Just be prepared for any emergencies or changes that have to be made if the attendant suddenly has to drop out of the wedding. (If one of your attendants is pregnant, you might consider having a Lamaze-themed shower!)

As a wedding consultant, I have always asked the bride's and the groom's attendants to assist me in gathering the wedding couple and important members of the family, as well as one another, at important points on the wedding day. For instance, having instructed them beforehand when the time for the cake cutting approaches, I am always grateful to the attendants for helping me gather the bride and groom and bring family members up close so that they can view the ceremony and even be in the pictures. This is so much more comfortable, and more efficient, than the bride and groom having a stranger tugging at their elbows. I have had many brides tell me as they view their photographs, "I didn't know my mother was nearby; she's in so many pictures." It always makes me feel proud that I have done my job correctly.

While it is true that the wedding day is *your* day, the attendants, whether yours or the groom's, should feel that it is an honor to share it with the two of you and should do everything possible to make it a happy day. This includes running errands throughout the months of planning. No doubt one of the most important requests you can make of your attendants is that they be on time for the rehearsal and other events and especially for the wedding day. It's a fact of life that when there are such a large number of people traveling from different parts of the city or country, they are going to be on varied schedules. It's also a fact that some people are forever late for appointments. But it's also a fact that people in responsible positions—your priest, rabbi, or officiant, the musicians and the caterer—are on a schedule themselves. Starting late will affect their ability to perform their duties and obligations, especially at the rehearsal and on the wedding day. You don't want to upset or rattle these people. Your wedding consultant will do everything possible to keep the schedule flowing as planned, but even she can't work miracles.

Maid/Matron of Honor or Honor Attendant

The role of the maid/matron of honor, or honor attendant, can be as broad as you and she agree. In a day when wedding consultants, calligraphers, and computerized mailing lists and Internet gift shopping have decreased many responsibilities of the maid/matron of honor, you don't want her to feel that she has nothing to do except show up for her fittings and the wedding day. You might ask her to help you in deciding the style and color scheme of the attendants' dresses, and see that they receive the proper instructions for fittings; if she lives in the same city where you are purchasing your gown, you may invite her to go shopping with you and help you make a decision or to give you advice about your veil. She can also give you her opinion about the gifts that are to be presented to the attendants. She's going to be the ringleader for the attendants in choosing a proper gift for you, so make certain she has good taste!

The maid/matron of honor should attend at least one of your fittings (along with one additional attendant) so as to learn how to bustle your gown. You need someone who knows what she's doing. As a matter of fact, I suggest having a backup, just in case.

Your maid/matron of honor and her backup should also learn from the gown salon what to do in case something goes wrong with the outfit (the beads begin falling off; the hem comes undone; someone spills wine on it). Ask her to help you prepare an emergency kit (to include pins, a couple of needles and some thread similar in color to your gown, black thread, a bottle of club soda, a clean white rag, an extra pair of pantyhose for you, and other items that could be helpful).

It is permissible for the maid/matron of honor or any of the other attendants to give a shower or to do so collectively. On the wedding day, the honor attendant should arrive as early as possible and see that everyone is having their makeup and hair done in proper order. She may also help you into your gown, though this task should be shared by the mother and grandmother. It is tradition that she hold the groom's ring and the bride's bouquet and assist you with your veil and train during the ceremony. She may or may not be one of the witnesses who signs the marriage license. She should help bustle your gown after the formal pictures have been taken or after the ceremony. If there is a receiving line, and we urge that there not be, the maid/matron of honor stands next to the groom (see chapter 9).

Other duties might include assisting the photographer and videographer to make certain that any special guests are not missed. If you do not have a wedding consultant, then have your maid/matron of honor assist you in creating and distributing copies of the wedding day schedule to all vendors and family members, as well as be the "director" on the day of the wedding to make certain everything stays on schedule. She may, if you desire, present a toast at the reception or dinner. Finally, she and another attendant may help you out of your gown and into your going-away clothes. Depending on the size and bulkiness of the gown, she and another attendant, along with your mother, should see it is properly wrapped in a clean white sheet or muslin garment bag and that the rented items (such as the slip) are packed separately. If there is a bachelorette party, usually the maid/matron of honor helps organize it. While out-of-town honor attendants pay for their travel expenses and attire, you pay for their accommodations.

Bridal Attendants

Traditionally, the bride's attendants are called bridesmaids. In a day when brides sometimes have male friends in their wedding party, we prefer to use the more politically correct term *bridal attendants*. As with the honor attendant, these persons can do as much or as little as you ask or as they are capable of doing. Their tasks can run the gamut from helping you address and mail invitations to hosting showers for you. If there is a receiving line, they should be there to support you.

Flower Girl

The flower girl is the only one who dares to upstage the bride. One of the things we often do at our weddings is suggest that the flower girl have her dress made in the same design as the bride's gown—same fabric, same color.

Let her look the role; she's in a play. Make it fun for her. Give her a single long-stemmed flower, its stem wrapped in a ribbon. Let her carry an unusually shaped basket, or present her with a lovely nosegay that matches your bouquet. Why not? The more she stands out, the more people are going to talk about your wedding.

Best Man or Groom's Honor Attendant

In the past, the best man was always a male who helped with the travel plans and the honeymoon. As we've said earlier, this is not necessarily true today. First of all, a groom may have a gal pal for his honor attendant. If the groom's honor attendant is a woman, she should dress appropriately, similar to but not a duplicate of the bridal attendants. Plus, in a day of travel agents and making travel plans over the Internet, usually the bride and groom see to any travel responsibilities themselves.

The best man, however, is still responsible for organizing the bachelor party. He is also to take the lead in deciding on, purchasing, and presenting the groom a gift from his attendants. One of his most important roles is to make sure the other groom's attendants have been properly fitted for their tuxedos, that all of them have sent in their measurements on time, that they are correctly dressed (inclusive of formal black socks if the event is to be black or white tie; also make sure everyone has the proper studs and cuff links, bow tie, and cummerbund). He should check to make certain the groom has all his clothing correctly laid out for the ceremony.

Besides being entrusted with the marriage license (and the officiant's fee or gift), which he should present to the officiant as soon as possible on the wedding day, he holds the bride's ring and may or may not sign the marriage license. He is responsible for offering the first toast at the reception (usually after the cutting of the wedding cake) and dancing with the bride and her attendants. If there are any telegrams or the like, it is the best man who reads them at the reception. A nontraditional role is for the best man to help corral the bride and groom, their parents, or any other special relatives as well as both groups of attendants during important parts of the wedding, especially when photographs need to be taken. With the maid/matron of honor, he can take the lead in quieting people and assembling them at the rehearsal. Most importantly, he should be early for any and all events and wait with the groom before the ceremony. His additional duties are to make certain that the groom and his attendants are on time for all events.

Groom's Attendants

If the event is black or white tie, the groom's attendants should be fitted for their tuxedos in a timely manner. This is not difficult. The formal-wear shop in the city where the wedding is to be held will provide the groom with the style and/or order number of the requested attire on a postcard; he only has to send that information to his groomsmen and they can go to a tuxedo shop in their area, be fitted, and the measurements sent back on the postcard to the designated shop. While it is recommended that a larger formal-wear shop that has stores in other cities be used, this is not mandatory. Any formal-wear shop will provide these preaddressed cards. Some formal-wear places will allow the attire to be picked up two or even three days before the wedding. Ask, and be certain that you know if additional costs will be incurred.

Advise the groomsmen that before leaving the store, they should try on the attire to make sure it fits (yes, this includes the freshly starched and ironed tuxedo shirt). Make certain the proper accessories are there. While the best man and the groom's attendants, when traveling from out of town, are responsible for their own attire and travel expenses, the groom traditionally pays for their accommodations.

Ushers

Ushers are part of the wedding party, even though they may not stand up at the front during the ceremony. While it is tradition to seat the bride's friends and relatives on the left side and the groom's on the right, more couples are simply asking that the distribution of people be even. Of course, if the guests request to be seated on a particular side, then by all means don't disagree.

The ushers and groom's attendants often combine funds to buy a collective gift for the groom. Ushers should be ready to seat the arriving guests about thirty minutes before the ceremony is to begin. Mothers of the bride and groom might prefer to be escorted and seated by a special relative or friend. The usher offers his left arm to a female guest as she enters the ceremony site and walks her down the aisle. If she is with a male friend, that person normally follows behind the two of them. Unaccompanied male guests seat themselves.

Ring Bearer

Ideally the ring bearer should be a friend of the groom. He can be attired in a fashion that follows the groom's lead or differently, whichever manner you desire. Either way, it should be in keeping with the formality or informality of the wedding. For example, knee britches with suspenders, a bow tie, long white socks, and jacket are fitting for a garden setting. Whatever you do, do *not* attach the real rings to the pillow he will be carrying.

Gifts for the Wedding Party

The bride and groom should give each other a special gift on the day of the wedding. This can be something small but significant. It should be romantic. Both sets of parents receive gifts from the couple. Gifts from the bride and groom are presented to their attendants at a pre-wedding party or at the rehearsal dinner.

A fun contemporary gift for your attendants is available through Catherine M. Cavanagh's Nuptial Bliss (Amawalk, New York): The Wedding Phone Card. Be an attentive bride and give this gift long before the wedding—for those long-distance phone calls your attendants will be making to you to discuss the wedding plans!

We will say more about gifts in chapter 8, but we do have a few additional pointers here. Just because someone is invited to the wedding doesn't mean they are obligated to send a gift. They need only send a gift if they attend the event. Gifts should be sent to the bride's home before the wedding and to the couple's new home after the wedding. The address printed on the flap of the invitation envelope is the address used for sending gifts. If you received an engagement gift, do not expect to receive a wedding gift from the same person. Also, anyone who has hosted a shower or other party is not obligated to give a wedding gift. All gifts are to be acknowledged as soon as possible upon receipt.

Showers and Other Pre-wedding Parties

Showers

People not invited to the wedding should not be invited to showers, unless it is an office shower, where the guests don't expect to be invited to the wedding. Try to keep records so that the same person isn't invited to more than one shower.

Showers can be hosted by anyone who wants to give you a party. Though not required to, your wedding attendants will probably want to host a party for you. It is their way of showing their love and friendship for you, so don't deprive them of this pleasure.

 Remind the person presenting you with a shower to let the invited guests know where you are registered for your wedding gifts.

—CELE GOLDSMITH LALLI, FORMER EDITOR IN CHIEF, MODERN BRIDE

More couples today are being creative with their showers. A popular option is a couples shower, attended by both the bride and groom along with male and female friends and relatives. The host or hostess should check with you and the groom about the kind of shower you would like.

Showers take place up to two months before the wedding. Gifts at showers, unlike wedding gifts, are opened in front of the guests. That's part of the fun of the party! Traditionally, the bride keeps the ribbons from the gifts and makes herself a bouquet to carry at the rehearsal.

TYPES OF SHOWERS

Paper: gifts of money (not paper towels and tissue).

Kitchen: items for the kitchen.

Tools/Garden Equipment: an ideal couples shower.

Lingerie: a shower for ladies only.

Honeymoon: another fun couples shower idea, with gifts like film, pool towels, and traveling overnight kits.

Bed and Bath: inquiries should be made as to the bride's favorite colors and fabric textures.

Computer Software: for the high-tech bride and groom.

Party for the Bride's Attendants

Hosted by the bride and/or her mother and held a few days before the wedding, this is your opportunity to let your attendants know what they mean to you and how grateful you are for all their help during the past months of planning. It is permissible to invite other female relatives and friends. If there is no rehearsal dinner, this is the proper time to give each attendant a gift from you and your groom. Traditionally, the gift is a piece of jewelry or something the attendants will wear the day of the wedding.

Bachelor Party

Hosted and organized by the best man, bachelor parties have a notorious history and are surrounded with a lot of secrecy. In reality, they are usually quite tame. According to Michael R. Perry's book, *The Groom's Survival Manual* (a must-read for all grooms), "the creation of the wild bachelor party story is a closely guarded male tradition, and the entire gender is dependent on each new groom to carry his own weight by maintaining the myth. In other words, lie like a rug about what really happened!" Lies or no lies, under no condition is the bachelor party to be held the night before the wedding. It should take place the week or so before; even men's eyes sag after a wild night of debauchery and womanizing. (Just carrying on the myth!) The only hard and fast rule for a bachelor party is that the bride be excluded. If the groom's honor attendant is

female, the exclusion policy holds for her as well. One of the male attendants can in that case sponsor the bachelor party.

Bachelorette Party

In a sense to share the spotlight with the groom's bachelor party, more brides are opting to have a bachelorette party, hosted by the maid/matron of honor. This is essentially a "girls night out." As if the already female-dominated rituals of the modern bride aren't enough, another party is given by and with her gal pals—watch out guys, there's no winning!

Belated Wedding Party/Reception

This is self-explanatory. For whatever reasons, you get married in a different city and come back from the honeymoon but have a party in another site where it is easier for people to travel. Whether or not you should wear your wedding gown remains controversial. We say, do what makes you feel happy; etiquette is being rewritten. Just have it freshly cleaned and pressed.

The Rehearsal Dinner

Folklore has it that close relatives and friends would gather for dinner on the eve of the wedding, and afterward smash the china and crystal against the wall in an effort to ward off the presence of evil spirits. Nowadays, a more sensible party is arranged for the parents, wedding attendants, and sometimes out-of-town guests. The officiant and his or her spouse are invited too. The rehearsal dinner is traditionally hosted by the groom's parents, though another close friend or relative may choose to sponsor it.

While it is certainly allowable for the bride's parents to host the rehearsal dinner, before offering they should check with the groom's parents, who might be offended if not given the chance to decline.

TIPS FOR A PERFECT REHEARSAL ❧

- Get all the attendants in place at the ceremony spot, that is, put them in the positions where they will actually be for the ceremony. You and the groom should take a moment to step back, look at the attendants facing forward, and make any necessary adjustments. The way the attendants are now standing will affect your photographs. Then step back into place and allow the officiant to go through the ceremony; have the musicians, photographer, and videographer available if possible and affordable.

- After the officiant announces you, recess to the back of the site with your attendants following behind you. When you get to the back, reverse the order of appearance and get in place for the entrance.

- Do the entrance/processional. By your attendants assuming their positions for the ceremony at the start, they will now have a focal point.

- Go through the vows again.

- Exit and reenter. This should be done a couple of times so you all feel comfortable. Remember, weddings are theater. And the problem is, you can't have a full-dress rehearsal!

CHAPTER 6

Where, Oh Where?

❧ Selecting the Site, Officiant, and Tradition

SEVERAL FACTORS ARE GOING TO COME INTO PLAY WHEN YOU BEGIN SELECTING your sites (yes, I did use the plural; you may very well decide on different sites for the ceremony and the reception). Even if you haven't completed your guest list, you at least have an idea of the number of guests you will be inviting. Still, deciding whether to have a religious or a secular setting is more important than how many people will attend. You can always be creative with your setting. For instance, we have produced many weddings for 150 people in cathedrals that were built for a thousand or more; we simply used a side chapel or gathered the guests near the front. So, first decide if you prefer a religious or nonreligious setting for the ceremony.

Think about the kind of mood or ambience you desire. What's the climate if yours will be an outdoor wedding? Is there a sufficient indoor facility to accommodate guests in case of inclement weather? What are the dictates of your religion, culture, or ethnicity? Consider, too, if you want one site for the ceremony and a different one for the reception.

The Religious Site

Many religions (including Roman Catholicism and Judaism) require certain rituals and rites, and there may be seasons when wedding ceremonies aren't permitted. Proper etiquette dictates that candlelit ceremonies occur only at dusk or afterward, but think first and foremost of the experience *you* want to have. If your ceremony is in the afternoon and you want candles along the pews, and if your site will allow them, then by all means, have candles—as many as you desire. Make it a point to see the types of candles that your site allows and that your florist uses. Because of fire codes, most candles are required to be enclosed in hurricane lamps or the florist must use tapers that are enclosed in metal containers; some are even battery-lit and have a very pretty "glow."

Beginning Your Search for a Religious Site

It is easiest to start with your own affiliation when considering a religious site. Because of the increase in the number of first- and second-time weddings, availability is more restricted today. Parishes, churches, and synagogues are naturally going to give their own members first rights of use. Given that, plus the fact that nonmembers are increasingly seeking a reli-

QUESTIONS FOR THE
RELIGIOUS CEREMONIAL SITE MANAGER ❧

- What are the restrictions or guidelines we must adhere to for the ceremony?

- May we write our own vows or have secular readings/music during the ceremony?

- Can we incorporate cultural or ethnic customs or traditions into the ceremony?

- How can we include our family or children?

- What is the appropriate clothing or attire?

- What are the restrictions regarding music, photography, videography?

- What is the appropriate fee for your services? (You may feel more comfortable asking the site secretary or wedding consultant. Even if the officiant declines a fee, one should be given. The officiant may simply be embarrassed or even have disdain for discussing finances.)

- How many witnesses are needed?

- If there is a communion service, may nonmembers partake? Is it possible to have communion without having a mass?

- Are aisle runner, chuppah, decorations, or candelabra available? Is there a fee for the use of them?

- Must the bride's guests sit on the left (her side) and the groom's on the right (his side)? (Few couples are acknowledging this tradition as it seems to imply that the guests are choosing sides.)

- Are candles allowed, and if so, how must they be contained?

gious setting for their ceremony, you'll find the possibility of discovering the perfect site for your ceremony more difficult. Thus, securing your site at the earliest possible date is a priority.

If you are not a member of a particular church or synagogue, begin creating a list of places that fit with the type of ceremony you desire. Look in your telephone book and call the local conventions and visitors bureau or chamber of commerce, or hire a wedding consultant to give you referrals of officiants and sites for ceremonies and receptions. Bridal trade shows offer a very good opportunity to pick up brochures and meet site managers. Ask your friends and relatives too.

Put all of this information into your resource binder. Once you have compiled a lengthy list, simply go through the materials, call the secretary or officiant, and explain your situation: that you are of the religion but not a member of their particular place of worship and that you would like to have your ceremony there. Give the preferred date and an alternative and see if the site is available. Go down the list until you have exhausted all the possibilities. Fridays and Sundays may be popular "off days," although Jewish weddings are not performed on the Sabbath. Be as flexible as possible. If you have no luck finding the appropriate religious facility, then consider other alternatives.

Officiants, Premarital Instruction, and Ceremonies

Did you know it is easier to find a minister, rabbi, priest, or other officiant to perform a wedding at a secular site (such as a Victorian mansion, hotel ballroom, museum, or town hall) than it is to find a religious site? I call this "bringing the mountain to Mohammed"!

Fortunately, there is a greater variety of enlightened religious officiants who will preside over wedding ceremonies at nonreligious sites than ever before. Many are not only intelligent and good-spirited but also "interfaith friendly." Some officiants, such as the Reverend Ed Holt (A Wedding Ministry, San Carlos, California), the Reverend Robert Dittler, OSB (The White Robed Monks of St. Benedict, San Francisco, California), and the Reverend Heron Freed Toor (Beautiful Weddings, San Francisco, California), see their roles primarily as spiritual leaders at the service of people who recognize the spiritual

commitment of marriages. They have solem-
nized vows within the context of faiths that
expand beyond the traditional scheme of
Christianity to include members of the
Muslim, Zen, Taoist, Eastern Indian, and
Jewish faiths, among others. Having membership in a particular religion is less important
than having a spiritual kinship with an officiant. As Reverend Dittler says: "A marriage is
the wedding of two individuals who surrender
to learn to accept each other just as the other
is, in love and compassion." According to
Reverend Toor, "A tip in selecting the person

who is going to officiate at your wedding is to select someone you feel a kinship with, someone who has a spirituality you respect. After all, while the wedding ceremony doesn't have to be of a particular religious persuasion, it should
reflect the spiritual bond that the bride and groom feel with each other."

While many Protestant denominations do not, the Roman Catholic,
Lutheran, and Episcopal Church consider matrimony a sacrament. Jewish
wedding ceremonies are derived from Judaic law and culture. If you are
having a religious ceremony, understand that there are going to be rites and
rituals you will need to perform. Furthermore, the site may have specific restrictions regarding music, photography/videography, readings, and flowers/
decoration. You may need to explain to the officiant not only why you want
to get married at a particular religious site but also how you plan to conform your life and family to meet the expectations of that religion. That's
really not as serious or frightening as it sounds!

Most religions or religious officiants require some sort of premarital
counseling. Take advantage of it. You are not going to be whipped into shape;

rather, you more than likely will learn some important communication skills. Expect to meet with your officiant three or four times. In the officiant you will probably meet the one person you are interviewing who is most concerned about your marriage and not your wedding.

People today seem more willing to seek out some religious affiliation and structure, or at least some semblance of spirituality, in their lives. Though the celebration of weddings changes from generation to generation, it is always seen as a serious commitment to enter into, and couples do not take it lightly. The idea of "the two becoming one"; the analogy of the couple, as members of the church, being the bride of Christ; the custom of getting married under the chuppah (symbolic of the nomadic lives that Jewish people have lived and also the safe haven under which the family gathers) all signify the sacredness of the institution of marriage.

 The goal of these sessions, besides enhancing communication skills, is to pinpoint potential problems and emphasize the need to use counseling as a lifelong tool.

—THE REVEREND ED HOLT, A WEDDING MINISTRY (SAN CARLOS, CALIFORNIA)

In ancient times, *wed* meant the property the groom used to purchase the bride; in time, the word came to signify the dowry the father's family was to provide the groom. The only one who seemed an inactive participant in this process was the bride. Isn't it interesting that today it is the bride who is the primary and sometimes only active participant in organizing and managing the wedding? Demonstrating further evolution of society's recognition of this celebration marking two people's union, we find commitment ceremonies, though they are still limited in their occurrence. Gay and lesbian participation in ritualized and celebrated commitment ceremonies (which are not imitations of heterosexual marriage ceremonies) attest to the desire for order and structure. The wedding is a private commitment a couple is sharing with relatives and friends. The couple is saying: "We are taking on a different role in society. We are committing ourselves to each other for life, and we want you to know that. We are now a couple." The latest generations of weddings are once again increasingly set in religious settings as people seek to affirm the spiritual nature of their commitments.

TIPS FOR THE CEREMONY ❧

- Officiants are legally responsible for mailing the marriage license, so once the ceremony is concluded and you have signed the appropriate document with any required witnesses, you do not have to worry about it.

- If it's a Jewish ceremony, sign the marriage license and/or ketubbah before the ceremony.

- There are many interfaith ministers who will officiate at a ceremony in a variety of settings.

On-Site Wedding Coordinators or Consultants

Most synagogues, churches, temples, and other houses of worship have a person who is the "keeper of the gate." They may call themselves wedding or bridal coordinators, banquet managers, catering directors, or even wedding consultants. Don't be confused by the title; just make certain you understand what exactly it is that this person does (review chapter 3). Make friends with him; he is the one who knows the site's rules, regulations, and restrictions. He will inform you if and how the officiant wants the rehearsal and ceremony conducted. He may even be present to conduct the rehearsal or to get you down the aisle on your wedding day. He will let you know about the music, readings, and other aspects affecting the liturgy or service that are permitted.

If you find that dealing with this "gatekeeper" is difficult, that he doesn't have the most pleasant personality, don't worry. Have your finance minister (the person writing the checks has a certain power) or your wedding consultant deal with him. Typically, he does have a difficult position. Sometimes, the site is like another home for him, and he has seen what goes on when people don't respect the site enough to take care of it. If you wish to bend the rules, ask your officiant—he has the real authority.

The Nonreligious Ceremonial Site

The same guidelines listed above apply to seeking a nonreligious venue. The availability of secular sites, with a wide range of costs, is greater, however. Again, some places to do your research are the local convention and visitors bureau or chamber of commerce, wedding consultants, wedding fairs and trade shows, and wedding supplements in your local newspapers (these are usually published in January and in May, June, or July). Plus, books are being published that not only list sites but also give detailed descriptions of the facility, information on the number of people it can accommodate, and restrictions regarding music or time (for example, *The San Francisco Wedding Guide* or *The Wedding Pages*). The best places to find such books are local bookstores, jewelry stores, or bridal fairs/trade shows.

The Reception Site

Consider having the ceremony and reception at the same site. This is the best of all possible worlds in terms of comfort and convenience. As with secular sites for the ceremony, the availability of secular sites for receptions is not only larger but much more varied and exciting. You can have both your ceremony and reception on a yacht, in a garden or park or on a beach (though you may need to get a permit), a hotel ballroom or suite, a school gym, Masonic or Elks lodge (if you don't mind dead animals staring down at you as you eat), Knights of Columbus hall, or even an aquarium (we once served sushi at the San Francisco Aquarium). The possibilities are limitless. What's more, such sites may have "packages" that include a photographer/videographer, flowers, music, and an officiant, not to mention an abundance of interesting props.

Be aware that reception sites have a "preferred" or even "required" vendors list you must select from. While it is true that some sites require a kickback or commission from the vendors on their lists, more often than not these lists include professionals who not only have credentials but also experience working in that facility. If you have a favorite vendor who is a professional, has the appropriate licenses, along with insurance and health permits, the site manager usually will allow that company to provide their services at your wedding.

- Do you have a preferred/required vendors list? What are the criteria for these vendors to be on your list? Will you allow the services of a vendor not on your list?

- What are your restrictions regarding photography/videography, music, and decoration?

- Exactly how long will we have the site booked, and does this include time for the vendors to set up and break down? If not, what charges or arrangements are required?

- Will we be able to meet the site manager who is to be on duty at the wedding, and how do we know that that person will be familiar with all the details of my wedding? Will the same person be on duty from beginning to end?

- Will we be informed in advance of any changes at the site (for example, construction, remodeling, change in important personnel)?

- If the site is a hotel, does it offer a complimentary bridal suite and complimentary parking for your guests?

- If there is a changeover in the ceremony/reception room, are additional charges incurred?

- Does the site have tables, chairs, linen, china, flatware, props (arches, platforms, dance floor, lighting, votives, etc.) available for use? Is there an extra charge? May I see what they look like?

- If any part of the wedding ceremony or reception is to be held outside, are there alternative plans in case of inclement weather?

- Are handicapped facilities available?

- What are the emergency procedures?

- Do you have a floor plan drawn to scale?

- Is the site available for the rehearsal, and will a site manager be present to conduct or oversee the rehearsal? Is there an extra charge for rehearsal time?

- Can you provide a map showing how to get to the site from nearby major roads?

- Do you have private facilities to be used as dressing rooms?

- Find out if any major events or celebrations will be held near the site of your wedding on your wedding date.

- Most places prohibit rice and birdseed (a person could slip and fall, and rice is not environmentally correct); some places may not allow flower petals.

- Hotels or restaurants may charge a "turnover/turnaround fee" if the same room is used for the reception. Otherwise, a room rental fee may be charged.

Your Contracts with the Sites

All site contracts should spell out in detail what they encompass. If something happens and another event is booked, will the site manager assist you in finding another site and even pay for any necessary mailings to alert your guests? If any civic or other public events are to be held nearby, will precautions be made so your guests enter and depart the site safely and easily? If the site receives commissions from its referred vendors, you should know this. Handicapped facilities should be noted and described in detail.

Here are some other points to look for in your site contract.

- The exact date and time that you have booked the facility (this should include the hours for setup and breakdown).
- The insurance required and the party responsible for taking out the policy.
- Any and all restrictions clearly delineated.
- Payment and refund policies as well as security deposits clearly stated.
- Procedures in case someone becomes ill or there is a power failure or other major difficulty.
- The name of the person and other staff who will be working your wedding.

CHAPTER 7

When Dresses Become Gowns

❧ The Bridal Gown and Mothers' and Attendants' Dresses

WHAT WOMAN HAS NOT GROWN UP WITH CHILDHOOD DREAMS OF HER wedding day? Love is magical and special, and so are wedding days. And though you may have no clue regarding a specific style and shape of gown, you no doubt have a feeling of how you want to look on your wedding day. Let your imagination run rampant!

What other opportunity do you have to be so bold as to walk into a shop where prices of gowns range from a few hundred to several thousand dollars and say, "I want to find a gown that I feel good in, that flatters me. I want to try on different styles and fabrics until I find something that really is the most beautiful possible gown for me." While it's true that you may have a restricted budget, there is simply no reason you shouldn't try on some of those high-priced designer gowns. After all, you may find a style and cut that suits you perfectly. From there you can always back off and say,

"This is perfect! Do you have the same style in a fabric that is not so expensive?" While you should give the salon consultant some idea of what you are able to spend, your main goal is to see multiple styles and fabrics. Let the salon consultant be concerned about getting you to the point where you are able to work within your budget; after some experience, you will know the costs of gowns that you like and thus make an informed decision about what you are going to spend.

While we will talk about the mothers' and attendants' gowns later, let me give you an illustration of the attitude you should have. We were once shopping for a gown for the mother of the bride. When booking appointments at some upscale Dallas specialty stores and finding out the names of the salespersons I would be dealing with, I explained that we were looking for a lovely gown for the mother of the bride and gave a brief description of what we wanted to see. Also, I briefed the bride, her sister, and her mother that they were absolutely not to say anything about prices, costs, or a budget. Moreover, they were not to look at price tags!

We walked into the designer evening gown section of one store. I introduced myself and my clients to the saleswoman. I explained to her, "We're shopping for a gown for the mother of the bride. She thinks taupe, a champagne pink, and pale pastels look good on her, but they don't. As you can see, she is short, she's got big hips, and she's lean in the breast department. But she has a beautiful face, a wonderful neck, nice slender arms, and good shoulders. We'd like to see her in some things that will complement those areas, and bring out some bold colors. She can handle them." The salesperson slowed her pace, glanced at me with an expression of horror at my bluntness, turned to the mother, and in a loud whisper that was meant to be overheard, asked: "Is he your personal shopper? And you let him talk that way?" Not breaking her stride, the mother, Loretta, replied: "Well, he's right. What can I say? That's why I hired him." We spent the next two hours trying on some incredible Versaces, Diors, and Bob Mackies— gowns like you see in the movies. (San Francisco's nationally syndicated television show *Evening Magazine*, along with *The Wall Street Journal*, did dub me "the Cecil B. DeMille of weddings"!)

The salesperson brought out several gowns within the parameters of my request, and as I looked through her selections, I narrowed down the number to three or four that I wanted Loretta to try on. Loretta would then go into the dressing room, put on a gown, and come out feeling luscious (and she was). I would stand back, look at her to size up the full picture, turn her around, check out the gown from all sides, glance at her face, study her body, and either give the thumbs-up or the thumbs-down sign or point out features that were good about the gown to help the salesperson know if she was on target.

After repeating this performance two times at other fashionable couture evening wear salons, we were able to find exactly the fabric, cut, and color that Loretta liked. It was at our third stop; the saleswoman knew me well since I had brought many clients to her, and she had made some considerably good commissions from many of those sales. She also knew how I worked; that while some of my clients could not afford the gowns they were trying on, there were others who spent a lot of money and became lifelong customers for her and the store. She looked at me to get the nod as to which type of client this was. There was no need to look at the price tag; I knew it wasn't within my client's budget. I simply turned to the saleswoman and said, "This is exactly everything we want in an evening gown. But, it's *très cher* [expensive, for you non-French-speaking readers]. Can you possibly help us find something very similar but with not such large numbers on the price tag?" Her eyes sparkled, a smiled crossed her face, and she took Loretta by the hand and said, "Come with me, honey." She led us to a different department of the store and after disappearing for about thirty minutes, came out with three gowns that were similar in style to the Versace we had liked.

The primary difference in the couture gown and the three that she was now showing us was the fabric. The Versace had been a heavy satin; the gown that we selected was a polyester blend that actually draped Loretta's body better. Whereas the Versace had emphasized her large hips, this poly-

ester blend had more texture to the fabric and didn't cling to the body so much. We stayed for alterations; the salesperson wrote up the ticket. Loretta was ecstatic. The saleswoman was happy; she had made a sale for the day. Although it was certainly less than she'd hoped for, she knew she would make it up with another client I would bring in. In just one day, having gone to three stores and trying on less than a dozen gowns, we had found the perfect gown for this important participant in the wedding day, second only to the bride!

This story illustrates several important points. First is the teamwork that went into finding the right dress. When making and arriving at each appointment, proper introductions were made by phone and in person; the salesperson was informed about what we desired to see; the client tried on several dresses out of her price range, but in doing so found something she liked that looked good on her. The salesperson was knowledgeable enough to find a dress similar in design and color but less expensive. Together, we had worked as a team with a goal!

The second point is not to be intimidated by shopping for the perfect gown. Allow yourself to be creative in the way you shop. Find something you like in a style, fabric, and design; *then* worry about costs.

If you can't afford what you find, see if you can find a clone in another fabric or with some minor differences—that's the third point. When you go shopping, preferably take someone who knows fabric, design, colors, and styles and who can be objective and tell you truthfully how the gown looks on you and who knows, too, how to shop creatively.

Fourth, don't worry that you are not being completely honest with the salesperson by trying on gowns you know you can't afford. The price tags might surprise you. Designer gowns are not always unaffordable; you won't know until you shop. And if it's not affordable, the salesperson might be able to steer you to a gown in the same store that *is* within your budget, now that she knows what looks and feels good on you. Remember, your wedding day is once-in-a-lifetime, and you should look at it in that way. It may be the one and only chance you have to purchase a specialty gown. You will buy many dresses in your lifetime, but not very often will you invest in a gown. As I said in chapter 1, when it costs that much, it magically becomes a *gown*. Get used to the terminology; it will help you to remember you are shopping for a gown and not just a dress.

 There are no hard-and-fast rules about what a woman should wear to her wedding, whether she's marrying her sweetheart straight out of college, is tying the knot for the second time with a couple of toddlers in tow, or has found the love of her life well into her fifth decade.

—MILLIE MARTINI BRATTEN, EDITOR IN CHIEF OF BRIDE'S MAGAZINE

Researching the Gown of Your Dreams

Later in this chapter, we are going to give you some technical terminology that may or may not be necessary for you to remember. Most women have no idea what blouson, Basque waist, juliet, gauntlet, and leg-of-mutton are. Then there's Battenberg, Point d'Esprit, Schiffli, Brussels, Venise, Chantilly, and Alençon. These may sound like places where battles were fought (and certainly battles have been fought when selecting a wedding gown), but in truth these are geographical terms to describe where various laces were created. Don't memorize these terms; it will only confuse you. Besides, you will often find that salon consultants refer to one fabric by different names.

Put sketches, notes, and magazine pictures into your resource binder behind the tab labeled "Gowns." Afterward, go back to the gown salon where you felt comfortable and where you received intelligent and friendly service. Take those pictures with you. Show them to the salon consultant and see what she comes up with for you to try on.

Remember, a wedding is like a jigsaw puzzle: You have to get all the right pieces (vendors) to fit together before it can be completed. It's the same with your gown. You may find that you will like features of five different gowns while not liking the whole of any one gown you try on. That's where gown salon professionals come in. They know their products. They know what already exists and what can be done with alterations to create the perfect gown for you. In all likelihood, a gown designer (of which there are more than two hundred prominent ones: just look at any *Modern Bride* or *Bride's* magazine) has already put the same five features together and the gown is already hanging on a rack somewhere in the salon. Rely on your salesperson for her expertise.

The best place to start looking for a gown is in magazines. Bridal gown ads will not only give you a picture but also identify the designer or the line and, possibly on the same page, provide the names of stores where the gown can be purchased. Bridal magazines, even the major ones, are compiled for specific regions of the country. This means that the issue you buy off the magazine rack will advertise the industry in your area. The top bridal magazines are *Modern Bride, Bride's,* and *Bridal Guide*; their largest issues are on the stands between November and February (publishers and advertisers know that the greatest number of brides get engaged at Christmas, New Year's, and Valentine's Day). Since many brides start in October to plan their summer weddings, the September and October issues are fast becoming as thick as these other issues.

The biggest mistake brides make is treating these magazines like the Bible or some other sacred book. It is not uncommon to see a bride walking into a salon, magazine in hand, with literally dozens of "stickies" poking from the magazine's pages. Don't do this! Instead, go through the magazine; when you see a gown with a particular sleeve, neckline, bodice, or whatever other feature you like, tear out the page and circle that part of the gown. Get out your hole puncher, punch the page, and put it in your resource binder behind the tab labeled "Gowns." (Be sure to write down the name and date of the particular magazine.) All your preferences will then be in one place. If you subscribe to the belief that bridal magazines are sacred and you simply cannot imagine tearing out pages, then buy a duplicate of the magazine to put on your library shelf.

While you are going through the magazines finding "gown parts," do the same for veils, shoes, stockings or pantyhose, and other accessories. Add these pages to your resource binder.

Another good place to shop for gowns is bridal fairs or shows. These can be overwhelming in that they *are* trade shows; you are going to encounter all kinds of different wedding professionals (and some not so professional). There are smaller, "boutique" bridal shows (with less than a hundred vendors), and then there are huge extravaganzas (where you will encounter hundreds upon hundreds of vendors). We in the trade dub the huge fairs "cattle calls"; these are spread out in a convention center or other type of arenalike building or tented parking lot. Not a few brides get the impression that they are the modern-day Christians thrown to the lions in the Coliseum!

Grooms aren't the most patient companions at a bridal fair. Some fairs take place in the summer, but most are held in January—even on Superbowl Sunday! It confounds me that no trade show producer has yet come up with the idea of installing a big-screen television at one end of the room, so the men can lie around in comfortable chairs, while their honeys enter the lairs of the wedding vendors.

Be sure to wear comfortable shoes and clothing, ladies! Try to get a friend to go with you so you don't feel alone and adrift in this unknown world. Do plan to spend the day; call in advance to inquire when the fashion shows will be held.

While we do not suggest you go to a bridal fair to seek out *all* of your vendors, it is a good place to find a number of them. In this chapter, we are concerned with wedding gowns, attendants' dresses, and other attire. Nearly all bridal shows have a bridal fashion show. Sometimes this is done formally on a stage and runway, other times more casually, with the models walking through the crowds. Take a notepad and listen to the person describing the gowns. Write down the things that you like about a particular gown, just as if you were looking through a magazine. Often the models will carry numbers, and a list of gowns shown will be provided in a handout. Pay attention to the store or salon that is putting on the show so that you can do your follow-up.

In larger cities, department stores often put on bridal shows. These are usually more enjoyable in that the show is smaller and limited in the number of vendors present. Often it will take place in the bridal registry, stationery, china, crystal, flatware, and gown departments of the store. Emphasis is on the gowns the store offers.

Now for a wake-up call as to the potential cost of your gown. Remember, you're not buying a dress but a *gown*. Authors Cele Goldsmith Lalli and Stephanie H. Dahl (*Modern Bride Complete Wedding Planner*) say that the average cost of gowns, accessories, shoes, and veil ranges between $780 and $1,000. In today's economy, that is increased to between $900 and $1,400. Surprisingly, the purchase of your gown, even including alterations and accessories, is not that costly of a venture, considering the cost of other aspects of the wedding (factor in about 7 to 15 percent of your budget). Be truthful to yourself as to what you can afford. It may take some time making the rounds of salons to determine how much the gown you want actually does cost.

GOWN STYLES ≫

A-line: fitted bodice that flares wider to the hem.

Ballroom: full skirt, off-the-shoulder, natural waist (think Cinderella); great for the full-figured bride.

Basque waist: waistline begins below the waist, forming a curved U or V shape; slenderizing; flatters the bride with wide hips.

Empire: cropped bodice, high waist, slightly flared skirt; large-busted brides should avoid this style, along with clingy fabrics and heavily decorated bodices.

Miniskirt: hem falls above the knees.

Princess: slim-fitting bodice with emphasis on the waist.

Sheath: no waist; fabric continues down the body from the shoulders for a close-fitting look.

COLLARS AND SHOULDERS ❧

Band: very traditional; a beaded band and fabric create a collar band at the base of the neck; can be open in the front; gives the bride with a short torso a great look.

Boat: fabric flows with the collarbone, from shoulder to shoulder in front and back.

Jewel: circles the base of the neck, dropping gradually at the base of the throat.

Keyhole: open teardrop shape in front.

Portrait: fabric forms from the back and comes around to the front, above the bust, framing the shoulders; terrific for the bride with beautiful shoulders and arms.

Queen Anne: high at the back of neck, flows in front in a way that bares the upper chest.

Queen Elizabeth: high collar at the back of the neck; bodice has a V shape.

Sweetheart: the bodice comes into a point over and between the breasts and curves to create a heart shape on the bodice and front of the gown.

V neck: comes to a point in front.

GOWN SLEEVES ❧

Ballroom: full, billowy, and ending at the elbow.

Gauntlet: covers forearm and wrist; detachable.

Juliet: long poufed top, fitted around the arm and wrist (think Romeo's Juliet).

Leg-of-mutton: full and rounded from shoulders to elbow, then tapered from elbow to wrist; think sheep's leg.

Pouf: short full sleeve, gathered at the shoulder; may be worn off the shoulder.

Lace is an appliqué, that is, it's sewn onto or into the fabric (think cutouts or clip art).

Alençon: French; designs needlepointed on sheer net fabric.

Battenberg: wide, open, loopy designs; made with coarse threads.

Chantilly: French; hexagonal mesh ground with scroll or floral pattern; delicate.

Point d'Esprit: patterns of dots woven into fine net fabric.

Schiffli: delicate embroidery designs sewn or woven directly into fabric.

Venise/Venice: raised embroidered lace; three-dimensional motif; thick cording.

Shopping for Your Gown

Ready to go look for that must-have gown? Get out your resource binder and find where you have the date, time, and place of your ceremony and reception written down. It is very important that you communicate this information to your gown salon consultant so that she can advise you on any customs and proper etiquette. She will also want to be familiar with the climate where the ceremony and reception will take place. For instance, the humidity of Houston is going to affect the comfort level of some fabrics, while outdoor weddings in June in San Francisco will usually require a heavier fabric.

Now gather your drawings and notes taken at bridal fashion shows and your list of questions, and let's go shopping. Granted, you are going to be a little nervous; it's an important decision. But don't worry. A good salesperson is going to be able to educate you about terminology and to answer your questions.

The most commonly mislabeled fabrics are satin and raw silk. The word *satin* does not indicate the fiber content, merely the finish of the fabric, which is flat and shiny. A shop may call it "Italian satin," "bridal satin," or "silk satin"; the newest I've heard is "cloud satin" to indicate the soft-to-the-touch feel of it. Always be sure to distinguish whether it is silk or polyester; bottom line is that fine silk can cost a whole lot more than polyester. But an inexpensive silk can be comparable in cost to a very refined polyester.

—LILY DONG, LILY DONG COUTURE BRIDAL (CUPERTINO, CALIFORNIA)

Although appointments are advised, don't be surprised if salons don't require this, especially if you are just browsing. Call ahead and check. As with all of your vendors, the most important thing to pay attention to from the onset is how you are greeted by the salesperson. If she isn't being attentive or isn't able to answer your questions, ask for someone else or go to a different salon. You're paying not only for quality; you're paying for service with a capital *S*. Successful salons are dependent on word of mouth for their business and have staff that are known for their patience and listening skills.

Don't be hesitant to look at gowns of all colors. Yes, you heard me correctly. "I've designed and made navy, chartreuse, deep-red, peach, and silver wedding gowns, and countless others which included a lesser proportion of colors for embellishment," says Lily Dong, owner of Lily Dong Couture Bridal (Cupertino, California). In the 1990s, pastels and soft colors have taken their rightful places on the racks alongside white gowns, made traditional only after Queen Victoria wore white at her wedding. Interestingly, more "marrying again" brides are wearing white than first-time brides.

While few, if any, salons are going to let you take pictures in different gowns unless you have placed an order, most won't have any difficulty with you taking notes while you are in the salon. Afterward, go for coffee or tea with your mom, groom, or accompanying friend. Sit down and review your notes about what you liked and disliked while the experience is fresh in your memory.

Don't schedule a trip to more than one gown salon per day. It's a wearing task, so to speak, to crawl in and out of those cumbersome gowns. You need to be fresh and relaxed for each visit. If you feel that you have already found the perfect gown in a magazine ad, let the salesperson know when you call to make inquiries. Make certain the salon carries the particular line and has the specific gown in stock. Don't make needless trips.

I advise brides to shop around: Go to salons and try on gowns, paying attention to different parts of the gown that you like and that look good on you. For instance, if you like the shape of a sleeve, ask the salesperson what it's called, or later draw it out in a sketch; find a picture in a bridal magazine that shows that same sleeve. Tear out the page and circle that part of the gown. Do the same with other gowns that you try on. If you see a bodice that you like and it feels good on you, then find a picture of a gown in a magazine that shows that bodice, even if the rest of the dress is different; tear out the page and circle that bodice. Do this until you have all the parts of your gown!

—DENICE D'ANDREA, GOWN EXPERT (LAS VEGAS, NEVADA)

In the beginning, you may find you are simply gathering information about the products and serviceability of the salon. Eventually, you may be so bold as to ask to meet the seamstress on an initial visit! With time you will gather more knowledge about the styles, colors, and fabrics (as well as prices) that flatter you most. A good salon consultant will make the effort to educate you about fabrics, laces, and styles. Be wary of the salon salesperson who gushes, telling you that you look great in every gown that you try on.

QUESTIONS FOR THE GOWN SALON CONSULTANT ✍

- Do you carry the designer gowns that I am interested in? Or, whose gowns do you offer?

- What are your price ranges?

- How are payments to be made?

- Do you work on a commission? If so, what does this commission include (accessories, alterations, undergarments, etc.)?

- What is your refund policy?

- How long will it take for the gown to be in? Can I get a written guarantee that the gown will arrive when you say it will?

- How long will alterations take? Will the dress be ready for my wedding/bridal portrait, that is, four to six weeks before the wedding?

- Can I meet your seamstress before I order my gown?

- What services (steaming, ironing, delivery, repair work) do you offer?

- Do you have a staff member who can be at my wedding to help me put on the gown and handle any possible snags? What are the costs for such a service?

- What is the fabric of my gown? What are the cleaning instructions? What should I do immediately if there are spills or stains?

- Pay attention to bridal supplements in your local newspaper. These usually come out in January and in May, June, or July and will have ads about bridal fashion shows in your area.

- Call a wedding consultant to find out when and where bridal fashion shows are in your area.

- While at the gown salon, if your mother has an opinion that is contrary to yours and there is no hope for compromise, let your salon consultant know. She has dealt with many a mother who wants to "have her own wedding" for her daughter. She will often know how to smooth over any difficulties.

- Take a couple of your attendants along at one of your last fittings so they can be taught how to bustle your gown and remove your veil properly. Don't count on your wedding consultant for this. It can be a laborious task, and your wedding consultant's time can be more effectively spent overseeing the setup of the reception or dealing with last-minute emergencies.

- Ask specifically if the beadwork comes off and what to do about it. We once had a bride whose very expensive designer gown began to shed its beads in long, continuous strands. The bride's mother screamed in horror. I grabbed my emergency kit, pulled out the superglue, and simply dabbed the spots to stop the flow of beads onto the floor. The mother was aghast, but it did the work and the beads remained intact. I suggested to the mother that she talk to the gown salon on Monday. When you pay that much for a gown, such a disaster shouldn't happen. Recognize that unless you are paying a fortune for a gown, beads are not going to be sewn on individually. A long-standing tradition on the East Coast and in the South is for the bride to sew the beadwork onto the bodice of her gown; however, you do want to know what to do if such a situation arises.

- Pay attention to which of your features you want to accentuate and which you do not. When you try on gowns, pay attention to the bustle. Have it bustled so that you can determine if you can sit in it comfortably.

- The length of the train is determined by the formality of the wedding, but you should see, too, what looks good on you given your height and weight.

- Talk to your seamstress about medications (inclusive of birth control pills) that you are taking, especially if you are experiencing swelling. Don't be embarrassed!

- After your last alteration, have the gown pressed before you pick it up. This can be scheduled as much as a month prior to the wedding.

Trans-shipping, or "We Can Get You Any Gown"

Federal law requires that all clothing be properly labeled with tags that include the name of the manufacturer or their "registered number," assigned by the Federal Trade Commission, along with fiber content and country of origin.

There's no need to be unduly suspicious if a salon says they can get a gown they don't normally carry. Gown salons are required to carry a minimal representation of a contracted designer's line. Salons pay a hefty price for exclusivity but in reality can't carry all designers' lines. Therefore, they often engage in cooperative purchasing. This means they can get a gown from a neighboring salon carrying that line. This is sometimes called trans-shipping.

Denise and Alan Fields, authors of *Bridal Bargains: Secrets to Throwing a Fantastic Wedding on a Realistic Budget*, state that trans-shipping is not illegal per se. Just be wary if a salon says they can get *any* gown in. Ordering directly from just any manufacturer isn't possible—a salon must carry that designer's line to begin with.

Some brides shop for gowns similar to the way they shop for florists or caterers. They go to full-service retail salons and take up hours of the gown consultant's time trying on gowns, then order the gown from a mail order service or from a discount bridal service. This method of purchase is unfair because of the high overhead that retailers must maintain and because the salon must commit to buying and stocking the samples for service. If a bride doesn't want to pay the going salon rate, she shouldn't take advantage of salon services.

Veils

While it is not necessary to have an elaborate head dressing, you do want to have some kind of headpiece that ties in with and complements your gown, even if it is simply an elegant comb with some bugle beads, small feathers, or fabric. After all, this is dress-up time!

A nice and simple touch is to have the creator of your headpiece attach the blusher (that veil that hangs over your face, worrying you that it is mussing your makeup) under the actual headpiece so the headpiece can be seen. We see so many brides with the blusher draped over the headpiece as well as the face, dampening the elegance and luster of the headpiece and thus its effect.

More often than not, the bride may have two veils, either incorporated into each other or entirely separate. Just before the reception, either the longer of the two incorporated veils or the entire veil is removed, and a shorter veil draping down the back is substituted so as not to get into the way of your walking and dancing. It is strongly advised not to continue wearing a long veil after all your important photographs have been taken; it will simply get in your way and is too burdensome to be draped over your arm.

STYLES OF VEILS ❧

Garden hat: an open crowned hat, sometimes decorated with flowers.

Headband: a strip of fabric that hugs the top of the head.

Juliet cap: a bridal cap that covers the crown of the head.

Mantilla: a lace or netting fabric that drapes over the head, often down to the shoulders or longer; sometimes covers the face, but not always.

Picture hat: a glamorous broad-brimmed hat.

Pill box: a small, flat hat that sits high or slanted to one side on the head (think Jacqueline Kennedy).

Wreath: a crown or circle of flowers, beading, and/or fabric that rests on top of the head.

VEIL LENGTHS ❧

Ballet (or Waltz): below the knee.

Blusher: covers the face and may fall to the waist.

Cathedral: fabric drapes 9 to 12 feet.

Chapel: extends beyond gown up to 2 feet.

Fingertip: falls to the tips of the fingers.

Royal: falls 2 yards along the floor.

Sweep: barely brushes the floor.

Being Measured for Your Gown

Contrary to general thinking, you are not getting a custom gown; rather, you are special ordering a gown. Lalli and Dahl compare this process to "making a costume."

Once you have selected your gown, get ready to have that figure measured, shoes and undergarments in hand! Many salons will rent an appropriate slip when you pick up your gown. Having the correct slip is of major importance, since the overall look is going to be affected; the gown may "crawl" through your legs when you walk, or sunlight can show through. Before you rush out to buy that sexy lingerie, consult your gown salesperson. Usually bra cups are sewn into the gown. If the gown is "clean," that is, sans lace, you don't want to wear laced and detailed bras or undergarments, as they will show through. Stockings can be pantyhose or thigh-highs. Undergarments in nude or beige may be advised, as white may intensify the whiteness or starkness of a gown, says our gown expert, Denice D'Andrea of Las Vegas, Nevada.

 If you simply must be a size 2, get a size 2 label and sew it into your gown. Though there is no logic to it, wedding gowns are cut in sizing charts different than ready-to-wear. Your adept salon consultant knows that gowns are notoriously cut on the small size, although some manufacturers are cutting truer to ready-to-wear today.

—DENICE D'ANDREA, GOWN EXPERT (LAS VEGAS, NEVADA)

The bust, waist, and hips are the measure points. The gown will be ordered for the fullest part of your body. Additionally, especially for tall women, it's important to be measured from the "hollow," or base of the neck, to the floor. Don't be offended that you're not going to be the same size you normally wear. Salons may only carry up to a certain size. For instance, Demetrios gowns stop at size 20, so the salon would have to order additional fabric for larger sizes—it's important that the salon consultant explains this to you up front. Also, it is better to have more fabric than needed and be able to cut back. It's not possible to water the gown and make it grow! "Any fabric removed during alterations should be given to the bride. Even if it is only a 1-inch square," advises Christine Morrissey of National Gown Cleaners & Archival Products (San Jose, California).

 If anybody knows, besides your doctor, your seamstress will if you are pregnant, because of body changes, however subtle. So be up front with your salon consultant about any changes that may affect the final fit of your gown.

—DENICE D'ANDREA, GOWN EXPERT (LAS VEGAS, NEVADA)

We once had a client who called and tearfully complained that she had gained weight (indeed, she was pregnant). "I can't fit into my gown! What are we going to do?" she wailed over the phone line. I laughed and replied, "Don't worry. We'll go to Tents for Events and find something for you to wear." The bride wasn't pleased. However, she was relieved by the salon's reassurance that the seamstress would be able to add fabric—but don't count on this.

Petite Sizes

Petite sizes do not indicate the size of your body but rather the length of the body from the neck to the floor. This is generally measured from the neck to the waist as well as from the base of the neck to the floor. It is two separate measurements. Either one will determine if the bride is a petite size.

Be prepared for the style of the gown to affect the sizing. Some bodies don't fit into some styles. For instance, big hips won't necessarily fit into a sheath. Again, pay attention to what flatters you.

Special Concerns

When deciding on the style of your gown, consideration should be given to potentially awkward moments. Remember, on the day of your wedding, you are not merely walking down the aisle and standing around in your wedding gown. You are going to be crawling into a limousine or horse-drawn carriage, kneeling, bending, going up and down stairs, dining, and dancing. You may be lifted high in a chair while hanging on to a cloth napkin or handkerchief with your groom, who is also being held aloft as guests twirl and dance you around in a sometimes dizzying spin. As crazy as it sounds, I recommend when trying on gowns that you do some hugging and turning and swinging your arms around; after all, you're going to be doing all kinds of body movements at your wedding. Think about kneeling in your gown if this is going to be required at your ceremony. The weight of the gown is another factor to take into consideration. Remember, you are going to be standing for hours on your wedding day. If you don't have the body strength for a heavily beaded and layered gown, consider something simpler.

Once you have seen and tried on enough gowns and narrowed your choices, be sure to enter their prices into the realistic costs column of your overall wedding day budget spreadsheet.

Placing Your Order

You should order your gown at least four months before the wedding, though six to eight months is a better lead time. In some situations, "rush" service may be a lifesaver, but if possible, avoid this as it cannot be guaranteed. If you are going to have a formal bridal or wedding portrait to be displayed at the reception, the gown should be ready and completely altered anywhere from six to eight weeks before the wedding. Consult your wedding photographer.

When you place your order, that is the time to get your first picture of you in your gown. Take several full-body shots, along with close-ups of sections and detail work. These pictures are important for you to verify the style when your gown arrives, but they are also important for the florist designing your bouquet. You may even consider ordering some extra fabric, the same as your gown and/or your veil, to be used in your bouquet.

Some final changes can be made when ordering the gown, such as trains being lengthened (this depends on the manufacturer) or laces added or omitted. Communicate any desired changes so they can be specified on the original order and you can be advised of any additional charges involved. It's almost impossible to make any changes once the order is in process. The good news: Usually there is no charge for normal shipping.

At some point, check in with the gown salon to make sure the order has been placed properly. Sales staff are professionals, but mistakes do happen. Write down the date, time, and who gave you this assurance, if for no other reason than to relieve any stress you may be feeling.

When the gown comes in, check its tags. Compare the information with your order form and the notes you took while shopping. You should also use the photographs you took of the gown when you had your first fitting. Compare the sections with the close-up pictures and the overall pictures. Make sure they match. It should really be the actual gown you ordered. All you have to do is look at the tags and compare the photos.

—DENICE D'ANDREA, GOWN EXPERT (LAS VEGAS, NEVADA)

Your Gown Salon Contract

Your contract is, as always, an important document. A nonrefundable minimum 50 percent deposit will be required, the balance due when the gown arrives. Sales tax will be applicable. Any additional charges by the manufacturer should be made known to the salon consultant and to you in advance. This information should be on your document. Your salon might be willing to commit to a "guesstimate" on these additional charges, but don't expect this, since your weight and proportions might change by the time the gown comes in. Also listed in the contract should be

- the size ordered, color, name of the manufacturer, and style number
- any customized or special services or requests
- the estimated delivery date and any special order requests
- the refund policy

Have the salon consultant give you a receipt of "confirmation of order." Keep a copy of this receipt in your wedding day binder, and give the original to your finance minister. Go to your overall wedding day budget and put the actual cost of the gown and accessories into the proper column.

Alterations

Remember, this is not a custom gown you have ordered. It's a "costume" being created for you. If a seamstress is to take in one part, she more than likely will have to alter another proportionally. Since nearly all gowns are lined, several layers are going to be affected and need adjusting. Beadwork and appliqués may need to be adjusted.

As stated earlier, think about body movement when you have your first fitting. You are going to be dancing, throwing a bouquet, and entering and exiting a limousine. Try kneeling, bowing, and any other positions that can be awkward in a cumbersome gown. You may want to take a clean bedsheet to your fitting so that you can try out these different positions (spread the sheet on the floor to keep your gown from getting dirty). The seamstress isn't going to think you are having visions as you kneel on the sheet, while you will feel more confident that you are going to be fitted properly for your wedding day.

Alterations will be scheduled starting at least a month before the wedding. Plan to have three to four sessions, and get some rest before each; the early sessions can take up to several hours. If you are dieting, this is the time to level off. Additional alterations are not only costly but also can compromise the integrity of fabrics. Alteration costs, by the way, are usually not included in the cost of the gown.

Though the cost of alterations is relative to the geographical region, you are always paying for the expertise of the seamstress. The professional seamstress will be able to give you an approximation of costs for known alterations (for example, sleeve length, hemline, length of gown train and veil). The fee is usually determined by the task rather than by the hour.

When the gown is completely altered and you've had your final fitting, schedule the pickup date. Before you leave the store, look at the gown and make certain that everything is as it should be. Pay attention to details.

The day before your wedding, if you are unable to hang your gown properly, the gown should be pressed. Be careful where you hang the gown if you are dressing in a hotel or other public room. We once read of a bride who hung her gown onto the hotel's safety fire sprinkler head, triggering the entire sprinkler system! Not all sites or places are going to have the

ACCESSORIES ❧

- Crinoline underskirt or slip
- Bra and other undergarments
- Shoes
- Jewelry
- Gloves
- Stockings/pantyhose/knee-highs

sort of height needed for a long gown. It is better then to simply hang it off the back of a door and drape the remaining fabric onto the floor. A simple sheet on the floor will protect the garment against dust and dirt—after all, you don't want to walk down the aisle with fuzz balls attached to your elegant lace! If you are worried about wrinkling, you can stuff some white fabric or lots of tissue into the gown.

Custom Designed and Made

Do you have nerves of steel? Can you stand the stress of being held hostage on the morning of your wedding while the hemline of your gown is still being sewn? Can you bear for your diet in the months of planning to be nails and water? If not, then think twice before even considering having a gown designed and made for you. And don't even think about reproducing a design you saw in a magazine.

In all of my twenty years in the business, I have found that most independent or freelance gown designers create more havoc than anything else. I've seen a bride dancing with her breasts more out of the gown than in simply because some designer didn't have the professionalism to tell the woman that the style she selected was not a good idea for her body. I've even had one "designer" just about follow a bride in the processional ceremony, still sewing the hemline of her gown. Don't think these are not true stories. I might add that these brides had contracted a gown designer *before* they came to us for our services.

My experience with most custom, one-of-a-kind gown designers is that they are dreamers. Not only are they incompetent at designing, creating, constructing, and *delivering on time*, but they are not even capable dressmakers. That's not to say that competent and even talented designers and makers of original wedding gowns do not exist. They do—but they are rare. Even in large cities such as San Francisco, there was no gown designer for years I could or would refer my clients to until Lily Dong, owner of Lily Dong Couture Bridal, started her gown design company, in Cupertino, California.

 The designer must be creative both visually and technically, especially in cases where the idea is new; she must be a problem solver.

—LILY DONG, LILY DONG COUTURE BRIDAL (CUPERTINO, CALIFORNIA)

A key factor to keep in mind if you are one of the bold brides who do elect to have a gown designed for them is to give yourself (and your designer) plenty of time. The more complicated the design and construction, the more time will be needed. Figure that you will need anywhere from a minimum of three to six months to have the finished product. Recognize, too, that as the gown is under construction, there will possibly be changes that you desire or that the designer will suggest. Pay attention to what your designer tells you; after all, she's the expert and can give you an objective opinion on how the gown looks on you. All good designers are able to make reasonable changes while the gown is still being made—"provided that the changes are an enhancement and do not dilute the original design idea," adds Dong.

Be aware that there is a distinction between dressmakers and custom dressmakers. Hire a dressmaker to make a beautiful outfit for your flower girl, but don't entrust her to your wedding gown. Dressmakers often make a garment from a commercial pattern bought at a fabric store; they will likely not know how to custom fit it or to make any change to the design. A professional designer, however, should be able to execute the design and create the gown merely from a picture she creates in her mind.

GOWN FABRICS ✒

Bridal satin: very lightweight; the intensity of the shine creates a silvery effect; generally polysatin is selected.

Brocade: heavy, with interwoven, raised designs.

Chiffon: free-flowing, with a lot of movement; cannot be put over crinoline without a proper slip or lining.

Chintz: slightly glazed, finished cotton.

Crinoline: stiff, open-weave fabric; used to give more body as underskirting.

Embroidery: weaving or sewing done directly on the fabric.

Linen: made from flax (think high maintenance when it comes to ironing).

Matte satin: silk-faced; heavier weight than either silk or bridal satin.

Moiré: silk taffeta with a wavy pattern.

Organza: sheer like chiffon but it has more body and doesn't drape as well.

Shantung: textured, plain-weave silk or man-made fibers.

Silk: a fine, textured fabric; raw silk is very textured, with slubs.

Taffeta: crisp, shiny fabric with a crosswise rib (think traditional attendant's dress).

Tulle: stiff, like crinoline; French tulle, on the other hand, is very soft.

Blusher: the veil that comes over your face, usually made of tulle; may be required by some religious or ethnic groups.

Bustle: a difficult piece of fabric that needs to be gathered at the back; supposedly gives the wearer a more feminine look.

Train: fabric that may hang from your shoulders (Watteau) or as a continuation of the back hem from the waist.

Cathedral train: 3 yards long, measured from the waist.

Chapel train: 1⅓ yards long, measured from the waist.

Brush train: barely touches the floor as it flows behind the gown.

Short-Term Care of Your Gown

You have looked at hundreds of gowns; you're exhausted from trying them on. It seems that your world has become a nightmare of tulle and organza. Don't worry! You have made the decision that will guarantee that you will be the most beautiful bride possible on your wedding day.

Now that you are ordering your gown (don't forget to get those swatches of fabric and lace), ask your salesperson how it should be cared for. Find out its fabric content. Ask especially about the immediate cleaning of makeup, wine, and food stains.

Once I walked into the "cry room" of the church where the bride and her "ladies-in-waiting" were dressing. A sister of the bride was standing off in the distance, sobbing. Another sister was standing over a distraught and weeping bride, patting her on the back, saying, "It'll be all right, Becky. No one will ever know." I remarked, "Ladies, I know this is a cry room, but aren't we overdoing it?" The bride looked up at me, and as she unfolded the lap of her wedding gown, she pleaded, "Don't tell Momma." There were dabs of a burnt-red shade of lipstick down the front of the gown. My training kicked in. I ran out to my car (I call it my "Bridemobile"), grabbed my emergency kit, and returned to the cry room. I took out a bottle of club soda and a clean white rag and began dabbing at the gown. Sure enough, most of the lipstick was absorbed away from the gown and onto the rag. We got a hair dryer, put it on cool, and blew the gown dry. The bride by this point was feeling a little giddy. I then dusted the gown with body powder (I make it a point in my kit to have some talc that is as close as possible to the color of most gowns). Afterward, one could hardly see the stain. Moral of the story: If it's possible to care for stains immediately, do so. Club soda is usually a good stain-buster.

 All of our artists have makeup hoods that can be worn if the bride *must* pull the dress over her head. If she is wearing a petticoat, we have a hint that works most often: The petticoat can usually stand on its own or with a little help; pull the dress onto the free-standing petticoat and step into both at the same time.

—JENNI TARVER, JENNI TARVER STUDIOS (DALLAS, TEXAS)

Gown Preservation

You've wedded your true and eternal love; you've partied with your family and closest of 300 friends; you've been toasted by the groom's best man, your parents, your grandparents, your maid of honor, your great uncle who came all the way from the old country; you've danced the night away. It's finally over! Not!!! You've got another obligation—to your gown. While we realize you aren't going to toss it into the closet or laundry hamper, we do want to emphasize the importance of having the gown professionally serviced as soon after the wedding day as possible.

Look for a cleaner who is an expert in caring for specialty, quality gowns. Just as you wouldn't take your cashmere sweater down the street to any dry cleaner, you certainly don't want to take your gown to someone who doesn't know how to properly care for and preserve it. Don't rely solely on the suggestion of your gown salon, and be wary of a salon that offers to have the gown cleaned for you. Not only may they be dealing with unreputable people, they also may not be properly insured to act as an agent for you; such a salon would need to have a bail policy.

Additionally, you will want to see a copy of the salon's, or even the gown cleaner's, insurance policy to know what is or is not covered regarding loss, damage, or failure in the preservation process. Ask for a copy of the policy and then take it to your family's legal adviser to have it checked. The policy should also cover loss in shipping or handling.

So, what's the difference between a dry cleaner and a specialty gown cleaner? Normal dry cleaners service "everyday" clothing. Gown cleaners and preservationists service only bridal, christening, communion, and social gowns. Regular cleaners use a solvent called perchloroethylene, which can be especially damaging to gowns with beads, sequins, and glued-on ornamentation. Professional gown cleaners use solvents and wet-cleaning methods unique to the process of caring for these specialty gowns. One such company is National Gown Cleaners, which has its own laboratory in San Jose, California. National Gown Cleaners uses conservation equipment found only in the best museums in the world. Not only will they "provide a phone consultation to answer your questions about technical matters, [they] will also arrange a no cost, no obligation, insured pickup of your gown from anywhere in the United States. International customers are charged the cost of shipping and insurance," assures National Gown Cleaners' Christine Morrissey. A red flag should go up in your mind if the cleaner asks for a release or disclaimer to be signed before services can be started. National Gown Cleaners is so convinced of their services that they only require such a release when it is a matter of restoration.

As soon as possible after the wedding day, the gown should be placed in a garment bag, preferably made of muslin—at the very least, a clean, freshly washed sheet. Your mother or a trusted relative or friend should take it to the selected gown cleaner and preservationist, and a thorough inspec-tion for food, beverage, dirt, grass, and other stains should be made. Pay special attention to the hemline of the gown. "Also, look for makeup stains not only on the outside, but also on the inside of the gown," says Morrissey. (Where was she at Becky's wedding?) Spot cleaning is done where stains are known to be, so it's important to point out any other stains to your cleaner.

After the gown is cleaned, it needs to be stored. The gown should be packed in an acid- and lignin-free paper box that is of archival quality. To prevent wrinkling, acid-free tissue is used between the folds of the gown and in the bodice. Avoid cleaners who use a box with a Mylar window; Mylar or other plastic will give off fumes or gases as it deteriorates.

Wearing white cotton gloves, you should take the gown out of the box every five to seven years, gently air it out and then refold it, using the same or new acid-free paper, and close up the box again. Store the box in a cool, dry place (under the bed seems to be the most recommended spot); it should be kept in a room that doesn't rise in temperature above 70 degrees.

Under no condition allow yourself to be talked into a vacuum-sealed box; the gown must be able to breathe. Vacuum sealing can trap moisture inside, causing mildew. A greater danger to fabric than air is light. Exposure to light is one of the culprits responsible for the yellowing process. If your gown is currently stored in this type of box (one with a plastic window), then take it out, refold it with acid-free tissue, and place it in another box. (Proper materials can be purchased from National Gown Cleaners for less than $150. The complete package includes an archival lignin-free box, a pair of cotton lab gloves, and archival buffered or unbuffered tissues.) Some cleaners such as National Gown Cleaners also provide indefinite storage facilities for their clients.

If you are going to wear a gown that has been handed down as an heirloom, then you will definitely want a professional trained in restoration to provide his services. Restoration technically means attempting to return the garment to its original appearance so it can be used. Modern fabric and materials might be utilized to replace damaged parts. Whatever your needs, seek out a professional long in advance of your wedding day.

 Generally, most cleaners are covered at only 50 percent of the cost of purchase or up to $500 of the value. This is not good for the consumer or agent if there is damage. Get a letter from the cleaners that says they are responsible for any results in cleaning and storage.

—CHRISTINE MORRISSEY, NATIONAL GOWN CLEANERS & ARCHIVAL PRODUCTS (SAN JOSE, CALIFORNIA)

Mothers' Dresses

Mothers, both of them, should wear dresses that are appropriate to the formality of the wedding day—and that flatter them. Both mothers should make this a special occasion to go out and purchase something that makes them look and feel elegant. It's not necessary that they "blend in with the flowers" or wedding decorations so as not to detract from the bride. An elegantly attired mother of the bride or groom can only complement the bride!

Tradition has it that the mother of the bride selects her dress before the mother of the groom chooses hers. Both dresses should be the same length. Mothers, do yourselves a favor and avoid peplums, or what we call in the trade "Dumbo dresses": the ones where that silly piece of fabric hangs from the waist like a microskirt. Dong notes that these ill-proportioned, off-the-rack dresses are made with the assumption that "one proportion fits all," meaning the length of the peplum is cut the same for a size 10 dress as it is for a size 20. The result is that the peplum for a size 10 is too long and for a size 20, too short. If you have large hips, a suit with a long jacket or a tunic over a skirt will drape better than a peplum. Also, fabric that is soft and flowing will drape over the hips more gracefully.

Have your mother be bold enough to consider *not* purchasing the usual pastel, plain-Jane dress found in bridal stores in the "Mother of the Bride" section. Most of them are poorly made and, trust me, your mother will never wear the dress again. Suggest that she go to a better department store or salon and specialty shop. If yours is a formal wedding, taking place in the evening, urge her to look for an evening gown that will bring her much pleasure not only when she wears it at your wedding but on future occasions as well.

As brides should be concerned about their menstrual cycle, mothers, and yes, even some brides, should be attentive to menopause. Let the gown salesperson know if you are having hot flashes and experiencing retention of water or swelling; she and your seamstress will give you excellent advice as to fabric and fitting. For instance, consider a three-piece suit so you can "cool off." Often a seamstress will not do a fitting during this time, preferring to wait a week or so.

—DENICE D'ANDREA, GOWN EXPERT (LAS VEGAS, NEVADA)

Attendants' Dresses

Attendants' dresses, no matter how expensive, can never be called gowns. They are usually very unflattering mis-creations of polyester or faux satin. Authors Denise and Alan Fields describe them as "throwaway gowns and disposable dresses." However, designers are beginning to offer more styles that actually can be worn again with little or no adjustments. You will have to look long and hard to find them, though.

More often than not, you are going to have problems when it comes to your attendants' dresses. Don't expect the dresses you see in magazines to look anything like the ones in shops. Magazine ads use slender models, whose makeup and hair have been done by professional makeup artists. The models are photographed in studios or at on-site locations with all sorts of props and technical equipment to give the best lighting. (This is true for wedding gown ads too.) Be ready for potential discontent from your attendants. Don't imagine that all your attendants are going to look good in one style, much less the same color. Here again, for some reason, manufacturers use sizing charts similar to those used for the bride, which means the sizes are out of proportion to ready-to-wear. So, if you think *you* are having a difficult time shopping for your attendants, you can imagine how they feel. Ginger Barry, in the article "Taking Measure of Your Maid's Business" (*Vows: The Bridal & Wedding Business Journal*), advises taking the largest attendant in for a fitting first—adding the caveat "make certain the salon has her size" when making the appointment.

Many attendants are young, new to the workforce, or still in school; they cannot afford to go out and buy an expensive dress, especially one that will probably be worn only once. Yet the average attendant's dress costs $130, with the added cost of about $30 for alterations. While matching dresses are the tradition, I feel that brides should be willing to try something new. If a bride and her attendants put some extra energy into shopping and don't simply settle for tradition, some interesting ensembles can be found. The beauty of this approach is that the attendants will likely be able to wear the dresses again.

By the way, who says you can't get a second wear out of attendants' dresses that aren't particularly desirable? They can be wonderful attire at Halloween or a costume ball. Dolores Enos, JWIC (Larkspur, California) relates the story of a bachelorette party during which her client invited the attendants to wear their ugliest ever bridesmaids' dresses. There was one stipulation: The dress could not be the one to be worn at *her* wedding!

Normal order time for attendants' dresses is two to four months before the wedding, but gown salons are notorious for ordering late and making out incomplete orders with last-minute add-ons. This is not always the fault of the salon. To avoid confusion and possible late delivery, order all the gowns at the same time. If there are changes in the order (an attendant gains or loses weight; she becomes pregnant), notify the salon, *in writing*, at the earliest possible date. Any changes in the order should be made by the bride.

It is an honor to be asked to be in the wedding party, but this is the bride's day, and if the attendants are so unhappy about the dresses they are asked to wear, they should bow out of being in the wedding party.

—DENICE D'ANDREA, GOWN EXPERT (LAS VEGAS, NEVADA)

The colors of the decorations and floral arrangements should be taken into consideration when selecting the dresses. Alternatively, color and fabric swatches should be taken to the caterer and florist. Season, time of day, and formality of the event are also important considerations. Madeline Barillo, author of *The Wedding Sourcebook*, suggests the bride think about the photographs that will be in her wedding album; the dresses' color and design should enhance the entire picture. Barillo reiterates that the final decision in selecting the dresses should be the bride's.

While a bridesmaid's dress is an expense, it's a one-time expense for a very special occasion. When the attendant accepts the honor of being in the wedding, she also accepts the terms, and one of the terms is that she may not be able to wear her dress again or recoup anything except happy memories. But what is more important than that?

CHAPTER 8

Invitations, Notes, and Things

❧ Your Stationery

MOST WEDDING BOOKS AND COLUMNS SAY THE INVITATION MAKES THE FIRST impression of the event. There is a great deal of truth to this. While looking through voluminous catalogs of stationery, you will see all sorts of expressions of moods and lifestyles. Your task is to find stationery that best expresses this life passage for the two of you. Any decision made at the stationer's shop will reflect the kind of life together the two of you are choosing for yourselves. Each is an important decision that should be made together, not by the bride alone.

You want to find stationery that fits your personality, your lifestyle, and the event you are about to celebrate. The style can be fun and frivolous; it can be so personal that the invitations are written out in longhand; or it can be ultraformal, with emphasis on the solemnity of the occasion. It may be conveyed by the color, the wording, or even the typeface.

Remember, you are sending a message in more ways than one. In your invitations, RSVPs, table assignment cards, at-home cards, thank-you notes, and wedding announcements, you are confirming your relationship with the person receiving your correspondence. Take time to reflect how you want your thoughts and feelings worded. I once had a colleague tell me she had never received a personally handwritten letter from a fellow colleague. I was astounded until I remembered that she is of the generation who cut their first teeth on a Gateway 2000. Now is your opportunity to actually reach out and touch someone in a way that Ma Bell never really could, in a way that is fast falling to the wayside.

So, when you think about your stationery, think first of your wedding day. What kind of impression do you want to send to your invited guests? How do you want to announce this important event? What's the mood or tone you want to convey to someone receiving your invitation?

Placing Your Order

You won't need to order your stationery until your guest list is almost complete. Then, once your guest count is established and you have decided on the site, the date and time for the ceremony and reception, and your menu, as well as on the style of your stationery, you should place your order. Give yourselves anywhere from three to six months for enough time to proofread and prepare the invitations for mailing, whether you hire a calligrapher to address the envelopes or you address them yourselves. You don't want to rush this. Unless your wedding date is near a holiday, especially Thanksgiving or Christmas and Hanukkah, mailing should be done five to seven weeks before the wedding. During the high holidays or summer, give yourselves two extra weeks. You're not only facing a backlog of mail during party or holiday seasons, you are also dealing with people's social calendars.

Types of Printing

Engraving

This is the most elegant, formal, *and* expensive way to go. The wording is cut onto copper plates, which in turn actually cut into the paper. The lettering can be felt on both sides. Engraved invitations are usually on a white or off-white stock. If yours is an ultraformal or formal wedding, you will want all of your stationery needs engraved. Consider purchasing your engraved plates as a memento.

Thermography

This process is considerably less expensive than engraving, but you get a similar impression. The look and feel of engraving is simulated by the application of a powder compound onto the paper as the ink dries.

Elements of the Invitation

The Invitation

When considering your invitation, first thought should be given to who is the formal host or hostess of the wedding. Contrary to some contemporary thinking, the person who serves as host or hostess is not necessarily the same person fronting the major expenses. There are as many options as there are perceptions of proper etiquette and decorum. Traditionally, the host is one or both of the custodial parents, or the custodial parent and his or her current spouse. The biological parents may be the hosts even if they are divorced and remarried. Or, the bride and groom may choose to be the host and hostess. Older couples can ask their children to issue the invitations. The essential message is to talk to all concerned parties before you determine the actual wording of the invitation. Be sensitive to possible hurt feelings and determine other roles for parents if you decide not to go the traditional route.

Here are other general rules for wording invitations:

- Spell out all names (first, middle, and last); do not use nicknames or initials. This includes dates, times, addresses, and the word "and." (Exceptions are: Mr., Miss, Mrs., Dr.).
- British spellings are traditional and formal. (For example: "honour" —*honour of your presence* is used to invite someone to the ceremony, and "favour"—*the favour of a reply* and *the pleasure of your company* are used as regards the reception).
- Information about the reception may be included in a bottom corner of the invitation or on a separate enclosure card.

Excellent sources for other information regarding wording are *Modern Bride Complete Wedding Planner* (by Cele Goldsmith Lalli and Stephanie Dahl) and *The Wedding Sourcebook* (by Madeline Barillo).

The Envelopes

The envelope without the "glue" is called the inner envelope. On it, you will write your guests' surnames with their appropriate title, for example, Mr. and Mrs. Smith, or Mr. Smith and Dr. Smith. If you are sending an invitation to a single person, then it is on the inner envelope that you write "Mr. Smith and Guest." The word *guest,* however, should not be written on the outer envelope. Neither should the word *family.* If children are invited, their first names are listed, in alphabetical order and on separate lines, below those of the parents. "By not including children's names, you are sending the message that they are not invited," says Linda Hiniker of Carlson Craft Stationers (North Mankato, Minnesota). Cele Goldsmith Lalli and Stephanie H. Dahl, authors of *Modern Bride Complete Wedding Planner,* say that "children over age eighteen each receive his or her own invitation." This is true for any adults that live in the household.

The invitation, with the tissue, the response card in its own envelope, and all other cards, facing upward (that is, facing the flap), is placed in the inner envelope; the inner envelope is slipped into the outer mailing envelope, face toward the flap. On the outer envelope, which has your return address on the flap, you write the name and address of your guest.

 Cohabiting couples receive one invitation with their names written on separate lines in alphabetical order.

—CELE GOLDSMITH LALLI AND STEPHANIE H. DAHL,
AUTHORS OF MODERN BRIDE COMPLETE WEDDING PLANNER

Save-the-Date Card or Letter

If you are planning a wedding around the holidays or during the summer, think about sending a save-the-date card or letter. This simply says: "Don't make any other plans; we're getting married, and we want you to be there!" People will love you for this; if they live out of town, they can purchase less expensive travel packages by booking in advance. A save-the-date mailing should go out as soon as you have set the date and decided on a site; the formal invitation comes later. If for some reason the wedding is called off, don't forget to send a simple announcement informing your invitees.

The Reception Card

The very formal bride will want to include a reception card, which gives information about the reception. Otherwise, the same information can simply be put on the invitation. An important point when ordering invitations, by the way, is to ask your stationer to assemble a full set of possible elements and actually weigh it to determine mailing costs; one additional card could put you into the next price range for postage.

The RSVP or Response Card

Many people who receive RSVP cards don't "get" them. Some think that because you invited them, you surely understand they are coming. Others think it's okay to bring their children or a couple who happens to be visiting them on the weekend of your wedding.

Without making your invitees feel they are etiquette deprived, you can help them out. In the place where the stationer would normally put an *M,* which is supposed to stand for *Monsieur,* instead, put "Name(s)," and then leave a blank for your guests to write in their own name(s); this should be followed by "will/will not attend" (they will circle one or the other).

If your response card contains a choice of entrées, then leave a blank before each entrée so that your guest can write in the number desired. Or you may ask them to circle the entrée of their choice. For multiple guests in the same party, you can enclose separate response cards for each individual so that each person may indicate the choice of entrée. In any case, an RSVP card is placed in its own envelope, facing toward the flap.

Some couples are smart enough to specify something like "The Favour of a Reply by May 31, 2002 Is Requested" or "Please Respond/Reply by

May 31, 2002." Another tip is to write a number in the upper corner of the back of the RSVP card that corresponds with a name on your A list/response spreadsheet. Then if your invitee fails to write her name on the RSVP card, you have a means of determining who the anonymous responder is.

Following is a sample of a response card that Linda Sue Abbott of Sentimental Reasons (Las Vegas, Nevada) and I created for the Kimberly Stokely and Ronald Longley wedding:

KINDLY RESPOND BY SEPTEMBER 14, 2002

NAME(S) _____

_____ DECLINES WITH REGRET

_____ NUMBER OF PERSONS ATTENDING

Please indicate number of entrées

_____ PORTOBELLO STUFFED BREAST OF CHICKEN

_____ TOURNEDOS OF BEEF FILET

Some stationers and wedding consultants are opposed to this manner of printing RSVP cards. They suggest that the bride write in the names of the invited guests, but this presents a problem if you have more than one person's name on the invitation and only one can attend. Also, leaving blanks and allowing people to write in the number of entrées might prompt a guest to write a number larger than the number of guests invited or even to invite an extra guest; however, asking them to simply "check" the entrée desired may not give an accurate count. Admittedly, there doesn't seem to be a perfect solution to the RSVP card, but I opt for getting as much information as possible from the guests.

The At-Home Card

A nice addition to the announcement or invitation is the at-home card. This is sent to let people know when you'll be returning from the honeymoon and available to receive guests. More importantly, it is an opportunity for you to communicate your new address and what name each of you will be using. Tradition has long since changed the rule that the bride takes the groom's last name. Not only are many of today's brides retaining their own name, but there have been instances of the groom taking the bride's surname as his own. And, of course, there is the endless hyphenating of names. The at-home card—again, included with the announcement or invitation—is placed in the inner (unglued) envelope, facing the flap.

The Map Card

Given the fact that some of us spend half our lives in automobiles, it is always a blessing to receive a map card with an invitation. Don't rely on your feeble drawing or a crude sketch. At least take a city map and have the section showing the main arteries or highways leading to your ceremony and reception sites photocopied and enlarged to the size of an index card to include in your invitation packet. Better still, have your calligrapher make a master to be sent to your stationer and printed or engraved on the same style and color of paper as your other

enclosures. Don't make the mistake of putting the map on the back of your RSVP card; hopefully, all of your guests will be mailing these back to you.

Tissues

We are not talking about bathroom or facial tissues here; we are talking about the tissue papers that are nearly the size of your invitations. These sheets of paper were created in days when engravers needed to place something over the newly engraved invitations to keep the print from smudging. In the past, the bride, not knowing the reason for the tissue, assumed that it was to be packed along with the cards, so she stuck the tissue into the envelope and—voilà!—we have the enclosed tissue. The tissue is placed directly over the invitation before it is slipped into the inner envelope with your other enclosures.

The Rain Card

Will your guests know what to do in case your outdoor wedding is rained out? On the face side of your map card, write out directions to and the name and address of the ceremony and/or reception site if moved indoors at the last minute.

The Pew Card

Pew cards are pretty much a thing of the past unless you are having a very large wedding. Certainly it is possible to have "assigned seating," without pew cards, to assure that those nearest and dearest to the couple will be closer to the ceremony area. It is important then to provide the ushers with a list of the names of these favored guests, indicating, too, just where they are to be seated.

The pew card (or within the ribbon card) is to be presented to the usher or, in some instances a security guard, upon arriving at the ceremony and signifies the special relationship to the bride. Closer seating to the front, nearer the ceremony area, means that you are with the in crowd.

—DOLORES MILAM, NUART (BEDFORD PARK, ILLINOIS)

The Gift Registry Enclosure Card

I'm not known for my conservatism, but when it comes to enclosure gift registry cards, I draw the line! Many department stores incorrectly inform brides that it is perfectly all right to include cards with your invitations, letting your guests know where you are registered for wedding gifts. While informing the bride that listing such information directly on the invitation is a serious breach of etiquette, in the same breath, salespeople will say, "But look at these precious little cards that state ever so simply and elegantly the stores of your registry." One can almost hear the cash registers ringing in their minds.

No information regarding the gift registry is to be included in the invitation packet. Shower invitations, save-the-date cards, letters from your wedding consultant, or word of mouth are the only proper vehicles for this information—no matter what you might read in the latest bridal magazine!

The Place Card

The place card has the guest's complete name(s) with appropriate titles (for example, Mr., Mrs., Miss, Captain, Dr., etc.). The card may have a couple's name or each guest may have his own separate card (for example, Mr. and

Asking your bridesmaids and close family members to discreetly spread the word is the appropriate way to let guests know what you'd like as a gift. It is a serious breach of etiquette to include information about the bridal or wedding registry on the invitation or on an enclosure card that is included in the invitation packet. It has always been my stand, and that of *Bride's* magazine, that this is highly improper. Just as you would not invite someone to dinner and let it slip that there's a florist conveniently located two blocks from your home where they can pick up a hostess gift, it is inappropriate to enclose information with the wedding invitation about where one is registered. A wedding invitation is a request to witness and participate in a celebration of love and commitment—no strings attached. No matter how expedient or nicely worded, it is impolite to infer that a gift is expected at the moment you're requesting the pleasure of someone's company. Most guests know it's customary to give a wedding gift to an engaged couple. They'd like to think, however, that it was their own idea to do so.

—MILLIE MARTINI BRATTEN, EDITOR IN CHIEF OF BRIDE'S

Mrs. John Naylor or Mr. John Naylor and Mrs. Anita Naylor). Also written on the card is the table assignment number. Usually, the place cards are set out onto a table in alphabetical order alongside a guest list. The most convenient place for these is on a table in the reception room so that guests may retrieve them while they are having cocktails. If guests are assigned specific seats at the table, then a duplicate card needs to be in place at the table (though it is not necessary to have the table number on this duplicate card). It is proper, however, to have a separate card at the table for each person. If you do not have seat assignments, then guests are free to pick a chair and sit alongside whomever they wish. However, in this case, you should have someone standing next to the place cards to inform the guests that they should take the card with them to their tables. Either way, you will need to indicate which entrée (chicken or beef) the guest has chosen. This can be done by writing a small *c* or *b* on the corner of the card or by placing a sticker that indicates one or the other. Just be certain to alert the chef so that he can inform his waiters how to interpret the stickers.

Thank-You Notes

In my book, thank-you notes weigh equally on the scale of importance as the invitation. I'm talking about nice, formally printed thank-you notes. We are not saying here that a "canned" thank-you response is to be printed. I remember a bride who actually thought she could have cards printed saying:

Dear _____:

Thank you for the lovely _____. Mike and I are enjoying it so much. It has a place of honor in our _____.

Sorry, it doesn't work that way. The only printing you should have on your thank-you note or card is described here.

- If you're using folded notepaper, you may have your full name or a monogram printed across the middle of the front or folded-over part.
- When the bride is using a monogram, her surname initial is printed in the middle and slightly larger than her first initial, which appears on the left. Her second initial appears on the right. Cards printed in this manner are to be used by the bride when

sending thank-you notes before the wedding. After the wedding, thank-you notes should be sent by the bride and groom.

- When the bride and groom are using a monogram, the married surname initial is in the middle, the bride's first name initial is printed to the left, and the groom's first initial is printed to the right. The surname initial is printed in a larger font.

I don't suggest printing "Thank You" itself on the card. Your note will make it obvious that it is a thank-you card. Besides, you can then use the notes or cards for other occasions.

You may choose to have your names and address printed on the flap of the envelope. Again, use your return address (that is, the bride's) before the wedding, and use the address that you will be sharing as husband and wife on envelopes to be sent after the wedding. Any other writing on the thank-you note is to be done by you and/or your groom.

If you anticipate receiving a large number of gifts before the wedding, you may want to consider sending a simple acknowledgment card. This is especially helpful for people who sent a gift via mail, courier, or the wedding registry. They will feel more relaxed knowing that the gift has arrived safely, even if you haven't had time to open it or formally thank them for it.

However, this doesn't mean you are off the hook. After the wedding, you must sit down and write a personal message. If you are each sharing in this responsibility it is not necessary that you both sign every note. Referring to one or the other will suffice, for example, "Kimberly and I especially liked the yellow-and-red-striped umbrella stand with its fuchsia dots. We already have it in a place of honor in the entranceway of our new home. [Signed] Ron."

Thank-you notes should be mailed no later than four to six weeks after the gift is received. On your A list/response spreadsheet write in the thank-you column the date that you actually mailed the card.

The Wedding Announcement

What happens when you want to invite someone who you know cannot attend? You simply send what is called an announcement. Happily, you have already created the relevant list.

The wedding announcement is of the same style, color, and paper as the invitation; thus, it conveys the same mood. Wording for the announcement is similar to that for the invitation, but instead of saying "request the pleasure of your company" or "request the honour of your presence," you say "have the pleasure to announce." As on your invitation, this appears on the line following the name of the person(s) issuing the invitation/announcement.

Just because you send an invitation or announcement to someone does not mean that you should expect that person to send a gift. Likewise, if an invited guest does not attend the event, he or she is not obligated to send a gift. Some experts, including Madeline Barillo (author of *The Wedding Sourcebook*), say that the announcement should include the date but not the place so that people don't confuse it for an invitation, and this certainly makes sense. However, if you do want to mention the wedding site, then be sure to use the past tense, for example, " . . . were married at Saint Joseph, Husband of Mary Catholic Church."

Announcements should be put into the mail only *after* the ceremony has taken place and the license has been signed by all required persons and recorded at city hall. Mailing them after the ceremony not only will save addressees the dilemma of trying to figure out if they are invited to the wedding, but it also will avoid unnecessary phone calls to you and your parents informing you that you mailed the invitation too late for them to respond. Remember, many people don't know the difference between an invitation and an announcement.

Other Stationery Concerns

Proofing the Paperwork

A "proof" is a photocopy of the layout of your paperwork, once it has been set up in the computer or by the printer. It's *not* an actual sample of your invitational materials, though such a sample can be ordered at an additional cost—sometimes as much as $50 per piece. Since you are ordering at least seven separate pieces, you may want to think twice before asking for a true proof sample.

When you have your count for the number of each printed piece, a list of the items to be ordered, and the wording of each piece, you are ready to place your order. The stationer will write out precisely the wording, spellings, and addresses you give her. Often, stationers will draw arrows to indicate the placement of a word somewhere else, or they will write in instructions such as "indent" or "center." That's well and fine for the manufacturer, but you want a clean copy (no editorial remarks or instructions, no arrows, no periods changed into commas) of each piece ordered so you can compare it with the finished piece when it arrives. You will be asked to initial or sign the final proof before the order is placed.

Another hint for "proofing" your entire order: Take the separate and individual pieces home (*before* signing off on the order) so you can study them at your leisure. Make photocopies and give them to both sets of parents, your groom, and your maid or matron of honor, or another attendant (that will make them feel more involved), and have them study the proofs for a couple of days and then report back to you if there are any errors. It is possible to read something a dozen times and still not catch the tiniest of errors until it has gone to print. If such errors occur and it is your fault, be prepared to shell out costs for reprinting and even possible rush charges.

After the pieces have been studied carefully and any errors noted, then and only then should you agree to sign the final proof and the order placed. If several corrections are needed, then ask for another proof.

After you have placed your order, enter the figures into the actual costs column of your overall wedding budget. On your disbursements sheet, record the date and amount of the deposit and when the balance is due. Put a copy of the receipt and order into your wedding day binder, behind the tab labeled "Stationery." Go to the vendors list at the beginning of your binder and record the name, address, contact person, and phone number of your stationer.

Have Your Stationer Assemble Some Guides

Once you have determined all of your stationery needs, ask your salesperson to show you how the invitation packet or announcement packet is to be assembled. When your stationery comes in, ask a second time for direction on its assembly. Have the stationer assemble five or six sets for you. Use one as a guide; keep two separate and in a different place so that you don't accidentally use them. Give a set to your parents and to the groom's parents. Certainly, the groom should have a set too. (Men are more sentimental than we let on.) Ask your stationer to weigh the completed set so that you will know how much postage will be required.

The Ceremony/Reception Program

A ceremony program is a nice thought, and it doesn't have to be costly. Your guests would probably like to know the names of the participants. Just as importantly, they will be able to look ahead and figure out how much longer the ceremony is going to last! Both sets of parents or other significant family members, the wedding attendants, the officiant, the musicians and readers, ceremony assistants (including acolytes), and any other people involved in a major way should be listed.

The ceremony program is an appropriate place to note the memory of a recently deceased family member. Sometimes, a couple will experience the death of a parent or other relative in the midst of planning their wedding. Having encountered this situation on more than one occasion, I have always urged the bride and groom to continue with their plans, as difficult as that might be. Indeed, the commitment ceremony and joyous reception that followed have had an even greater impact on the couple, knowing that their parent or relative or friend would have wanted them to celebrate their lives.

One such occasion nearly threw me for a loop. I once had a bride whose father died six months before the wedding day. The anguished daughter wanted to commemorate the memory of her father by issuing the invitation with the following wording: "The Late Mr. John Smith and Mrs. Smith request the honour of your presence . . ." I talked with the bride extensively, trying to explain that this not only would be in very bad taste, but it would cast a pall over the entire wedding planning and even more so over the wedding day. The daughter was relentless. There seemed to be no hope for convincing her of an alternative. Finally, after one of our planning consultations, I brought up the matter of the invitations and their wording. The bride dug in her heels; she was adamant. I just said as gently as possible, "But think about it. A dead person can't invite someone to anything, except maybe the beyond. He certainly can't invite people to a wedding." All of a sudden she began to sob uncontrollably. After some comforting by her fiancé and mother, she turned to me and said, "I know, I know. I just want him here." My heart went out to her. I told her to go home and think about it. I told her to talk with her fiancé and her mother and, after a couple of days, make her decision. I assured her that whatever she decided, whatever she wanted, we would do.

To be perfectly frank, I was quite willing to support her in her decision. Though the stationer had told me that there was no way she would print such an invitation, that she would be the laughingstock of the business, I had already found another printer who would abide by the bride's desires. Three days later, the young lady telephoned me and said that she would not press the issue, but that she wanted to do something to remember her father on her wedding day.

We dedicated the ceremony program to him, and upon her return from the honeymoon, we had the florist make up a replica of her bouquet, which she took to the cemetery and placed at her father's headstone. Years later, the bride and I still talk about that decision, and she still feels that we took the more positive route.

Additionally, in the program you might have a few sentences expressing gratitude toward your guests for arranging their schedules to be present at this special moment for the two of you.

Guest Registry

Besides your photo album, your guest registry will be one of your most important keepsakes of your wedding day. There are a lot of ugly, cheap-looking guest registries; you know the kind—the ones with the equally unattractive white feather plume pen. Think of finding something more special to commemorate the event.

One of our JWI members, Sherry Richert of Mad Moon Creations (San Francisco, California), makes wonderful guest registries and/or memory books that are handcrafted and professionally bound. She gathers stories and pictures about the bride and groom from relatives and friends, then has them professionally reproduced to create a "life story book" for the couple.

Some of her productions contain lined pages for the guests to sign at the ceremony and reception. It's a simply marvelous keepsake.

Personal Stationery

For the life of me, I can't understand what has happened to etiquette. Most people do not write letters nowadays, but worse still, they do not send even thank-you notes after having been sent gifts, been guests in people's homes, been taken to dinner, and the like. Here's your chance to remedy the situation and make the world a better place.

 If you prefer the personal touch, the sense of ultraformal, that's when you want the invitation to be addressed by an expert calligrapher who actually handwrites the names and addresses.

—ADRIENNE KEATS, ADRIENNE D. KEATS CALLIGRAPHY (SAN FRANCISCO, CALIFORNIA)

When you order your invitations, order some personalized note cards and/or stationery. These can have both your name and your soon-to-be-husband's (Mr. and Mrs. Ronald V. Longley). Or, they can have your monograms as described above in the section entitled "Thank-You Notes."

Get Envelopes Early for Calligraphy

Ask your stationer to get the envelopes to you early so you can begin addressing them; you don't need to wait until you have the invitations themselves to begin this task. Besides professional calligraphers, some stationers are able to do calligraphy via computer software. Ask your stationer about this.

Done in calligraphy, place cards, menus, and table numbers, in addition to the invitations, are a nice touch.

Divvying Up the Invitations

There are different thoughts on how to determine how many invitations go to the bride's family and how many go to the groom's. Hopefully, by the time you are ready to order your stationery, that question has been answered. Some people advise an even split; others feel the groom's family should simply be told how many they are allowed to invite. However you choose to solve this dilemma, do communicate openly with each other so there is a clear understanding before placing the order.

OTHER TIPS FOR MAKING UP THE GUEST LIST ❧

- Draw up a list of relatives and friends who are important to you (consider each name and ask yourself, when was I last invited to their home or they to mine?).

- Get a zip code directory from the post office; use full nine-digit zip codes.

- Invitations should be mailed four to six weeks before the wedding date; they should all be mailed at the same time.

- Find out how many extra envelopes will be included in your order.

Schedule Time for Follow-up Phone Calls

As a precaution, schedule your RSVP date several days before you really want the cards returned. It is not unusual for people to mail the RSVP card on the actual date requested on the invitation (that means it is going to arrive at your address three or four days later than expected).

Deciding on a cutoff date in advance will be the signal for you to schedule a party for your groom, attendants, and parents (actually anyone willing to help), and get logged on to your e-mail or get on the telephone to contact your etiquette-challenged guests to inquire about their intentions to attend. When making your twentieth phone call for the day, avoid the temptation to be short or curt with your invitee. Try to be sympathetic as you listen to her lengthy explanation, attempting to figure out if she means yes or no. Be patient with the person on the other end of the telephone line; she doesn't realize you still have fifty or sixty other people to call. If she will be attending, while you have her on the phone, determine the number of guests and the entrées desired. Write in the information in the appropriate spaces on your A list/response spreadsheet. Don't depend on the mail if your guest says she will return the RSVP with the necessary information; it's too late for that! Make certain that a guest who hasn't returned the RSVP is checked with by phone before you replace her with someone from your B list.

Other phone calls you, your parents, and attendants will be making are to those who think your wedding is an opportunity to invite all of *their* nearest and dearest. Some people will actually write in that they are bringing other people. (Be happy they are forewarning you!) A phone call needs to be made to the invitee, politely informing him that, due to the limitations of your facilities, you are only able to accommodate those you sent invitations to. Similarly, you will need to phone those guests who have added their children's names to the RSVP card, if yours is to be an adult wedding.

Inviting Boyfriends/Girlfriends/
Domestic Partners/Cohabitating Couples

Recognize that while you are not obligated to invite a friend's significant other, if you really want a particular friend to be present at your ceremony and reception, you should consider inviting his date. Today it is not only appropriate but is expected that a guest's significant other or steady boyfriend/girlfriend is invited. You should also take the time to call the guest and ask for the full name of the special friend so that person will feel welcome. Both names should be written on the invitation and inner envelope. From my experience, such an expansive gesture on the part of the host and hostess won't inflate the guest list that much. If, after exhausting all attempts, you are unable to learn the name of the friend's guest, then it is permissible to write "Mr. Smith and Guest" on the inner envelope.

Presidents and Popes

Even if the president of the United States is not among your nearest and dearest, you might, just for fun, include him (or her) on your guest list. Just send the invitation to the President of the United States, The White House, Washington, D.C. (I guarantee the post office will know the address). There's no need to send a contribution; he'll get that elsewhere. While the president won't show up, unless he *is* numbered among your nearest and dearest, you might get a congratulatory letter. Before you go out and have the letter matted and framed, check the signature carefully to make certain it is not a facsimile, in other words, a stamped signature. If it is a facsimile and you want a true signature, send a note to the same address, requesting a letter with the actual signature.

Barillo suggests sending an invitation to the pope (don't forget to include a small fee; usually $20 is acceptable, though reportedly no amount is too large), requesting a papal blessing. At some point, you will receive a lovely piece of parchment with the pope's picture and your names and the date of the wedding. You should write out exactly how you want your names to appear; the pope, after all, is only infallible in regards to matters of faith and morals. Barillo advises that you contact your diocesan office (or archdiocese office; just look in the business section of the white pages under "Diocese of [your city]"; or look in the yellow pages under "churches, Catholic") to obtain the correct address. Your diocese will send the request for you along with others that might be in the hamper; plus, you will get a quicker response if the diocese sends it for you. (Not that the diocese has better connections, which it does, but their return address will alert the recipient that this is not just a fan letter.)

Gifts

Again, I want to reiterate the proper etiquette for when and where gifts should be sent. Gifts should be sent to the home of the bride, or the bride and groom if they are cohabiting, or to the home of the parents of the bride. The outside flap will have the address of the person issuing the invitation, and gifts should be sent to that address. Under no condition should guests bring gifts to the wedding and/or reception. Besides the fact there may not be a suitable place to keep them in security, the gift could easily get misplaced or damaged. Furthermore, the card, if not properly attached, may fall off and be lost and the bride and groom have no idea who sent the wind chimes of seashells and driftwood. Alas, many of your guests will bring gifts to the wedding, so you should have a plan for how they are to be handled.

While it is not a breach of etiquette to display the gifts, my suggestion is to be more discreet. Have the coat-check person or a dear friend accept the gifts. Scotch tape should be available so that the person can further secure all cards to the packages. Do this even if the cards look as if they are firmly attached. Stack the gifts on the display table or in the coat closet at the reception site.

Once all the guests have arrived, ask a relative to accompany the site manager or an employee to take the gifts to a secure place (a locked coat-check closet, your hotel room, a nearby relative's home, etc.; it is advised *not* to have the gifts taken to your or your parents' home). Believe me, the site employee will appreciate knowing he is relieved of responsibility for them himself. It is not a good idea to leave the gifts on display throughout the evening or to put them in an automobile. Rarely will wedding consultants take this responsibility on their shoulders, so plan ahead to make appropriate arrangements.

Don't panic if you don't receive a gift from your closest friend or relative. She may be of the school that counsels she has up to a year to send a wedding gift. However, for your peace of mind, and theirs, it is not improper to call those who you just *know* would have sent a gift. Simply explain that you are writing your thank-you notes and are concerned that if she sent a gift, it didn't arrive.

In some parts of the country it is fashionable to display the opened gifts in the home (this should never be done at a reception). In such a case, it is nice (as well as an aid to the memory) to tape the greeting card to the gift. This will also allow you to make certain your list of received gifts matches the items on display.

Record Your Gifts

Your computer software organizer will be your most valuable tool in keeping up with your gifts and thank-you notes. If you do not have a computer, use 3 × 5 index cards that contain your master guest list. Use your A list/response spreadsheet and write in a brief description of the gift. Even if you are sending an acknowledgment card, keep daily track of gifts received. It is too easy to overlook someone and fall behind on this laborious but very important task.

CHAPTER 9

"Cocktails, Anyone?"

≈ The Wedding Reception

ONE WEEK YOU ARE GOING TO BE THINKING AND TALKING ABOUT INVITATIONS, the next week your gown. One week your floral decorations, the next your ceremony. Into this melee comes thinking about your reception, which includes the food and beverage and your wedding cake and how they all fit together. Let's be honest—you surely don't think your guests have gotten all dressed up in their best duds just to bask in the glow of your happiness! They expect a really good time!

One of the nicest remarks I heard expressed by two of my favorite clients, John and Anita, was that they wanted their wedding reception to be memorable for everyone. After their honeymoon, the couple called to tell me they had received many thank-you notes *from their guests*. The guests had enjoyed themselves so much that they actually took time to write to the bride and groom, expressing their delight and appreciation. Now, that was a successful party!

Types of Reception Sites

Visualize and Learn to Articulate Your Vision

Selecting the mood and ambience for your wedding reception isn't as difficult as it may seem. You already know many of the various segments of the day; now all you have to do is create smooth transitions to connect them into a natural flow. As you begin to talk with site managers, florists, and caterers, be attentive to the language *they* use. Listen to how they describe certain possibilities, and you will gradually be able to find the words that will help you articulate your own dreams. For instance, if you are concerned about having to be at different places at different times of your wedding day, consider a hotel for your ceremony and reception. Besides some pampering (many hotels have spas as well as makeup, hair-care, and exercise facilities), a suite can be reserved for the night preceding the wedding.

Write down descriptions of the images that occur to you, using the language of your vendors. Do a mental walk-through of your wedding day and sites. If you are not a particularly visual person, return frequently to your site so you can clarify the details in your mind. It's especially important to visit at the same time of day as your wedding; if you are marrying a year down the road, check out the site in the same month, too, so you can observe the lighting and get a sense of the place. Be aware of changes in daylight saving time (spring forward; fall back) so you are not imagining a candlelit evening that will actually occur in the brightness of the afternoon.

Return as many times as you need to until you are able to create a clear, detailed picture in your mind. Get a feel, too, for the degree of formality or informality you want your wedding day to have.

 You can have all your service providers and guests come to you. You simply have to prepare yourself, step into your gown, and take the elevator to the ceremony to meet your handsome knight.

—LORI KENNEDY, FOUR SEASONS HOTEL (LAS VEGAS, NEVADA)

Sites That Are All-Inclusive

As we said earlier, some reception sites, like hotels, restaurants, and country clubs, may bill themselves as "all inclusive." To be all-inclusive simply means that the site not only offers the setting but also the caterer and possibly the florist, music, and so on. In other words, the site may provide all or some of the ancillary professionals needed to have a wedding.

Other sites (museums, mansions, art galleries) may have a "preferred" or "required" list of vendors you must select from. A site that has a required list of vendors may allow little or no choice of vendors except from its list; you're stuck hoping these vendors are competent and creative, whereas a site with a preferred list of vendors tends to be more flexible. These latter sites may allow you to bring in your own vendors as long as they are professional and have the proper credentials, insurance, and health permit; such credentials should be verified when interviewing prospective vendors. Having some leeway in the selection of your vendors is very important to creating a natural flow. By having more options, you will be able to select people who work well together and produce an event that runs smoothly.

Be careful when selecting a hotel room for your wedding. Some brides think that a suite of rooms can serve them well for a small ceremony and reception. The reality is they can't. Suites and private rooms are furnished for homey intimacy. To have many people in a suite for a ceremony or reception can be cumbersome; these rooms are simply not made for that kind of traffic. Staff persons can't move around with the ease that is needed to serve the guests. However, Four Seasons can still re-create the intimate, residential atmosphere, the homey environment that a bride desires but do so in one of our facilities situated close to the kitchens and storage spaces that may be needed by our staff.

—Lori Kennedy, Four Seasons Hotel (Las Vegas, Nevada)

Types of Receptions

Among your choices for the type of reception are a simple reception or a reception followed by a luncheon or dinner. If you are on a restricted budget, or the time of day isn't a mealtime, then choose to hold a simple two-hour reception. This kind of reception can be formal or informal, while the reception followed by a luncheon or dinner is usually formal or even ultra-formal. Consideration should be given to the time of day and to your guests too. Most of them have spent several hours getting dressed and attending your ceremony. No matter how short your ceremony is, your guests who arrive on time or even early will have been sitting for as much as an hour or more. Folding chairs and pews (even the ones with seat and back cushions) aren't recliners. Your guests may want to walk around, to have something to eat and drink. If you are serving alcoholic beverages, whatever the time of day of your reception, provide food to offset the beverage consumption.

It is very important to let your guests know in advance what type of reception you are having. This is done on the response or reception card, for example: "Cake and Punch Immediately Following" or "Cocktails and Hors d'Oeuvres Immediately Following."

The caterers you are interviewing will also need to know the mood or tone, the formality or informality, of your wedding. The formality will be influenced by the decisions you make regarding your gown, the men's attire, and the setting. You want the formality or informality to be carried all the way through the function so there is some consistency. (Even kegs of beer can appear to be elegant; just drape a moiré "peplum" around them!)

Simple Reception

A simple, or limited, reception lasts about two hours and is a good way for the bride on a limited budget to entertain her guests. It can be a cake and punch reception, a champagne reception, a cocktail reception, or a tea. These vary in style as well as substance.

A cake and punch reception is just that. After mingling with their guests over exotic punch, the bride and groom cut and serve the wedding cake. The music is usually background music, but if the bride and groom want to dance, they certainly should do so.

A champagne reception differs only in that there is champagne and perhaps hors d'oeuvres on lovely trays, served butler-style. The cocktail reception is similar except that hard liquor is served in addition to beer. At all of these, nonalcoholic beverages should be available.

A tea is usually a more formal reception; while wine may be served, the beverage of choice is tea and coffee. Tiny finger sandwiches and canapés should be served. Seating is to be provided for all guests.

Reception Followed by Dinner

The reception and dinner consists of a cocktail party that lasts about forty-five minutes to an hour, followed by dinner, which is in the form of either a buffet or a sit-down, plated dinner.

After your photographer shoots the post-ceremony formals (that should take only about twenty minutes), you will still have time to mingle among your guests for about thirty minutes. You may choose to use this time to freshen your makeup, leaving the mingling to the parents and the wedding attendants. This is a good time, by the way, for you, your mother, and a couple of attendants to bustle your gown and to remove the long veil; make certain these attendants went to your last gown fitting and were instructed in bustling the gown—the task can take as much as fifteen minutes for even an adept bustler.

The reception may provide alcoholic or nonalcoholic beverages or a combination of both. Food is presented butler-style, passed on trays or at food stations. Limited quantities and assortments of finger foods, canapés, cheeses, fruits, and crudités can be set on tables (these are called food or satellite stations) so your guests can serve themselves. Take into consideration the number of guests and the size of the room; food stations may not be practical due to lack of space. Ask the caterer to help you decide what food items and quantities would be appropriate. Ask, too, how many pieces of food per guest will be served. You should have anywhere from four to six per person, and they should be of a variety and type that will complement the dinner to be served later.

The buffet presentation may provide limited or full seating for all the guests, who either serve themselves or are served by waiters standing behind the buffet tables. The advantage of the buffet is that your guests are able to choose the food items they prefer. One disadvantage is that your guests must queue up for possibly a fourth time (once to sign the guest registry, another to get drinks at the bar, and a third time if there is a receiving line). Another disadvantage to the buffet is the probability of higher costs. Buffets require that food items be replenished constantly so the presentation looks good. Also, people do tend to take larger quantities of the more expensive items (for example, prawns); I always suggest that such items be passed on trays. By having limited seating, you may be able to save money on rental items (chairs, seat covers, tables, linen). However, your guests may be very uncomfortable. The fact is, juggling flatware and a drink, napkin, and plate of food is difficult. We suggest that when providing a luncheon or dinner, full seating be provided. "But," you say, "we don't want our guests to be stuck at one table all evening. We want them to move around and visit with the other guests." From years of experience I can affirm that guests do get up from their seats and go "table hopping" to visit with their friends. Most are protective of their assigned seats and place their napkins atop the back of the chairs to show the seat is taken. The guests who stay in one place really want to, so allow them to be comfortable.

Reception Followed by Lunch or Dinner Featuring Food Stations

One of the most popular trends today is to have "food stations" in various locations of the reception or dining room. These are simply tables topped with finger foods that guests can help themselves to while dancing or mingling. Sit-down dinners can be rigid, and often do not allow for the informality and relaxed ambience that brides and grooms may desire. Food stations also allow for continuous dancing throughout the evening. If you decide to have food stations at your wedding, it is important that this be communicated to the musicians as it will mean you will want continuous music, without breaks, and they should be contracted accordingly.

Beverage Service

Beverage service doesn't mean that you must serve alcohol. Also, a "non-spirits" party doesn't have to be spiritless. Jazz up the presentation; do something out of the ordinary.

Be conscientious when providing alcoholic beverages; you could be held liable for an accident caused by a guest who has been served too much liquor at your wedding—all the more reason to contract a catering service with responsible bartenders and proper liability insurance. Find out who is liable if a guest drinks too much and is involved in a DUI after the reception. I don't mean to put a "downer" on the reception, but we must deal with all possibilities. As more state laws lower the level of what is considered legally drunk, there is a greater consciousness about not drinking to excess. That doesn't necessarily mean alcohol has lessened in popularity. Rather, people seem to be more quality conscious, opting for premium-label liquor as opposed to a house brand. Or they'll do something extraordinary, like offer cigars and scotch after dinner!

Your budget is not necessarily what restricts the kind of beverage service you provide for your guests; rather it's the way the caterer spends your money. Let the caterer know what amount you have to spend, then let him be creative and come up with some ideas that will make you happy. Because the bar is always hosted by you and the groom or the one paying for the reception, under no condition is a no-host bar (where the guests pay for drinks) considered proper. Nor is there to be tipping of any bartenders. If you see a glass or tray on the bar or a bartender collecting tips, have your wedding consultant discreetly request that he not accept tips and that the "tip container" be removed. You are already being charged a gratuity or a service charge and often a tax on that gratuity or service fee.

When serving wine, ask the caterer what types would complement your food. Determine, too, if the site or caterer has any restrictions on what beverages can be served and how they are provided. For instance, hotels and restaurants do not allow you to bring in any beverages; if they do, then a corkage fee is usually assessed. Hotels and restaurants charge as much as $3 to $5 per drink (geography and size of the city make a difference)—in some cases, whether it's alcoholic or not. For specialty drinks that require blenders and mixers, the cost could rise considerably. A corkage fee can be anywhere from $10 to $15 per bottle. There should be no tax on corkage (since you should have already paid that when you bought the beverages), but study the proposal and contract. In some states, service is taxed. As with food, the gratuity or service charge (which most states have legislated into law) can be from 15 to 20 percent. Some establishments charge an additional tax on this amount.

Beverage

Champagne/wine/beer/nonalcoholic

Champagne

Full bar: premium brands (these are the top-of-the-line labels); house (while not necessarily inferior in quality, these are the more common labels).

Punch and coffee

Tea bar

Champagne toasts: champagne is served already in glasses brought out on trays by the staff, or the waiter will fill each guest's glass at the table.

Scotch and cigars

Coffee/cappuccino bar

Corkage fee: if you bring in your own beverages, often the caterer or site may charge a fee for opening and serving the drinks.

Food

Breakfast: late morning; service may be buffet or plated; seating should be provided for all guests.

Brunch: late morning to early afternoon; usually light fare; service may be buffet or plated; limited or full seating may be provided.

Lunch: noon to early afternoon; may be preceded by a light beverage service (wine/champagne/nonalcoholic).

Dinner: service may be full- or limited-seating buffet or plated.

Stations: food may be on tables distributed throughout the room or actual food preparation may occur at each station.

Butler service: hors d'oeuvres are passed on trays.

Buffet: guests may serve themselves or be served by staff standing on the other side of the buffet tables; limited or full seating is provided.

French service: two staff persons are used; one serves the portions while the other holds the serving dish.

Russian service: the same staff person holds the serving dish and serves from it.

Plated or sit-down service: each plate is prepared in the kitchen and brought out to the guest.

Punch and cake: usually served at a time of day other than lunch or dinner. Your RSVP or reception cards should state "Punch and Cake Reception Following" so guests will not expect a hearty meal.

Cocktail reception: can precede lunch or dinner or simply denote a short reception lasting only a couple of hours; if the cocktail reception precedes lunch or dinner, it often lasts from 45 minutes to an hour; some hors d'oeuvres served butler-style or limited food stations may be available; it's light fare, but any time alcoholic beverages are served, food should be provided; also, realize that your guests have spent time preparing and attending the event; they will be hungry; usually, seating is minimal.

Staff ratio: number of server staff to guests; depending on the style of food service, the ratio could be from one to two staff persons for every ten guests; consider your menu and style of service and confirm with your caterer that sufficient staff is provided.

Some caterers will allow you to bring in your own wine without charging a corkage fee. If you do provide your own wine, make certain it is delivered at the convenience of the caterer, since he is doing you a favor. Consider carefully whether or not it is really a savings to you to go this route; we have found that unless the client has been given the beverages by a friend or relative, not much money is really being saved. Also, last-minute worries about transporting the wine or liquors to the caterer or site, and then retrieving the leftovers, can be more of a hassle than you want to deal with.

Interviewing Caterers

When compiling your list of caterers to be interviewed, follow the formula we state in each chapter: Start with your wedding consultant or site manager; this professional will know if the site has a preferred or restricted vendors list.

Once you have obtained this information, you can check with photographers, musicians, and videographers about the quality of service, food, and presentation of potential caterers. These vendors are the ones who are actually present at receptions and dinners; learn from their experience. Bridal trade shows are another option; you can look through caterers' portfolios, gather their menus and references, and talk with them in person. While you could look on the Internet, this should be a last resort. Endless and often fruitless time can be spent surfing the Net; we suggest you wait until you have narrowed down your lists, and *then* go to the Web sites of those being considered for interviewing. Personal references are always the best. Ask your friends who have recently married if they have any recommendations.

Call the vendors on your list and ask if they can send sample menus and brochures. Be sure to inform them who referred you so you're not an unknown entity—you are a potential client. Caterers, and all vendors, need to know this. Provide the date, time of day, and site of your wedding, and ask if they are available and if they have worked at that site before; if so, how many times and for what types of receptions? What are the chefs' specialties and price ranges? Can they prepare unusual dishes? Vernon Jacobs of Event of the Season (Corte Madera, California) notes that "there is an increase in vegetarianism, and people are wanting something more complex than just varieties of pastas. People are interested

in more exotic herbs and spices." Speaking of vegetarians, do be sensitive to any guests who would prefer a nonmeat, nonfish, or nondairy dish or who have special dietary requirements. Make a note in the entrée column of your A list/response spreadsheet so these guests won't be overlooked. Let the caterer know what regions of the country your guests are flying in from and the type of food you think they will appreciate. Be direct about your budget and ask if it is a realistic one. Inquire about the possibility of coming by and seeing the staff actually set up for a wedding at your site. If the caterer agrees, be considerate. Don't "hang out." Make sure you leave long before the guests start arriving. Also, this is not a time to be quizzing the caterer or his staff.

After some time, you will have collected packets containing dozens of menus, brochures, and handwritten notes. Put these in your three-ringed resource binder, behind the tab labeled "Caterers."

Narrow your list to three caterers who have the proper credentials (insurance, business license, and health permit). Fill out a wedding budget according to vendor type sheet. It is important that the three caterers on your list be comparable in cost and menus; this is the only way you can get a legitimate comparison. For instance, Now We're Cooking! Inc. of San Francisco has fine Bavarian china, crystal, and flatware. They stock oversized damask (100 percent cotton) napkins. Instead of the usual chrome-framed table numbers, they use gold-framed ones. Thus, their bid, when compared with a caterer who uses Libby glasses and polyester regular-sized napkins, is going to be higher.

In order to prepare accurate proposals, the caterers must be acquainted with the site. Some sites have no kitchen facilities at all; this necessitates bringing in the proper ovens, hot boxes to keep the food at correct temperatures, and even cleaning equipment. Vendors who have never worked the site will require a visit to the premises. A vendor who has worked the site before is always preferable. He will know its particular hazards as well as assets. If a rental company is required, the caterer will know what instructions to give them for ordering and delivery.

When interviewing caterers, don't forget to ask if they know your DJ or band, the florists you are interviewing, and the photographers and videographers you are considering. If the caterer has worked with any of these before, give him a plus. Remember, you are hiring a team. In all of my years I have found that it is the caterer, the photographer/videographer, and the musician who step on one another's toes the most on the day of the wedding; if these people don't know one another's style and temperaments, they can cause chaos at your wedding. The photographer can hold up the timing of the caterer by taking too long for the group shots after the ceremony; the band leader or DJ can start the dance music too early and cause either a delay in the food service or the food might have to be taken back to the kitchen and reheated because the guests are out on the dance floor. This actually happened at one of my weddings at the Mark Hopkins Hotel in San Francisco, and I thought the catering director was going to have a coronary. As the entrées were being placed in front of each guest, the band started playing a wild dance tune. I looked toward the dance floor to see the bride and groom, with guests in tow, intent on getting the party started. The catering director was fuming. As he directed his staff to return the plates to the kitchen so the food could be kept warm, he stood to the side of the room, shaking his head in disbelief. (This would have been a good reception for food stations, by the way.)

Always be sure to seek the direction of the caterer or the wedding consultant long before you decide to make any last-minute changes in your schedule. Trust the advice of this professional and avoid interrupting the flow of the evening. While your guests may enjoy your impromptu and carefree attitude, you don't want them leaving your reception complaining the food was cold!

Besides the photographer and musicians, I also like to meet with the floral designer. If there isn't a wedding consultant, someone needs to get the timing down. This task usually falls to the caterer. Besides detailed planning, the key to a successful reception is to let the professionals do their jobs. Creating a full vendors list with names of the contact persons, phone numbers, and verification of all the details of each one's responsibilities is imperative. It makes all of us more organized.

—LAURENCE WHITING, NOW WE'RE COOKING! INC. (SAN FRANCISCO, CALIFORNIA)

I can't emphasize enough that your caterer be a team player. It's also essential that she can be trusted to go the extra mile to do everything she can to make your wedding reception a success. I once produced a wedding held in San Francisco's California Academy of Sciences' Natural History Museum. After getting the bride properly down the aisle, I went to the reception site, only to be greeted by varied catering staff with the question "Have you heard about the champagne glasses?" As I weaved my way around the tables to get to the kitchen, this question was repeated at least four times by different people. I found the catering manager, and I didn't have to ask. He immediately said, "I'm sorry, Robbi, but the rental company didn't leave champagne glasses when they made their deliveries yesterday." Of course

I was seething inside, but why humiliate this man and wind up only embarrassing myself? I simply said, "I guess you've done everything you can to try to get some glasses." I had worked with this caterer for years and knew him to be a perfectionist. I just reassured him, "Well, let's just hope the bride doesn't notice!" Fortunately, she didn't. She was more concerned that the caterer remove place settings for guests who turned out to be last-minute "no shows." A few days later, when talking to the caterer on the phone, I left him with: "You and I both know that this will never happen again to one of my clients. Next time, please have someone on-site when rentals are delivered, so that every item can be checked and counted." It never happened again, and I remained close friends with a valued professional. Even professionals make mistakes.

In the long months of planning, I tell all my brides and grooms and their parents that things may go wrong—you probably won't even know about them, but if you do see something amiss, relax. Don't let anything mar your wedding day. You've hired the best, and that's all you can do. If something happens, let it go.

 The temperament of your team is of the utmost importance. Are they grandstanders or do they realize their first responsibility is to the overall success of the event?

—VERNON JACOBS, EVENT OF THE SEASON (CORTE MADERA, CALIFORNIA)

Deciding the Dinner Menu

Determining your menu is not really as difficult as it may seem. Taking into consideration the type of reception and service as well as the time of day, you need only decide on the specific food items. To do this, simply make

QUESTIONS FOR THE CATERER ❧

- Do you also handle beverage service?

- What are the cost differences between a full bar (premium and house labels), a wine/champagne/beer/nonalcoholic bar, and a nonalcoholic bar?

- Can you draw up your proposal so it is segmented according to beverages, food, labor/service and rentals, taxes, and service/gratuity? (If the caterer is providing decorations, have these cost out separately.)

- Can you give recommendations about the length of the cocktail hour and the dining reception?

- Do you, or can you, provide seat covers, chairs, linen, tenting, lighting, plants or shrubbery, dance floor, staging, and other props or equipment necessary for our wedding?

- When is it necessary to give a final count? Do you give consideration to the guest count if for some reason there is a last-minute increase? What about last-minute rentals?

- Will you provide more simple fare for the photographer/videographer and musicians and let them know in advance how this will be handled?

- What are your requirements for setup and breakdown? Are these within the restrictions of our site?

- Can you arrange for food and beverages to be taken by the bride and groom at the end of the reception?

- Can we observe your staff setting up for a wedding at our site?

- Can we get a copy of the insurance policy, health permit, and business license?

- What is your cancellation policy?

- Is there a lesser price for children's plates?

lists of the caterers' more interesting fare, collect menus from your three caterers, and add these to your resource binder. From time to time, study the lists and menus with your fiancé.

Talk to your families about what kind of food they enjoy. Together, you and your fiancé then come up with your own menu to present to the caterers so they can start working on proposals. If children are to be in attendance, be considerate of them, just as you would be of any guests who require or prefer special diets. You may want to order simpler food and smaller portions for the young ones.

Today's brides and grooms are interested in greater variety and more interesting preparations of food than in previous years. People are more properly acquainted with haute or nouvelle cuisine, get bored more easily, and are more food-quality conscious than in the past. Brides and grooms therefore want to offer their guests more menu choices, sometimes as many as three or four entrées (actually the correct term for this course is *main course*, but the French word *entrée* sounds better). While such an extensive menu may be more costly, don't worry that this will create a nightmare for your caterer or for you.

Remember, *you have a plan of attack*. And your plan includes providing a properly worded RSVP card in your invitation envelope so your guests will be able to make their selection in advance. You're even going to instruct them to write in the number and the entrée desired (review chapter 8). What could be easier?

Once you've narrowed down the food items, ask your caterer to prepare a "taste-testing session." (Usually a tasting is done once a contract is signed or after the place and date have been reserved.) Invite your wedding consultant, your parents, and even your maid or matron of honor and best man; all of you get dressed up and go out to dinner! Make it a fun evening. Start off with samples of the hors d'oeuvres. Ask the chef to prepare servings (enough for all to sample) of the salads and/or soups and each entrée with appropriate vegetables. Have plates provided for everyone and treat this as a family-style meal. It is also advisable for the chef to have the wines available that he would suggest accompany the courses. If possible, ask the chef to be on hand to answer any questions you might have during the tasting; otherwise, call him in the days afterward. Make your final decisions, and voilà! You have your menu! By the way, if you don't pay for this meal afterward, it will certainly show up on your final wedding billing. Off-site caterers may be more restricted and may be unable to provide this extra service unless they have their own kitchen.

Weddings are a time for elegance, fantasy, that larger-than-life feeling. This is a time to feel luxurious, even pampered. We love to be waited on; that's why we go to nice restaurants on special occasions.

—LAURENCE WHITING, NOW WE'RE COOKING! INC. (SAN FRANCISCO, CALIFORNIA)

Rentals

Ask your site manager if they provide any of the necessities, such as chairs, tables, linen, dance floor, etc. Are there props (columns, pedestals, silk trees or shrubbery) available for use? If so, is there a charge? It is best to let your caterer deal with items not provided on-site. He will likely remember to include items you may not be aware of but still need.

Knowing someone at a party rental store won't necessarily get you a discount. Even if you can get items discounted, they still need to be delivered, counted, and inspected to make certain everything ordered has arrived. Plus, everything has to be set up and then broken down and returned to the party rental company, and you don't want to be responsible for having to replace any broken or damaged items. Also, your caterer will know the companies who have the best-quality rentals. Learn to depend on your professional. You may think you can save money by doing more things yourself, but in the end your savings will only add up to pennies.

The Caterer's Proposal

Once you have determined your rental needs (inclusive of china, glassware, flatware, linen, etc.), along with beverages, menu, and type of service, the caterer should have enough information to write your proposal. There is no uniformity on how caterers write up proposals, and sometimes it is difficult to determine the "bottom line." That's why you should ask that the proposal be sectioned into categories: food, beverages, labor and rentals, gratuity/service charge, and tax. Ask, too, that the proposal include setup and break-down times. Make certain that you have double-checked with your reception site and that the time needed for the caterer to set up and break down is included within the total amount of time that you have the site rented. Otherwise, you are going to run into overtime charges that could be extremely high.

As important as the quality and attractiveness of rental items and the food, is the ability of the staff and organization. A caterer can have great-looking platters and his staff can be the best-dressed in town, but if quality in preparing and serving the food isn't there, then looks just don't matter.

 We are so organized behind the scenes that it looks effortless. We have a team of professionals who are trained in what they do, and I'm not just talking about our full-time designer whose sole job is to make certain the food looks beautiful; our chefs and food preparers and our wait staff are among the most qualified in the Bay Area.

—LAURENCE WHITING, NOW WE'RE COOKING! INC. (SAN FRANCISCO, CALIFORNIA)

- Beverage service should be separate, with labels and brands listed.

- Food should be itemized as to count and its preparation described.

- Service and kitchen staff should be listed (don't forget to be comfortable with the ratio of staff to guests; a sit-down dinner should be one staff person per fifteen guests).

- Rentals, inclusive of china, crystal, and flatware, should be itemized and described.

- Labor may be itemized separately; if so, what staff persons will be doing and how many are being provided for each job should be indicated.

- Any extraordinary charges (room fee, lighting, sound technician, etc.) should be itemized and listed in a separate section.

- Any gratuity/service charge and tax (there may be a state sales tax and a city tax) should be stated.

- The date when the final count is due should be noted.

- Method and time(s) of payment should be clear; while it may be possible to put your first and/or second payment on a credit card, most places will require a check (possibly certified) for the balance.

- If the caterer has a refund policy or a security deposit that is refundable, this should be noted in the contract.

- The contract should state who carries the liability for damaged or lost items and for replacement charges.

- The name of the person who will be present to check off and inspect the rental items when they are delivered should be specified.

How does your caterer think about your event? The true professional looks at weddings as performances. The bride and groom are the foremost audience members; all the vendors are performers in a well-orchestrated event.

Negotiating the Proposal

It is highly unethical to take a proposal prepared by one caterer to another and ask if he can replicate the menu for less money. Shocking as it may sound, some brides actually do this. Don't be one of them. After you have narrowed your list to one caterer, you can attempt to negotiate the proposal he has prepared. He will already know how much he can cut costs and yet not compromise the integrity of your event; he will already have a concept of the money you have to spend and will do his best to keep that dollar amount in check. Negotiating doesn't mean only trying to get the costs down; it also means making decisions about the substance of the event and how the various parts will come together in a unified whole; you may need up to four "rewrites" before you arrive at not only what you desire but also what is within your budget. All this takes time, and professionals know that and will be patient.

I have always found it best to be up front with a caterer; this can save you both a lot of headaches. By genuinely working *with* your caterer, you will arrive at a proposal that pleases you and does not overextend your finances. Generally, be prepared for the catering bill to total between 50 and 54 percent of the entire budget for your wedding day.

Once you have your contract, go to your computer file and binder labeled "Wedding Day." Add the caterer to the list of vendors that you have determined to be part of your team. In your finances section, enter the amount to the actual costs column of your overall wedding budget spreadsheet; on your disbursements sheet, write down the date and amount of your initial deposit as well as the dates that additional payments are due, along with the amounts due. On your wedding day schedule, input the time of arrival for setup and the times for the different segments (reception begins, dinner is served, cake is cut, etc.). As an added help to your caterer, who will be receiving this schedule in the mail two to three weeks before your wedding, include the address next to the name of the site. Be certain that you have reviewed your contracts with your site, as well as with the musicians and photographer/videographer, to ensure that all times are coordinated. Have the caterer advise you about his reception floor plan so that you know the best spots to place the head table, dance floor, cake table, etc.

ॐ **The most important thing from a caterer's standpoint is the budget. I can always give clients more for their money if I know what I'll be allowed to spend. I know lots of ways to save them money.**

—SHARON GRAHAM, FINE CUISINE INC. (HOUSTON, TEXAS)

Transfer from your resource binder to your wedding day binder all materials that pertain to the caterer you have decided to use, along with copies of the final menu and your contract. Give the original contract to your financial minister for safekeeping. Congratulations, you have completed one of the truly major tasks in planning your wedding day! Hopefully, you have had fun along the way.

Your caterer will probably require anywhere from a third (with a second payment due closer to the wedding day) to half of the cost in her contract, with the balance being due as much as ten days before the wedding. You will also have to provide a final count of the number of guests about three to four days before the wedding day. While a secret of the trade is that most caterers will prepare as much as 5 percent over the contracted count, this is not always the case. Realize that the caterer may not have enough rentals for unexpected guests, so be as precise as possible when giving her your count; keep accurate records as your RSVPs come in.

Photocopies of the final proposal and of the contract should be placed in your wedding day binder; the original documents should be kept, along with your other important wedding papers, by your financial minister.

The Wedding Cake

The wedding cake is one of the four focal points of the wedding (the invitation, your bouquet, and your gown being the others). All of your guests will want to see your cake up close; then they will go to their tables and talk about it. The traditional tiered wedding cake dates back to the Victorian age, and—up until recently—most wedding cakes tasted as if they had been left over from that age! The modern wedding cake is tasty and can come in all sizes, shapes, colors, and flavors. The tiers may be made of poppy seed, carrot, nut, banana cream, chocolate mousse, Diva chocolate and truffle, or any combination of these. Today's wedding cakes are pieces of edible art, a fine dessert as well as a grand finale to your wedding. Your guests are going to want to stay and eat it.

White is still a prevailing color—by the way, if you want a white exterior to your cake, be sure to communicate this to your pastry chef; white does not always turn out white! Still, frostings can be as varied as white chocolate, marzipan, rolled fondant, ganache, or the traditional butter cream. Specialty cakes are finished off with delicate, hand-sculpted flowers that can be painted in edible gold leaf or other food colors that give them a true-to-life appearance. Some brides choose to have their cakes decorated with fresh or silk flowers. Be careful about fresh flowers, though, as some are poisonous. I'm of the mind that fresh flowers belong in a vase, not on a cake, though I have seen some cake tables decorated with an abundance of rose petals that make the cake look quite regal. When deciding on your cake ingredients, do talk to your pastry chef about the temperature of the site, indoors or out.

WEDDING CAKE TIP ❧

Having a "fake" or Styrofoam tier or tiers is not necessarily economical if the cake requires elaborate decoration. Ask your pastry chef.

Be sure, too, to ask the caterer's or site's preferences on where to set up the cake. You'll want to avoid having the cake sitting in the glare of sunlight through a window. Also, while setting the cake table in front of a large mirror sounds like a lovely idea, it is actually a photographer's nightmare, since the flash will show up as a reflection in the pictures. Having the table set up against the wall or in a corner is not practical either, as this offers no room for you and the groom to stand and pose for pictures while cutting the cake. And *never* allow your caterer or banquet person to put the cake on a table with wheels or in any way move the cake table once it has been set up. Every time a staff person rolls a cake table onto the dance floor, my heart skips a beat. Dance floors are definitely to be avoided as places for the cake table. The same goes for the entrance to the dining room. "Well," you ask, "what are we to do, suspend it from the ceiling?" Simply select a spot away from the wall, not in front of a mirror, and anyplace but near the dance floor or entranceway. Oh, and you want your guests to be able to view the cake from up close as well as from afar.

Obtaining Names of Pastry Chefs to Interview

As always, start with your wedding consultant, reception site manager, caterer, and friends who have recently married. Also, let the vendor know who referred you. After giving the date and place of your reception, ask her to describe her different types of cakes. Find out if she has worked with your caterer and site, and whether or not a cake cutting or service fee is charged. Inform her of your budget and find out if it is realistic compared with her costs. If she does specialty cakes, inquire about the designs and flavors available. Ask her to send you brochures and price lists.

Be attentive to the pastry chef's personality and level of interest in you and your wedding. Does she inquire about your other vendors? Does she ask what sort of statement you want your cake to make? Note how she describes not only her designs but also the setup and look of the cake table. Also, does she work in a professional kitchen or out of her home? Either way, she should have a business license, a resale permit, a health permit for her facilities, and a backup staff. It is important, too, to know what kind of vehicle will be used for transporting the cake.

Interviewing Pastry Chefs

When it comes time for you to interview pastry chefs (this should be done at least three months before the wedding; allow longer if you are ordering a specialty cake), read through the materials from your resource binder. Select those vendors you feel are most in line with your desires and budget. Try to narrow your list to the three you're confident can produce not only a delicious cake but also a design that is the most beautiful you can possibly imagine. Make appointments!

Once you have decided who is going to be your pastry chef, transfer all his materials from your resource binder, with your notes, to your wedding day binder. Ask him to draw up a proposal, which should include a sketch or at least a detailed description. After the bride and groom, the parents, and the financial minister have reviewed the proposal, sign it and return a copy to the pastry chef with your deposit (usually 50 percent) and your expected guest count. Put a copy of the proposal and contract into

QUESTIONS FOR THE PASTRY CHEF ❧

- Is there a cost difference to have different flavors for each tier?

- Will you set up and decorate the cake and cake table? Is there a charge for this?

- Will you provide a box for any left-over cake so it can be taken home?

- What is your policy about the tier plates and other cake parts?

your wedding day binder and give the originals to your financial minister. Go to the finances section of your computer's wedding day file and put in the actual costs. Note on your disbursements sheet the date and amounts of your deposit and final payment. A security deposit is usually required for the plastic plates and columns used (be sure to put this amount into the refundable deposits column of your overall wedding budget and disbursements sheets, as long as everything is properly returned to the pastry chef).

A suggestion: Ask the pastry chef to provide you with a box so the leftover cake can be taken home with your mother or a close friend. Also, if you are on a restricted budget, think about ordering a beautiful, fully decorated smaller cake to display at the reception and a large sheet cake that can be plated and served from the kitchen.

 When interviewing cake chefs, make sure that they are neat, that they move with purpose. Do you feel that you can entrust them with your precious cake?

—TSUKI CASPARY-BROOKS, DOLCI WEDDING CAKES (DALLAS, TEXAS)

Delight Your Guests by Serving Selections of Two Different Flavors

Since today's wedding cakes often come in diverse flavors, think about offering each guest two slices, each a different flavor. Your guests will comment all the more on how wonderful the reception was if they can finish it off with an exquisite-tasting cake! Ask your pastry chef what sizes to cut the servings (the norm for these rich cakes is 2 inches square). And remember, just because you may decide to serve the guest two different flavors doesn't necessarily mean you must order for twice the number of people.

Anniversary Layer

The top layer of the wedding cake is traditionally the "anniversary" layer. Believe it or not, some couples actually do freeze this layer and bring it out on their anniversary. Unfortunately, no matter how well you wrap it, it very likely is not going to be tasty. Ask your pastry chef to provide a box for the top tier, refrigerate it after the reception, and then take it with you for your honeymoon. A better option is to ask the chef to bake you a fresh tier, exactly like your wedding cake, on your anniversary. Many pastry chefs include this in their fees for the wedding cake.

Dessert or Not Dessert

I have actually been to weddings where, in addition to the wedding cake, an elaborate dessert was served at the end of the dinner. This can be a costly redundancy! We suggest that you forego the extra dessert and put that money somewhere else in the wedding. There is one exception. A tradition strong in the East and Midwest of the United States is to present a "sweets or Viennese table": a lovely and elaborate display of truffles, pastries, and cakes. Occasionally, a bride has preferred to have an abundant Viennese table and a smaller, symbolic wedding cake for her and the groom.

Cake Toppers

If you are thinking of using your mother's precious porcelain statue for a cake topper, or one that decorated her wedding cake, think again. More times than you might imagine, a lovely heirloom has slid off a wedding cake and abruptly crashed to the floor. If you would rather not gamble on the chance of losing a treasured family keepsake, keep it in the china cupboard safe at home.

A bride decided to forego flowers on top of the cake for a Lladro figurine that was a wedding gift from her mother. The cake baker delivered the cake. It was late afternoon and the frosting was warm and soft. The Lladro was placed on top of the cake. At a moment when no one was around the cake, the figurine fell onto the table. The leg on the groom broke off. I Scotch-taped it back on as a quick fix and settled it back on the table in front of the cake. As a replacement cake topper, I used ribbons and bows. Discovering the broken figurine, the bride cried.

—Victoria Rohrer, JWIC, Weddings Unveiled (Whitmore Lake, Michigan)

"Too often they're stolen," adds Deborah McCoy, author of *The Elegant Wedding and Budget-Savvy Bride*. This is of particular concern if your wedding is held in a public place, for example, a hotel or restaurant. I had my own near disaster when, sometime during the reception, the mother of the bride placed a tiny figurine of a dancing couple on one of the tiers of her daughter's wedding cake. Many of the guests recognized it as having been on her cake a generation previously. She hadn't alerted me beforehand, and when the cake suddenly disappeared into the kitchen to be cut and served, she said offhandedly, "Oh, don't forget my special figurine." Fortunately, I was able to get into the kitchen before the figurine became just a memory; it was about to be thrown into the trash! Don't do that to your wedding consultant. Let him know when you have such a treasure that needs to be protected or retrieved.

Our advice is not to decorate your cake with a precious heirloom or gift that has great sentimental value unless you can live with the possibility of something happening to it.

The Groom's and Other Specialty Cakes

While some brides like to surprise their grooms with what traditionally is called the groom's cake, many grooms are getting more into the wedding picture by selecting their own cake. The custom has been strong in the South from the time when people had to travel long distances to attend a wedding. The groom's parents would bake small cakes, often fruitcakes, wrap them appropriately, and distribute them to departing guests.

Speaking of getting in the picture, Cookies by Design, in Las Vegas, Nevada, has a new high-tech photography system, called the Jet Decorating System, that can scan and then digitize and transfer an image from a photograph to the decorating component, transferring the image right onto the cake. The resulting image is almost as colorful and sharp as the original photograph.

Have the pastry chef help you design a unique cake. There are all sorts of possibilities. We've seen wedding cakes shaped like gift boxes with all sorts of wonderful confections pouring from the top. A specialty cake we designed for a famous high-fashion model to serve at her rehearsal dinner was a pink "hat box" decorated with white polka dots. It looked so real that guests talked about it all during the entire reception.

Such specialty cakes can be expensive. Costs range anywhere from $3 to $15 a person. However, remember that the cake is not only a special part of the wedding, but it also replaces the dessert (in fine restaurants, desserts are comparable in price).

Another popular specialty cake is the croquembouche. This is a tall stack of profiteroles, or cream puffs, piled sometimes as high as 6 feet in a cone shape, and then festooned in beautifully spun candied sugar and corn syrup strands (also called angel's hair), ribbons, and bows.

We once had an interesting adventure with one of these 6-foot croquembouche "trees." After getting the bride down the aisle, I returned to the reception site to make certain that all was going according to schedule. When I arrived at the reception site, I learned that the croquembouche hadn't arrived. Upon calling the pastry shop, I received the response, "Don't worry, it's on the way; the delivery people left here over an hour ago."

"But," I replied, "your pastry shop is only ten minutes from here!" Getting nowhere with the shop manager, I called the owner at home. He immediately arrived at the reception site only to learn that the cake still hadn't. I overheard him talking on the phone with his employee in French; my understanding of French was not necessary, it turns out, since his gestures and body language spoke volumes. Meanwhile, I was praying that the truck was refrigerated. Profiteroles are delicate and can spoil easily, especially in an unrefrigerated truck driving around in the September heat of San Francisco.

Fortunately, realizing the search for the reception site was proving futile, the truck driver had the good sense to pull over at a telephone booth and call the shop to check in. The owner proceeded to get the phone number of the telephone booth, call the driver and, very loudly, give him directions to the site, first in French and then in English. The cake arrived, in its refrigerated truck, ten minutes later, and the owner set up his majestic confection while I stalled for time at the reception. The bride never knew that her beautiful croquembouche had been wandering the streets of San

Francisco for two hours. That cake might still be lost if the bride hadn't had a wedding consultant who was on his toes.

While there are no rules and regulations about having a rehearsal dinner cake, many couples are opting to present their attendants with this "teaser" the night before the wedding day. This idea is especially popular for theme and destination weddings. One of our clients, Deborah Quinn, who had flown her forty-three guests from Boston, Massachusetts, to Napa, California, presented a cake constructed in the form of a hot-air balloon at the rehearsal dinner. She also had hot-air balloon floral arrangements designed and placed in each guest's hotel room. The morning after the wedding, the guests gathered in the parking lot to witness Debbie and her new husband, Ron, climbing into the basket of a *real* hot-air balloon and then floating away through the clouds, bidding them adieu.

Another bride, who was having a "black and white" themed wedding (I call it the "Black-and-White Ball done right"), had the pastry chef deliver a zebra-striped cake to the rehearsal dinner site. For this same client, I suggested wrapping her attendants' gifts in appropriate gift paper, then in plastic wrap; for these the pastry chef, Susan Morgan of Elegant Cheese Cakes (Half Moon Bay, California), created boxes and bows out of white chocolate, which she then hand painted using the wedding colors. The delectable results were placed on dessert plates, which were brought out by waiters, who set one in front of each bridal attendant. After careful study, one of the attendants realized that the elaborately decorated pastry box was, indeed, just that; she lifted the lid and found her gift wrapped in black-and-white-striped paper. I immediately dubbed this dessert "Having your cake and eating it too!"—a phrase that has since become popular with writers describing specialty wedding cakes.

Be sure to input any appropriate information on your overall wedding budget sheet. On your wedding day schedule, note the time the cake is to arrive and be set up. On the reception floor plan, make certain the cake table is drawn in the proper place.

The Flow of the Reception

There is a secret to enjoying your wedding day and having memories to last a lifetime: Don't let the day rush past you so that it becomes a blur. Avoid thinking ahead about events that are coming up. Be attentive to the moment. When you are walking down the aisle with your father, really *experience* walking down the aisle.

Once, while taking my friends, Tom and Barbara, on a tour of St. Peter's Basilica in Rome, I noticed they were rushing from statue to statue, reading their *Michelin Guide* voraciously. Having lived and taught in Rome for many years, I was quite familiar with the Vatican, but this was a first trip for them. After going the full circle of the inside of the basilica, they were rushing for the door. I stopped them, and as we stood at the famous Bernini bronze doors, I said, "Tom, Barbara. Stop. Take a deep breath and calm your spirits. Look around the entire basilica, slowly. Take a mental picture of what you are seeing."

Even as your makeup is being applied, let yourself experience the luxury of being pampered.

—JENNI TARVER, JENNI TARVER STUDIOS (DALLAS, TEXAS)

I give the same instructions to my brides and grooms. Mentally take pictures throughout the day, so when you hear that special song you and your groom danced to, for example, you can clearly see yourselves sharing your wedding dance. I also advise you not to drink much alcohol. Indeed, if you can refrain from any alcohol, all the better. Throughout the day you are going to be surrounded and pressed by people. If you can grab a few minutes by yourselves, do so. The Jewish wedding has a beautiful custom obligating the bride and groom to be alone for about ten minutes immediately after the ceremony. They are ushered into a specially prepared room so they can reflect on the seriousness of the vows they have just exchanged. Ahead of time, I have the caterer provide a plate of simple food and a beverage laid out on a lovely, decorated table for the couple's private time. I urge all my couples to go alone in the limousine from the ceremony to the reception when these are at different sites. It's a wonderful time for them to *be* with one another.

Take a Peek

About fifteen minutes before the guests are to enter the dining room for the dinner and dance, I always make certain the musicians are set up and ready to play. I cue them to begin playing a predetermined song, often the wedding dance song. Then I gather the newlyweds and both sets of parents and grandparents and secretly whisk them into the room. I want them to see the room in all of its elegance before the guests are allowed in. As they walk into the room, each is offered a fresh beverage off a silver tray held by a waiter. I watch for their expressions. These critical seconds will tell whether or not the perfect team has been assembled and we have pulled off our jobs to perfection. Invariably, the bride and groom both have tears in their eyes. This is the moment *I've* been waiting for.

Take a good long look as you enter the room, so you can appreciate its enormity and yet, at the same time, its intimacy. Stroll around. Note how the flowers are arranged ever so elegantly. Notice how the favors or name cards are placed just so. Every vendor that has anything to do with a wedding thinks that his involvement is the most important, and that is as it should be. For me, it's seeing the whole thing come together so charmingly.

After the bride and groom and parents have taken their peek, I bring in the wedding party. This is important; these ladies and gentlemen have stuck with the bride and groom during the long months of planning. They are obviously close to the couple or they wouldn't be in the wedding party; it is with them that the bride and groom are going to revisit in conversation the moments of their wedding day, so it's important they, too, participate in this preview. After all, how many times has the maid of honor heard about the fondant wedding cake with its strategically placed tiny hand-sculpted daisies?

After their sneak preview, I gather everyone into a separate room (it's time to take one last look at yourselves and retouch that makeup) while the guests enter the dining room. The music continues until all have found their seats. As the stragglers are being seated, your wedding consultant will be lining you up for the grand entrance if there is going to be one.

Long before the wedding day, I have given the DJ or band leader the names of everyone to be announced. Packy Boukis, JWIC, of Only You (Broadview Heights, Ohio) suggests phonetically writing out the names so they are pronounced correctly. Don't forget to let the announcer know how you are to be introduced; you want everyone assembled to know how you will formally be addressed.

The order of the entrance should be: your parents (they are the official hosts of the wedding reception), the groom's parents, the entire wedding party. If special relatives will be announced at this time, it should be after the groom's parents. All remain standing for your grand entrance.

The doors are closed again; the bride's gown and veil are fluffed. The groom straightens his jacket. Suddenly, a trumpet voluntary for two trumpets blares (Henry Purcell's Trumpet Voluntary and C.P.E. Bach's March for

Trumpet are nice); the doors reopen, and you and your husband are announced by the names you will henceforth use as a married couple. You make your grand entrance to the applause and delight of your guests. It is truly a moving moment.

Toasting

Anyone presenting a toast should be asked to have prepared—and even written out—the toast in advance. Otherwise, they may ramble on. Usually, the best man presents the first toast (most often his toast is presented immediately after the cake cutting; but, hey, it's your wedding, and you can change things if you like). The father of the bride may offer a toast to the bride and groom and to the groom's parents, welcoming the union of the two families. The groom may toast his new wife and both sets of parents. These may be followed by additional toasts by the other attendants or special guests. There is certainly nothing prohibiting you from offering a toast to your new husband, your parents and his parents, your attendants, and to all your beloved relatives and friends gathered around you.

Cake Cutting Ceremony

Other good times for toasts are before or after the first course is served or after the entrée has been eaten. If the toasts are offered after the first course, then the cake cutting ceremony should be delayed until after guests have completed the entrée. Then, after the toasts, the newlyweds can go directly to the cake for the cake cutting ceremony.

Don't rush this part of the event; the photographer will want to get some good close-up pictures of you. Placing his hand over yours, the groom guides your hand as you two cut the first slice. The groom feeds the bride the first bite, and then she feeds him the second. The cake cutting ceremony usually sends the signal to guests with children or who are older that, except for the dancing, the party is near its end. They may want to leave after watching the two of you dance your first wedding dance.

While it is very tempting to shock your guests by smashing the cake into each other's faces, believe me, this can be—and often is—an unappetizing scenario. (Besides, you can ruin your gown by having cake all over it.) No one wants to see you play with your food. Have a dessert plate and fork at hand so that eating your cake remains in keeping with the elegance of your wedding. You should also have a couple of cloth napkins on the table in case you need them.

Once the photographer has taken the appropriate photographs is the best time to start your wedding dances. The transition is a natural one, unless you opt to have your cake cutting ceremony even earlier. Recognize that just because you are cutting the cake doesn't mean it will be served immediately; it will take time for the caterer to cut and plate each serving. Key to a successful cake cutting time is that it not be too early or not too late. All your guests want to share in this ceremony with you and will want to taste the cake. Don't put it off until your guests start departing.

The Wedding Dance

The first wedding dance should be to a song that especially evokes romantic thoughts and feelings for you both. Usually, the bride and groom dance the entire first dance with each other, alone, but if they are shy, they may invite the parents and attendants to join them.

"But," you say, "my groom doesn't know how to dance." *Not to worry!* To learn a simple dance "takes only one or two lessons," explains Kim Sakren of A Perfect Wedding Dance (Las Vegas, Nevada). Often couples want to

learn something complicated so they can perform and show off in front of their friends—and why shouldn't they! This is a special time when all eyes are on them. We do advise couples to stay with the lessons long enough to get a newly learned dance practiced so it becomes second nature.

After the bride and groom have danced, then comes time for the "round of dances." Here's the proper sequence. While the bride dances with her father, the groom dances with his mother-in-law; then the bride with her father-in-law and the bride's father with the groom's mother. The groom dances with his mother; then the wedding attendants are invited to take their turns with the bride and groom before the guests all join in. It is imperative that the wedding dances be reserved until most of the guests have consumed their entrées; we suggest they be delayed until after the cake cutting ceremony. The dancing continues while the cake is being served and eaten. After that, and only after that, should the musicians be allowed to crank up the volume. Make a binding agreement with the musicians: If the wedding consultant or a parent of the bride asks them to lower the volume, the musicians shouldn't have to be asked twice.

 Think about taking dance lessons. Even the parents can get in on this. Many couples continue their dance lessons long after the wedding day.

—SCOTT PATTERSON, CALIFORNIA ARRANGEMENTS (SAN FRANCISCO, CALIFORNIA) AND KIM SAKREN, A PERFECT WEDDING DANCE (LAS VEGAS, NEVADA)

Bouquet and Garter Toss

The bouquet and garter toss are usually done at the end of the evening. Because state-of-the-art preservation of flowers and bouquets exists today and many brides are choosing to have their wedding bouquets preserved, many have the florist make up a separate, smaller "tossing bouquet" that is kept on the cake table. A smaller bouquet can also be part of your bridal bouquet and attached in such a way that it becomes a "breakaway" bouquet for the tossing. The attendants assist in arranging the unmarried women, including themselves, into a small group. The bride goes to a strategic place, and, turning her back, tosses the bouquet over her shoulders.

Next the groom sits by his bride and, to the roll of drums or sometimes a striptease song, he salaciously slides his hand up her calf and thigh. Some grooms really like to be the star of this moment, moving slowly and deliberately; others remove the garter with their teeth. It is one of the truly lighthearted moments of the evening as the bride sits and blushes. A hint for the groom: Remove your wife's shoe before your hand starts to creep up her leg; it will make the garter easier to remove! After removing the garter, the groom turns his back on the assembled unmarried men and stretches the garter so that it shoots toward them. Sometimes the one who catches the garter will place it onto the leg of the lady who caught the bouquet. Other times he puts it on his arm and wears it as a band of courage (or possibly trepidation, since legend has it that the catcher of the bouquet and the catcher of the garter will be the next to marry, though not necessarily to each other). Your photographer will want to get pictures of both you and your husband with the people who catch the bouquet and garter.

The Last Wedding Dance

For obvious reasons, we prefer to call it "the last wedding dance" instead of the last dance. (We certainly hope that you will enjoy many dances in your new life together.) Since the last wedding dance signifies the end of the party, some couples go to their room or a room set aside for them to undress and change into their "going away" clothes before returning to the reception to dance "the last wedding dance." Ask your best man and maid/matron of honor to have your departure clothes set out and ready so you don't have to worry about what you are going to wear. While you are not going to be able to change in five minutes, you don't want to be gone from the reception too long or your guests will think you have secretly slipped away. Many a bride and groom have been startled by returning in their departure clothes only to find that most of the guests had left. Also, ask your attendants and your mother to assist you in getting out of your gown. Separate any rental attire and place them in appropriate garment bags. Don't forget the shirt studs and cuff links, and any rented slips and undergarments that need to be returned to respective salons or stores. And remember to have a clean white sheet or muslin garment bag on hand that the gown can be placed in to be taken to the cleaners and preservationist within a day or so after the wedding day. Before starting the dance you both should say your good-byes to your parents, the best man and maid/matron of honor, other attendants, and any other special close relatives and friends. The dance should be announced so that the guests' attention will be on you.

The photographer should always be alerted before these key moments are to happen. Even though more brides and grooms are remaining until the very end of the party, some still want to leave in a flourish. Have your best man and maid/matron of honor, or the wedding consultant, gather the parents and other close family members and special friends at the door or on the steps leading outside so they can be the last to say good-bye to you.

Don't forget to add the appropriate information to your wedding day schedule and the reception floor plan.

Video Montage

Some brides and grooms work with their videographer in the months of planning to create a video montage of pictures from the couple's past, their courtship, and family gatherings. Another idea is to gather slides that tell the "life story" of the couple. The video or slide presentation is then shown at the reception. Be certain to check with your reception site to make sure that outlets, a projector, VCR, extralarge monitor, or screen are available. Also, take care to tape the extension cords to the floor so no one accidentally trips on them; ask the site person if taping to the floor is permitted. Ask, too, about any setup or rental fees.

Portrait Display

Even if you don't do the more elaborate video presentation, consider having a bridal portrait or a wedding portrait displayed at your reception. This is another custom derived from the Southern region of the United States. Often, a very large portrait of the bride is displayed near the guest book table; it may be as large as 30 × 40.

If you choose to follow this custom, you will need to inform not only your photographer but also your gown salon. Your final fitting will be necessary before the portrait can be taken. A new twist on the tradition is to photograph you alone or you and your groom in more casual attire. This could also be the engagement portrait. The key is to have enough time to have the proofs processed and to select the favored pose as well as to have the photo printed and framed.

- Have a realistic concept of budget and guest count and know your reception site before asking for a proposal from a caterer. Be up front from the beginning as to what your budget is; if you really don't know, then allow the caterer to present you a proposal based on your dream wedding, with suggested ways to pare it down if necessary.

- If you have a large number of guests (any amount over fifty), think twice before you decide to have a receiving line.

- If you're having a buffet, make certain there is enough seating at least for guests not able to easily juggle a drink, plate, napkin, and fork.

- Some food items (especially for a reception) are cost out according to a rate per count (that is, number of pieces of the item).

- A full bar isn't necessarily more expensive than a wine/champagne/beer/nonalcoholic bar.

- Provide seating for your photographer/videographer in the room where dinner is being served so they don't miss something important while eating back in the kitchen somewhere.

- Provide at least some food (sandwiches and nonalcoholic beverages) for your musicians. Musicians who are treated to a meal are in a better mood, which translates into better music.

- Figure that each guest will have from two to three drinks during the reception. That doesn't mean they are drinking a lot; some people set their drinks down, go to the washroom, and return not remembering where they put the drink.

- In addition to the bar, have some drinks (wine, champagne, and nonalcoholic beverages) served butler-style.

- Be specific on your RSVP card about the kind of reception you are having.

- Don't be too creative with your RSVP cards when offering a choice of entrée (most people do not know that *boeuf* is French for *beef.* You don't have to go to the other extreme and say just "meat"; most people know the terms *filet mignon* or *rib eye.* Remember to offer a vegetarian choice.

- Note that hotels nearly always charge a city and state tax on the entire bill, along with a service charge, and they also tax the service charge; technically, though some call it a gratuity, legally it is a service charge, not a tip.

- Find out who on the catering staff will be coordinating the reception with the band, photographer/videographer, and wedding consultant. Make certain all these people are in communication with one another and go over the schedule for the event in advance.

- If the wedding is on a Friday evening and is not a formal sit-down dinner, plan for the probability of extra guests; your invited guests might extend spur-of-the-moment invitations to coworkers.

The Receiving Line

One of the most controversial choices in planning a wedding is whether or not to have a receiving line. A receiving line characterizes the most formal of formal events. (Think of how many times you've seen the president of the United States and other dignitaries standing in line shaking hands as someone behind them whispers the name of the person approaching.) In years past, the receiving line offered an opportunity for the bride and groom to be introduced to their guests. However, now that brides and grooms are taking a greater role in planning their weddings, receiving lines are falling by the wayside.

The difficulties with a receiving line are many; I'll offer a few. If many of the guests are strangers, you aren't going to remember their names; it's just another time when people have to queue up; time that would be spent enjoying the reception and dinner is taken up since guests may be in line for an hour or more—your guests, as much as they love you, want to get something to eat and drink.

Even if you don't have a receiving line, it's your duty to go around to each table to greet your guests after dinner so that you can hug, kiss, and thank them for attending. This act of "receiving your guests" also affords the photographer an opportunity to get some wonderful pictures of you and individual guests.

If you do decide to have a receiving line, despite all the arguments against one, it is imperative that you let your wedding consultant and caterer know well in advance so it can be scheduled. Moreover, you want to be certain you have sufficient room for it.

According to John Loring in *The Tiffany Wedding*, if the fathers stand in the receiving line, then the order is as follows: mother of the bride, father of the groom, mother of the groom, father of the bride, the bride and groom, the maid/matron of honor. An alternative is to have the mother of the bride as the first person, then the mother of the groom, father of the groom, father of the bride, the bride, the groom, maid/matron of honor, and finally the bride's attendants. Another way to set up the receiving line is to exclude the father of the bride and the groom's best man and attendants, leaving them to enjoy the tranquility of not having to be in the receiving line. However, if the father of the groom is going to be in the receiving line, it is proper for the father of the bride to stand by his side (misery loves company).

CHAPTER 10

We Walk into the Lily of the Valley to Create a Scene

❧ Flowers, Decorations, Lighting

GET READY! THIS CAN BE ONE OF THE BIG-BUDGET ITEMS: AS HIGH AS **20** TO 35 percent of the total, depending on where in the country you live and how elaborately you want to decorate. In places like Montana, for example, the percentage may be higher, whereas in Chicago it may be lower, simply because of greater availability of fresh flowers.

Decorating is also called "creating a scene" (which has nothing to do with the in-laws). Though it can be expensive—you may have to spend more than you realize if you want a showstopper!—it can also be one of the most fun and exciting components of your wedding.

Start by putting your mind into "relaxed" mode, and then envision the setting of your wedding. (At this point, you will have already contracted the sites for the ceremony and for the reception.) Focus on the basics: What colors do you see? What kinds of shapes and movement? What about the lighting? Do evening stars glow in the far horizon of your mental screen?

- Floral designer
- Wedding consultant
- Caterer
- Ceremony and/or reception site manager
- Cake chef
- Financial minister

If warm, bright colors like red, yellow, and orange appear on your color screen, then the ideal spot might be the sandy beaches of Baja, or even the hills of Connecticut in October. However, I have a feeling that most of you are going to get married in a spacious synagogue, lofty cathedral, quaint church, grand hotel ballroom, country town hall, luscious bed-and-breakfast, airy private home, billowy tent, rustic gymnasium—even a museum or aquarium. It's your decision, and the choices are limitless.

No matter where your wedding is held, no matter how intimate or large-scale the setting, the site nearly always needs some help to look its best. And don't think that decorating means paper streamers and rolls of crepe paper; nor is it necessary to recreate the Garden of Eden! Creating a scene means just that: creating an ambience that carries through the theme of your wedding.

You need a thread to weave in and out of every aspect of your wedding, and that is where flowers, ribbons, shrubs and trees, mirrors, fabric, and lights come in. Once you've decided on your site and the colors for your gown and the attendants' wardrobe (both men and women), you're ready to prepare a palette for painting the canvas.

If you are not good at mental imaging, then talk to the florists you are interviewing and see if they have someone on staff to be your personal artist. You want someone who will listen to you describe what you want for your dream wedding, even vaguely, and then reflect back a clear, coherent picture. If she can do sketches, all the better. In your description, you'll want to focus on the most important components, your bouquet, of course, being at the top of the list. Remember, this is one of the four focal points in a wedding, in addition to the invitations, the bride in her gown, and the wedding cake. People will gush over your bouquet, almost to the point of drooling. Gloria Gasser, owner of Floral Images (Las Vegas, Nevada) and one of the most caring and creative florists in the country, actually studies the bouquets she designs, having them photographed by professional wedding photographer Susan Gomez of Light Images by Susan (Las Vegas, Nevada) from every possible angle. Gasser is meticulous in crafting a beautiful bouquet: front, sides, *and* back.

In giving thought to the kind of person you want to paint the picture for your wedding day, your first and foremost consideration is to hire a personable individual, someone who is interested in the entire wedding and not just dropping off the flower arrangements. It should be someone you feel confident with. Additionally, the person has to be an artist.

Don't be satisfied with going to the floral shop where you order flowers to be sent to your mother on Mother's Day or to your best friend who just had another baby. While it's true that not all floral shops do cloned FTD-like arrangements, it's also true that not every floral shop has a designer or that every flower shop owner can decorate. Anyone can put flowers into a vase, but to be able to give simple elegance to a bowl of carnations by adding a rose or two, two or three gerbera, and a splash of French rolled ribbon requires talent. You want someone not only who knows the mechanics of preparing a bouquet so it doesn't fall apart but also who can express the vision of an artist. Talent and creativity may add to your costs, but remember it's your wedding and your decision.

A floral designer will want to talk to you about the site for the ceremony and reception. If decorating the site, she must be willing to go to the site with you, regardless of how many times she has done weddings there. She needs to experience the site with you to familiarize herself with your vision; she must do a walk-through with *you*. If she is only doing bouquets and corsages, then this trip obviously isn't necessary.

A good place to meet florists is bridal fairs, or you can obtain names from good friends or relatives who have recently married. A better idea is to ask your wedding consultant and/or your caterer. Obtain any preferred or required vendors list from the site where you are having your wedding. Once again, don't forget to ask the question "Is the site, or vendor, receiving commissions for the referral?"

When talking to floral designers, be sure they have appropriate facilities for storing flowers, for example a walk-in cooler, as well as enough space to comfortably arrange the flowers *and* proper vehicles to transport them to the site. Some florists who work out of their home will tell you they are more affordable simply because they don't have the tremendous overhead of a retail flower shop. To do large weddings and events, however, a florist must have access to facilities with adequate refrigeration so the flowers can be kept at proper temperatures.

 Don't clutter a natural setting. If you have a beautiful vista on a hillside, you don't need a lot of baskets filled with exotic flowers. Let nature work for you.

—JACK ROBINSON, CAFE EUROPE (SANTA ROSA, CALIFORNIA)

Meanwhile, you'll want to be tearing pictures out from magazines of flower arrangements that you like. Get a photograph of yourself in your gown, or at least of the gown itself. Collect flyers, brochures, and business cards while talking with florists at trade shows. Put an asterisk by the names of the ones you make a connection with, who sound creative and imaginative. All of these lists, notes, and pamphlets go into your resource binder. When the time comes for you to work on this aspect of your wedding, take all these materials out. Separate the ones who you've met or talked to on the phone who seem gracious and who make you feel important.

You'll also need a list of the names of people who will need flowers (anyone in the wedding ceremony, parents, grandparents, special relatives, the cake servers, soloists, and guest book attendants). Note, too, the different segments of your wedding day requiring floral arrangements (ceremony, reception, dinner). Keep in mind your budget for flowers and decoration— and keep this as flexible as you can.

 You want to know if the person you are meeting with is actually going to be your florist. How long has he been with the company? Moreover, is he a *wedding florist*? Is he knowledgeable about what he does, not only about flowers, but about design and the multiplicity of containers? Does he have letters of reference from recent brides?

—W. DONNIE BROWN, FIVE STAR FLORAL DESIGNS & EVENT (DALLAS, TEXAS)

Shopping for a Floral Designer

Set up appointments with the florists you have met who are best able to answer your questions, who seem the most knowledgeable, who come up with creative ideas, and who are realistic about your budget. Go to these first. If you have a wedding consultant, have him call the florist and give his "take" on what you want, along with information about the site, so the florist can begin thinking about your wedding.

Talk to the florist about the wedding you desire most. Pay attention to how she receives the information. Does she ask questions? Is she interested? Recognize that this is an introductory meeting. It's to see if you and the florist have a good rapport and to help determine whether or not you want to entrust your wedding design to her. After the meeting, you should jot down any of her ideas you liked. It is safe to let a few days go by before you call the florist to let her know what direction you want to go in, but don't wait too long. A specialty florist is telling you the truth when she says you must book within a reasonable time frame. A floral designer isn't a "cookie cutter" or assembly-line worker. Besides, she still needs to draw up a proposal for you. When you do call back, she will probably need more information from you. As you continue to go down your list of florists, interviewing others, follow the same format.

 Your wedding consultant can be quite helpful in communicating between you and the florist and also seeing that the florist stays within your budget.

—JOY NORTON, STANFORD DESIGNS (DALLAS, TEXAS)

As time goes by, try to be more precise about what you want. You'll find that the more information you give your florist, the better she will be able to guide you in articulating what you want. Keep in mind that some floral designers have very strong and even overwhelming personalities. Don't worry. You aren't going to be working intimately with the floral designer on the day of your wedding. You want to make sure she can provide a quality product, reputable service, and punctual delivery and setup on your wedding day; she and her staff are going to be working behind the scenes to set the stage for your entire event, so you don't have to be buddies.

Remember, your flowers should elicit the same response from your guests as you in your gown—they should electrify. When your guests walk into the ceremonial and reception sites, their mouths should fall open—Granny should be dropping her dentures. People will be delighted you have invited them to share in this fantasy of yours.

Now, don't get me wrong—I am not saying that you have to spend a fortune to have a beautifully decorated wedding. As we said above, even the most humble pink carnations can be made to stand proud and tall just by adding a rose or two to their company. You are, however, going to have to spend something. I can pretty well assure you that any proposal is going to be three to four times what you originally expected, because you are used to buying a single bouquet or arrangement. Flowers bought at the supermarket are not comparable in price with flowers bought for your wedding.

Ask if the florist submits an itemized and descriptive proposal. Many are willing to let you study the proposal in their office but will not allow it to be taken from the shop. This is because some brides will "price shop"; they will take the proposal to a second or even third florist and ask to get it cost out for less. Needless to say, any florist who would "steal" another's creation is unethical. Also, any florist other than the one who created the design may very well reproduce a watered-down version, and that's what it will look like: a less expensive and likely less than fresh grouping of flowers.

 If the client wants us to "redo" or "reshape" ceremonial arrangements so they can be used at the reception, we are delighted to, as long as the service is in our proposal and contract. But it takes a great deal of creativity to design arrangements that quickly and easily can be adapted to dual purposes.

—Domonie Mattson, Dom Unique Designs (Brooklyn Park, Minnesota)

Decorating the site for your wedding is where your professionals come in; you are paying someone for his artistic ability and also for his experience. The florist will know, given the availability of worldwide and global delivery services, how almost any "out of season" flower can be obtained at almost any time of the year (though you should be prepared for the quality of flowers that have to be "flown in"). A professional is going to know, too, when the various liturgical seasons occur—during which some flora, or none, are allowed on the premises of some religious sites.

You'll want to ask your professional florist a number of fairly detailed questions. Has he worked with your vendors before? If hired for the complete design effect, does he know what table linen, overlays, and napkins are available that would beautifully complement the floral decor? In fact, does he own linen, overlays, and napkins that would work better than the caterer's? Will he be responsible for advising on lighting, trees, and shrubbery? Will he have someone at the ceremony site or where the bride will be dressing, to distribute and pin on flowers? This most certainly will incur an extra fee, but do you really want to skimp here and have your untrained maid of honor or, worse yet, nervous mother, pinning on boutonnieres? You'll be wanting a professional around when that rosebud suddenly flops onto the floor or droops, pulling the lapel down with it because it's pinned improperly.

 Dye can not only come off on clothing, it can be seriously dangerous if ingested. Your competent florist will suggest flowers in real colors that will completely satisfy you.

—Scott Patterson, California Arrangements (San Francisco, California)

Another question for your florist is whether he will provide staff to transfer arrangements and redo them for the reception site. Some will be reluctant to simply because they may not have the time, especially if the wedding and the reception are back to back. Others prefer not to reshape a floral arrangement once it has been designated for a specific purpose. There is also the very real difficulty of having to remove flower arrangements while the photography session is going on after the ceremony, plus having to wade through your guests at the reception in order to set them up anew.

QUESTIONS FOR THE FLORAL DESIGNER ❧

- Can you give us some brides' names and phone numbers you have recently worked with?

- Are we able to come see your decorations for a ceremony and reception at a religious site?

- Are the flowers that we like seasonal at the time of year of our wedding? If not, what are the possibilities and costs for obtaining them?

- What will be your required setup and breakdown time? What time will your staff arrive to begin to set up, and then later to break down? Are these within the confines of the sites' requirements?

- Can you draw up a proposal that gives us choices in cutting back without compromising our desires or that gives us options in prioritizing elements? How long will it take you to deliver the proposal?

- Can you handle lighting, fabric, napkins, and table linen? Can these be cost out separately? If you do handle these items, will you coordinate setup with the caterer?

- Will your staff work with the caterer and cake chef to coordinate use of flowers for serving trays as well as the cake and other tables? If the cake or cake table is to have fresh flowers, will your staff take care of that or will the flowers be delivered to the cake chef early enough for her decoration?

- Will you be the designer for our wedding? If not, can we meet with that person to ensure he understands our vision?

- Is it more economical to use a mixture of preserved, silk, *and* fresh flowers? If so, are you familiar with such arrangements?

- Do you need the cake knife and champagne glasses in advance?

- Once we have firmed up our decisions, can you do a sample bouquet and table centerpiece in advance so we can see the overall design and color? Or will you at least provide a good sketch of these and the overall design of the rooms?

- Are there any additional costs, for example, delivery; having a representative on-site to distribute the individual bouquets and pin on corsages, boutonnieres, etc.?

All of these special touches may increase costs, but for the bride who has made decoration a priority, these options are available. Don't forget, there are marvelously lifelike silk and preserved trees and flowers today—

you don't have to settle for plastic. These simulations can be rented and save you a considerable amount of money.

After visiting your site with you, have the florist draw up a proposal in itemized and descriptive paragraph form, specifying how each segment of your wedding will be decorated: the flowers to be used, the size and extent of the arrangement, and the cost. Unless yours is a simple wedding, don't settle for one of those silly, bigger-than-legal-size forms that many florists are still married to. These forms have enough room only to write in some names of flowers and a column listing their price; the florist adds up this column to arrive at your total cost. By the way, you probably won't be able to read the florist's writing; sometimes I think some of them once practiced medicine, since they fill out these forms as if they were writing a prescription! Do be sure to ask for a legible and detailed proposal if you are planning an elaborately decorated wedding.

The Floral Designer Goes to Work

After reviewing the proposal and trimming it to your style and budget, let the florist go to work. When a budget is more extensive and the contract signed, florists will often agree to make up a sample of a centerpiece so you can see the colors and design together with the table linen and chair covers. Meet one or two times until you get the overall concept as well as the specifics ironed out.

As the wedding day approaches, check to make certain the florist can still get the flowers promised. For clients who desire full-scale decoration, Brown says some floral designers will give you the opportunity to change your mind about the flowers as much as ten days from your wedding. "Of course, the budget and contract can't change; but since I order my flowers three days before the wedding, I will often give the bride the opportunity to make changes if she desires," Brown adds. If you feel your budget warrants such service, ask for it.

Place a copy of the florist's proposal and signed contract in your wedding day binder. Behind the tab labeled "Florist," also include any relevant brochures, business cards, and drawings. The original of your contract goes to your finance minister.

YOUR CONTRACT WITH THE FLORAL DESIGNER ✠

Your contract with the floral designer should contain the following:

- Names, date, time, and address(es) of the wedding site(s).

- An itemized and descriptive list of each floral piece, no matter how big or small.

- The number of pieces and arrangements.

- The delivery time and place; the times to begin and complete the setup; the time to begin and complete the breakdown. Do these times match your site requirements?

- The names of your designer and the person who will be on site to distribute and pin on flowers.

- If the florist will transfer flowers from the ceremony site to the reception site, the flowers should be rearranged so they fit in with the new surroundings and don't merely look as though they were moved from one place to another. There may be a slight charge for this, so be sure it's stated in your contract.

- The total cost and dates when payments are due.

Decoration Trends

Remember to include the groom when designing the wedding set. More often than not, he feels left out of all of this planning. Having him give his opinions about the table arrangements and other flora will make him feel special.

Once a bride's mother provided me with a sample of the beautifully colored beads sewn onto the bodice of her daughter's gown. I repeated the look by putting a cluster of the beads in the center of the stephanotis used in her bouquet.

—JOY NORTON, STANFORD DESIGNS (DALLAS, TEXAS)

Many florists take a piece of lace or fabric that matches the wedding gown or attendants' dresses and incorporate it into the bouquet. W. Donnie Brown of Five Star Floral Designs & Events provides tissue-lined boxes for the client so flowers may be removed from the containers and taken home by the guests. See if your floral designer will do this for you.

Something that's *in* is interesting boutonnieres. Grooms want to wear something different too; we just did some for a New Year's wedding. The men wore a black magic rose, with pepperberry and dusty miller. The bride's bouquet was a hand-tied design with a slight teardrop effect, in different shades of red—black magic roses, Charlotte roses, America lilies, rapid red freesia, bouvardia, Italian ruscus, and plumosis. The design was about 12 inches wide and 18 inches long. French pavé style is really popular right now, the mixing of pale yellows and pale greens. Understated is what's in.

—W. DONNIE BROWN, FIVE STAR FLORAL DESIGNS & EVENTS (DALLAS, TEXAS)

Besides being a talented and creative designer, a florist must know how to care for flowers. "Just as modern travel has made unseasonable flowers seasonal, so has the industry given us products that help prolong the life of flowers and reduce browning," attests Joy Norton of Stanford Designs

(Dallas, Texas). You don't want your spring garden arrangements looking as if they've been through a summer drought. The flowers need to be cut and arranged as near as possible to the time of the ceremony and reception to ensure freshness; some florists even go so far as to cut the stems while immersed in water. Keep in mind your climate. Delicate blossoms like the irises, calla lily, or lily of the valley may not stand up to a 104-degree dry temperature.

Design Elements Your
Floral Designer Can Provide

Props

A floral designer who has an abundance of props, stands, and vases will be your best bet. Most floral designers, like Laura Little of San Francisco's Floramor Studios, have a huge inventory of napkins, tablecloths, and overlays too. Previously, a party giver had to depend on the rental company for such items, and even then had only the basic whites, off-whites, grays, and pastels. The braver and more innovative rental agencies, after years of encouragement by wedding and event planners, now carry a great variety of not only colors but also types of fabric. Give me organza!

Lighting

Often a floral designer will need to bring in the expertise of a lighting company. Great drama can be added to a country dance hall or school hall or even a gymnasium by simple uplighting and washing the walls in colors that complement your flowers and gowns. Baby Fresnels or pin spots can be shined on each table arrangement or the wedding cake to give it a life of its own.

Fabric

Fabrics of a similar hue or shade as your attendants' dresses and flowers can be draped on walls or along banisters or stairways or swathed along the rails of a yacht. Fabric can be draped over tables. Tulle and a shiny, inexpensive fabric interspersed with strings of white lights and draped on the pews down the center aisle can add splendor to a candlelit wedding ceremony; these can later be taken over to the reception site and used to drape the buffet tables or cake table or intertwined through the branches of trees and shrubbery. For a country wedding, we used the same design but substituted burlap for the tulle; big burlap bows with dried sprigs of wheat held the swag in place at every third pew.

Go to your local inexpensive fabric store, buy bolts and bolts of color, and just go wild (or at least as wild as the site manager will allow you). Later you can cut up the fabric and have it sewn into tablecloths and napkins to be given as gifts.

Shrubs and Trees

Plants and greenery are no longer used just to hide ugly table skirting or to create a border for the band's raised platform. Rather, florists bend them to their imaginations. For example, the Academy of Science in San Francisco has high, vaulted, curved ceilings that are just incredible, but the three-story headroom can feel excessive! To bring some intimacy to the space, we brought in huge palm trees; clear, twinkling lights rested atop the palm fronds. When the museum's lights were dimmed, it seemed as if twilight had fallen. The curvature of the palm fronds flowed perfectly with the curved ceilings and at the same time gave guests a greater sense of closeness.

One synagogue reception hall had powerful beams crossing the ceiling as well as massive right angles and squared-off corners. To offset the angularity of the place, we brought in rounded ficus trees, again using the twinkling lights. The contrast of the bushy, leafy trees against the straight lines of the room lent the space greater appeal.

Silk/Dried Flowers

Talk with your designer. Again, let him know your budget. Also let him know what you would like if you could afford it. Be firm, and be realistic.

OTHER FLORAL DESIGN TIPS ✎

- Have the florist bring an extra boutonniere or two and even some loose flowers matching those in the bouquet, along with floral tape and pins, in case something goes wrong.

- Have your "tossing bouquet" delivered to the reception site and placed on the cake table where you will later add your bouquet. That way, you don't have to worry about it.

- Be careful with the aisle runner. Consider having it set up in advance so that it is secure and stable. You can always "rope off" the area and have guests enter their seats from the outsides of the rows. Be certain that the aisle runner is thick enough so women's heels won't protrude. Don't even think about placing an aisle runner over grass unless it is supported by a platform or otherwise stabilized.

- Make sure the air-conditioning or heating system at the site is properly set before the flowers arrive.

- If you have your wedding on a yacht, pay a visit to your local flag maker— unless you're a Martha Stewart devotee who would prefer to make her own— and order a flag using your wedding colors and your monogram (remember, the initial of the bride-soon-to-be-wife goes on the left; the initial of the couple's surname in the middle, the letter a larger size, and that of the groom-soon-to-be-husband on the right, in the same size letter as the bride's).

Preserving Your Bouquet

What's a bride to do with her exquisite bouquet after the wedding? Put it in the refrigerator and once in a while glance at it at the same time as she is reaching for leftovers to reheat for dinner? Set the plastic holder into a jelly jar atop her dining table and prolong its life by daily adding water?

"To assure that your bouquet will last indefinitely, have it freeze-dried," says Linda Lee Sirmen, one of our floral preservation experts and owner of Special Arrangements by LL (Plano, Texas). Linda Sue Abbott of Sentimental

Reasons (Las Vegas, Nevada) has a member of her staff pick up the flowers about two hours into the reception so they do not become bruised or lose any more of their vitality. "If the bouquet cannot be picked up or dropped off at the preservationist, gently wrap it in plastic and put it into a refrigerator," advises Abbott. When the bouquet arrives at her salon, Abbott takes a photograph before she disassembles it, to make sure she can replicate the shape and size.

After being grouped into similar types of flowers, the entire lot is placed in a freeze-drying machine; the flowers come out smooth, colorful, and in full form. They then undergo a chemical process to make them more pliable so they will not shatter and fall apart. By using this modern technology, the bride's bouquet can become more than a memory; it can last forever (as much as anything can last "forever"), hanging in a beautiful airtight, decorative display container.

Let your floral designer know that you are thinking about having your bouquet preserved. She will be able to discuss which flowers freeze-dry well and which don't.

—LINDA LEE SIRMEN, SPECIAL ARRANGEMENTS BY LL (PLANO, TEXAS)

"Will my bouquet really retain its sharpness of color?" you ask. Even freeze-drying isn't perfect; the process could change the colors slightly (it depends on the flowers being preserved), and the colors could become muted just as your drapes or carpet do with time. Ask your preservationist for a brochure or other instructions on how to best care for your bouquet.

CHAPTER 11

Smile . . .
You're Gonna Be in Pictures

❧ Your Photographer and Videographer

I DON'T KNOW ABOUT YOU, BUT ONE OF THE THINGS I HATE MOST IS BEING photographed. Ever since I was a kid, I can remember being stood in groups while someone standing at a distance, holding a camera, would say "Smile!" I would try to smile but could only manage a stupid-looking grin.

It wasn't until I had occasions requiring a professional portrait that I discovered something important about being photographed. Why was it that in some photos I look handsome, with sparkling eyes, great posture (the head tilted just so), and most importantly, a beaming smile, but in others, I look awkward, dull, and uncomfortable? The answer: the photographer. It doesn't matter what kind of camera or how many lights, umbrellas, or sets of lenses the photographer uses. First and foremost, the photographer has to be skilled at making you feel at ease in front of the camera. In other words, the photographer is a "people person" who is also an artist at taking pictures.

245

Who will be spending the most time with the two of you on your wedding day? Who will be directing you? Your mom? Your wedding consultant? Think again. It will be your photographer (or videographer).

Let's first deal with the language of the camera. Why? Because photographers and videographers live in a world of their own. Remember, they work behind black metal boxes. It is necessary to know their terminology so you will be certain to hire the right one for the style you desire—there are at least six styles of professional photography to consider.

Portraiture Photography

This style, more often than not, is captured in a studio with powerful lighting and dramatic backdrops. The resulting portrait has a classical feel. The photographer is adept at controlling the image. Even without retouching, a negative or print can be made to look beautiful because of the skill and experience of the portraiture photographer. For example, a bald groom can appear less so simply by controlling a sort of flat, half-moon-shaped prop that creates a shadow over his head. Some facial wrinkles, even crow's-feet around the eyes, can be displaced with proper lighting.

If retouching is required or desired, it can be done directly on the negative or print via airbrushing or by fine artists under a magnifying glass, or even by a high-tech process called digital imaging, which we will say something about later in this chapter.

Professional portraiture is shot with what is called a medium-format camera. This produces a 2¼-inch-square negative that makes a 5 × 5 print. Retouching if done by hand is a simple but expensive task.

A custom in the South that has quickly spread is to have a professional portrait of the bride or of the bride and groom taken at least a month to six weeks before the wedding day, enlarged to 16 by 20 inches, and displayed at the wedding reception.

Many portrait or studio-based photographers can transport equipment similar to what they use in the studio to a site or "on location" session. Still, if you desire portraiture photography in the traditional sense of the term, it is more cost-effective to go to the studio than to have the studio come to you.

 When deciding on a portrait, think about where it will hang in your home.

—Pat Bruneau, JWIC, L'Affaire Du Temps (Milpitas, California)

Photojournalism

Photojournalists claim they do not do posed pictures; they simply document the day as it unfolds—or unravels. They shoot from afar with their telescopic lenses, and black and white is their favorite medium. Something to consider is that the photographer has to take a lot of shots to be certain he gets the one that will please you. This is why photojournalists tend to be so pricey.

There is little difference in the styles of photojournalists and candid photographers. Some photojournalists state up front that even their casual pictures (for example, those taken at the reception of guests sitting at the table) are somewhat posed. While one need not worry so much about the photographer who shoots lots of candids, one does need to be careful about the photojournalist. What I mean by this is simple: Be aware that if you hire a true photojournalist, one who really does not follow any sort of script, you could be disappointed when you end up with no photographs of groupings of parents, family, the wedding party, or the bride with her favorite uncle. A disaster occurred when I took an educated, sophisticated "marrying again" bride seriously when she said that she wanted a photojournalist for her photographer, that she did not want any posed pictures whatsoever. When her proofs returned, she was horrified there were no pictures of the wedding party as a group. Moreover, the picture of the bride and groom cutting the cake was a blur, because they hadn't "posed" for the shot.

If you want any "posed" pictures, then you do not want a photojournalist. You want a wedding photographer who shoots both posed and candid pictures. By the way, for "candid" shots, the photographer will often forewarn guests they are going to be photographed so he gets everyone in the picture (or so he doesn't catch Aunt Martha gnawing the meat off a chicken drumstick).

Candid Photography

Candid photography, more often than not, is a combination of the portraiture, photojournalist, and environmental (see below) styles. A candid photographer uses a 35mm or medium-format camera and film. You get pictures of people dancing, talking, or simply sitting at their tables—groupings of eight or ten at each table are asked to lean in and smile. You also get the usual formals and groupings before or after the ceremony. "I take about 20 percent posed pictures and 80 percent candids," says Ron Barbosa of Barbosa Studios (Dallas, Texas). Dolores Enos of Photography by Rusty and Dolores Enos (Larkspur, California) adds that while brides insist they don't want an overabundance of formals (Rusty Enos shoots about 12 percent), "they select nearly all of these for their wedding albums."

Environmental Photography

This style produces pictures, whether posed or candid, in natural settings. You may go to the local park or to the sand dunes of Cape Cod, walking along the beach in your wedding gown and holding your high heels in your hand, the wind blowing your veil. Or you may be astride a horse at the Kentucky Derby. It can be any natural setting, even if it's not natural for a bride in her gown, as long as it works for you—after all, it's your memory. Rusty Enos has a signature photograph of a bride walking around the reflection pool of San Francisco's Palace of Fine Arts; as her train flows in the breeze, a goose is following behind her, plucking with its beak at her gown.

Some of the best environmental photography done for JWI clients includes that for the three daughters of a Texas John Deere franchise owner. As noted elsewhere, in the South, the tradition of displaying a bridal portrait at the wedding reception is ingrained. Six weeks before the wedding, we dressed the first daughter, Kimberly, in her gown (which we had to order for early arrival), and posed her climbing onto a John Deere 340 tractor beneath a hundred-year-old oak tree. We posed the second daughter, Becky, right in the middle of a ready-for-harvest wheat field, clambering onto a John Deere wheat harvester. We handed a bouquet of cotton bolls to the third daughter, Melissa, and posed her mounting a giant John Deere cotton-picking machine *and* amidst all the John Deere implement equipment at the Central Texas John Deere plant. Now, *that* is environmental photography.

Progressive Photography

Jim Eagan of Eagan Photography & Video (San Jose, California) notes the rising interest in a style known as progressive photography. "Off-angle shots, cross processing (unnatural colors), casual compositions, and dramatic lighting techniques would best describe this photography," says Eagan.

Artistic Photography

The artistic style is associated with dramatic posing and creative lighting to evoke a particular feeling in the viewer. Plain and simple, it's the sort of picture you see on the front of *Bride's*—that is, it produces a "modeled" effect.

CURRENT TRENDS

- Environmental and candid photography (inclusive of wedding party and family formals) are fast becoming the choice of couples today.

- Black and white is definitely on the upswing and more affordable than in the past.

- Black-and-white photos with a matte finish and a "ragged" edge (a frame that appears rough and unfinished) have become a popular album presentation. Also, black-and-white photos printed on archival paper with a matte frame and prepared individually in an archival box are especially popular among photojournalists.

- More brides and grooms are doing many of the formal shots before the wedding ceremony.

Costs

For the services of the day, leading to a completed album, costs are going to start at $2,500 in a large city, where competition is high. Cost of course varies, depending on the format and style of photography and whether or not the photographer has an assistant to help coordinate posing. If you can afford to hire an assistant, do so; things will go a lot more smoothly—and in a more timely manner.

Other Important Terminology

Digital Imaging

Digital imaging is one of the most fascinating innovations in photography. The image is stored on a screen on the reverse side of the camera, meaning the photographer can immediately know if the image is a good one or if he needs to reshoot it; he doesn't have to wait to have the film processed in a lab.

Once the camera is plugged into a computer, the photographer can work more magic. For example, digital imaging solves the problem of a bride being photographed with her groom *before* the ceremony: Just take two separate shots of each alone, insert the groom into the photo of the bride, and voilà! You have a picture of the bride and groom together, and he didn't have to see her in her gown before the ceremony. Images can be preserved on a CD-ROM, though it is doubtful that CD-ROMs will totally replace the traditional wedding album.

35mm and Medium Format

The 35mm camera is no doubt similar to the one you have at home. It produces a negative about ¾ inches by ½ inch and a 3 × 5 or 4 × 6 proof. The downside of 35mm is that its maximum range for reprinting, without graininess, is 10 × 10. Some photographers, such as M. Christine Torrington of San Francisco, California, say this is inaccurate information; a 35mm can be enlarged to 20 × 24 without losing any of its sharpness. Fred Smith of Reflections of Love Photography (Irving, Texas) states that "more and more photographers are switching to 35mm because with recent improvements in film, there is no way a consumer can distinguish between medium format and 35mm, and 35mm is much easier and faster to use."

We think loyalty to a particular camera format has more to do with style and preference for the equipment than with the increased quality of 35mm film. While it's true that the quality of the photograph has a lot to do with the artist pressing the shutter, no one will dispute that the medium-format camera produces a higher-quality negative. And for the mother (or bride) who wants to erase those crow's-feet and trim that waistline, she is going to be happier with the larger negative, where retouching and airbrushing can be done more easily; retouching is practically impossible on a 35mm negative.

To sum up: All portraiture done in a studio should be with a medium-format camera. The 35mm camera is preferred by the photojournalist or candid photographer because it has a quicker shutter action; creates better shadow, color contrast, and depth; and is easier to operate in more casual situations.

Negative

A negative is the developed or processed film. It will be rectangular (35mm) or 2¼ inches square (medium format). More often than not, the photographer will not sell the negatives unless you live in another country. The photographer not only makes his profit margin via reprints but also has the facility and space to store negatives in a proper climate and environment.

Camera Originals/Proofs

These are the images you receive. They are automatically mass produced from the film roll onto color or black-and-white paper. Although not sprayed for protection against fingerprints, light, or dust, they still have a long shelf life.

The photographer should have *at least* two proofs or pictures of each group pose or special moment (both sets of parents, the attendants, the two of you cutting the cake, etc.). If there is only one proof, and it's not a good one, ask the photographer if there is any chance there might be another that wasn't developed, though, truthfully, this is unlikely.

Print/Image

These are the finished products that are yours to frame or put into an album. They will have been retouched and airbrushed if you so request. While they usually are sprayed for protection against fingerprints, dust, and light, they may not be. Ask your photographer how he handles this dilemma. Sizes of prints/images are usually 5×5, 5×7, 8×10, 10×10, 11×17, 16×20, 20×24, and 30×40.

The chemicals used in spraying prints do more damage than good, and flecks of dust can be caught on the print in the process of spraying. Besides, Kodak and Fuji film manufacturers guarantee their paper for a lifetime, and the paper used today is so advanced that spraying doesn't really protect against fingerprints, which is the usual reason given for spraying the print.

—AMI DAVENPORT, A DAY TO REMEMBER PHOTOGRAPHY (LAS VEGAS, NEVADA)

Panoramic

This refers to the use of a wide-angled or panoramic lens to capture a large group portrait or a background setting. Such a shot is most often reserved for the center of the album so the two inserts create one lovely photograph. It is often a difficult shot to get, but the effort is worth it when you see most, if not all, your guests captured in one photo.

Cropping

Cropping literally means framing the picture so part of the print is enlarged or someone or something is cut out of view before it is printed. I once noticed the tripod a photographer had been using showing up in the majority of his prints; the problem was that the angle the pictures were taken from and his use of 35mm made it impossible to crop the pictures so the couple would be centered and framed in the $3,000 neon-light archway they had made just for the ceremony.

Soft Focus vs. Out of Focus

This isn't as tricky as it sounds, though some photographers will try to pass off out-of-focus prints as being soft focus. A sharp eye can tell the difference. Notice the details of your gown, for instance, the lace or beadwork. Or look at people's eyes; if the print is in focus you will still be able to see the "catch light" in them. (The "catch light" is the reflection of the flash off the cornea of the eyeball.) Even though other parts of the picture may look fuzzy, the flash reflection, and the eyes themselves, should be sharp and distinct.

Airbrushing and Retouching

These are done on a negative or print, for example, to eliminate a second chin (it's cheaper than plastic or laser surgery). Glares or reflections on eye glasses normally need to be retouched. Such work may not be included in the price; ask your photographer and have it put into your contract if it is not included and also get an estimate of what the total cost will be per print or per hour. Airbrushing or retouching on a negative does not have to be repeated for additional prints, whereas on a print it does.

Black and White

Obviously, black and white preceded color prints, and—for awhile—people lost interest in them. Film producers and labs got lazy and simply created a color film that could produce a black-and-white print. Labs became either color or black-and-white specialists; the black-and-white labs could produce a black-and-white print from a color negative, but the quality wasn't as good. Finally, Kodak came up with a black-and-white film and paper that is of high quality yet affordable, so the photographer can take both by simply changing camera backs.

Sepia

Sepia is a term describing a brown-tone print, lending it an antique quality.

Natural Color

This film produces more of a neutral contrast, which is closer to natural sunlight and shade and without the use of artificial light.

Vivid Color

This produces very well-defined tonality in the colors of a print. The colors therefore stand out.

Color Film/Paper

This is used to produce color and lesser-quality black-and-white prints as well as sepia prints.

Engagement Portrait/Picture

The engagement portrait is of the couple; it may be a studio or environmental portrait. It is usually taken for the purpose of printing in the newspaper. Many couples also see it as an opportunity to have a black-and-white picture taken; newspapers can print from either a color or a black-and-white print. The backs of photographs sent to newspapers should not be written on, not even with blue pencil, as the photographs are often scanned to reproduce the image. If you want your picture returned, put a return address label on the back, though this is no guarantee you will ever see the photograph again. Make sure you have a duplicate if it's a favorite.

CREATING A KEEPSAKE ❧

Have your engagement portrait matted with a broad mat and framed without glass. Attach a pen and have guests sign the portrait during the reception. This makes a terrific keepsake.

Bridal Portrait/Picture

The bridal portrait is most often taken in a studio, where the photographer creates a mood or ambience with backdrops and lighting. However, it can also be taken along a lake, in the park, or at some favorite site. The bridal portrait is often shot six to eight weeks before the wedding to ensure enough time for development of proofs, selection of a particular pose, and then final production of the portrait. The framed portrait is displayed at the wedding reception. A tip from the experts: Have your final fitting at least a month in advance of the wedding date.

Wedding Portrait

The process is the same as with the bridal portrait except that the groom is also in the picture—literally. This means that he will have to see you in your gown before the wedding or that you'll have to get all dressed up again after the honeymoon; that is, unless your mother has packed your gown off to the cleaners and preservationists. Options are to have this portrait enlarged from one taken on the wedding day or to hire a photographer who shoots with a digital imaging camera.

Formals

These are the groupings of pictures taken before or after the ceremony. They're the ones of the two of you with your parents, with the groomsmen, with the bridal attendants, etc. They are *posed* pictures.

À La Carte vs. Packages

Be prepared for prices to vary. "The couple want to keep in mind that they are not just hiring someone to take pictures; they are paying for the creativity and the expertise of the photographer," says Dolores Enos, JWIC. Ansel Adams was once asked how long it took him to get a famous shot of the falls at Yosemite. He replied, "A lifetime."

Photographers will set up a package, or they may simply charge a shooting, or sitting, fee, and then charge additionally for each print, cost depending on the size ordered. Some photographers charge less for prints of the same size and from the same negative when ordered in quantity, but don't count on it. Ask!

Portfolios/Albums

Your album will contain the final prints you put together to tell the story of your wedding day. It can be stitched and bound or simply have clips that fit into sockets of the album folders; the latter is economical but of lesser quality. The album itself may be made of archival paper and have a leather or faux-leather covering, while the prints may have a mat around them or be flush to the edge.

It takes about forty inserts (prints can be put on both sides of an insert) to produce an album that is attractive and looks complete. The format or layout of an album may limit you to 8 × 10 or 10 × 10 prints, while others are made for a mix of 5 × 7 (two on each side), 8 × 10, and 10 × 10. Ask before you decide on your photographer, as he may produce one or the other album.

Some types of albums include the bride's and groom's (usually holds prints from 5 × 7 to 10 × 10, either matted or flush), the parents' (usually consists of 5 × 5 or 5 × 7 prints, either matted or flush), and the proof album, a book of unfinished camera originals put into plastic pages with an index page facing each print so orders can be written in. Albums are frequently monogrammed, with the name of the bride and groom and the date of the wedding and/or cameo picture on the cover.

Finding the Right Photographer

Now that you know the terminology, how do you proceed? Where do you start in finding Mr./Ms. Personality who also knows what he/she is doing?

Ask some friends who have recently married about their wedding photographer. Did they like him? Did she seem to enjoy her work? As you go through the wedding albums of friends or relatives, ask them about specific pictures. How did the photographer get this particular pose or expression? Why does this picture look fuzzy? What did it feel like "being on the spot" for so much of the day?

Bridal fairs are a terrific place to not only meet photographers to see how you "click" with them but also to pick up flyers, leaflets, and brochures that document costs, styles, and other information you will need to accomplish your comparative shopping. Web sites are possibly a step above the yellow pages, since you are able to see a sample of the photographer's work. The pictures selected for the site are certainly, or at least should be, what the photographer thinks are his best shots. You will at least have an idea of what the photographer *thinks* is his style of photography.

Remember to ask other vendors you are interviewing what photographers they work with *regularly*. Another source is the preferred vendors list that most synagogues, churches, hotels, country clubs, bed-and-breakfasts, and other sites have. But don't just get the list; ask the catering or site manager specific questions about the photographers listed. These professionals are a great source of information regarding the way a photographer works on the day of the wedding simply because they interact closely with him on the day of the event. You'll want to find out as much about the "person" as you can; save your technical questions for the photographer himself. Take notes, and put these, along with other pertinent materials, in your resource binder, behind the tab labeled "Photographers/Videographers."

Again, the vendors whose names come up the most in conversations with recently married friends as well as other vendors are the ones you should begin calling to "feel them out." You'll give the photographer your name, the date of your wedding, and the name of the person who referred you. Offer as much information as you can about how you envision the wedding day. Be up front about your budget.

As you do your telephone interviews, pay attention to the jargon the photographers use. Unless you are "photography equipment friendly," the jargon is going to be new to you, but you need to learn it to help you narrow down your list of vendors. Personality is important and so is talent, but equipment is high in the ranking too! Knowing and understanding what kind of equipment a photographer uses will ensure a constructive and fruitful interview.

OTHER TIPS ON FINDING A PHOTOGRAPHER ✍

- Do the people in sample photos seem relaxed?

- Look for creative lighting and composition.

- How many years of experience does the photographer have?

- It is your responsibility to obtain permission from the officiant and the sites for all photography and videography. Get it in writing. And get it beforehand.

The yellow pages are on the bottom of your list of where to find a good photographer. Rather, go to bridal trade shows or fairs and meet photographers in person. Not only will you get an idea of what they are like dealing with people, but you can also see their work and ask them questions without any kind of commitment. Moreover, if a photographer at a bridal show is congenial and upbeat even after talking with so many brides in one day, that's a real clue he likes what he's doing.

—RUSTY ENOS, PHOTOGRAPHY BY RUSTY AND DOLORES ENOS (LARKSPUR, CALIFORNIA)

Interviewing Photographers

When interviewing photographers, ask to see a proof album of one or two weddings. Don't settle for an album containing only one or two pictures each from a dozen or more weddings, or you won't get a feel for how the photographer shoots an entire wedding. Note the total number of proofs (there should be up to 200 for a small wedding of 125 people).

Get an idea of what packages the photographer offers and the prices. Write all of this information down and add it to your resource binder. Also, pay attention to how the photographer interacts with you. Does she seem interested in your wedding? Does he ask you questions about the mood, ambience, or the flow of the day? Does she willingly tell you about her price ranges? Be sure to ask for references of recent brides.

- Are you a member of the Professional Photographers of America association?

- Have you shot before at the site of my ceremony? At the site of my reception?

- Do you have an assistant?

- Will the photographer we interview be the one photographing our wedding?

- What is your backup equipment? (It should be the same format as the primary equipment.)

- What time will you begin photographing and how late will you stay?

- When will the proofs be ready? How long after ordering will the final prints and/or album be available?

- How long do you keep the proofs? The negatives? How are they stored?

- Do you use high-speed film to expose natural light?

- Do you have telephoto and wide-angle lenses?

- Do you work well with the wedding consultant, videographer, and catering director we've hired?

- Will you meet, or at least talk with, our videographer and catering director before our wedding day?

- Will you help us create a schedule so we will know what is going to be photographed throughout the day?

- Do we get to keep the proofs or camera originals?

- What will you be wearing the day of the wedding?

- Do you use a local or out-of-state lab or do you process your own film and prints?

- Will you come to the rehearsal? What is your fee for doing so?

- What are the percentage of formals vs. candids that you shoot?

- Do you have insurance that will make it possible to reshoot the wedding if something goes wrong? Exactly what does your insurance cover? Can we have a copy of your policy?

- What are the names and phone numbers of some recent wedding clients?

Be sure your contract contains these items.

- The name of the photographer.

- The starting and ending time for the photographer at your wedding.

- The number of proofs you will be able to view for your final order.

- The size and description of the completed album.

- The refund or cancellation policy.

- A list of the prices, quantity, and sizes of prints included in the package or a list of prices for à la carte ordering, along with an indication of how long prints will be available at those prices and whether or not there is a service charge for prints ordered at a later date.

- Is there an additional charge to complete the album, and if so, how much?

- An explanation of nonperformability and insurance policies.

- The dates and amounts of the deposit and future payments. (Usually the final payment is due when the album is ordered.)

 The entire wedding is of great concern to me, not just my role. It's very important that my clients and I like one another (I only work with clients I like!) and that we have a rapport.

—SUSAN GOMEZ, LIGHT IMAGES BY SUSAN (LAS VEGAS, NEVADA)

Should You Assign a Friend to Assist the Photographer?

Every photographer we interviewed said absolutely not. Assigning a friend to follow around the photographer is not only an imposition on your guests, but also an insult to your photographer. Recognize that you have hired a professional. In fact, your friend may not know exactly what you want, whereas your photographer will have met with you in the weeks before the wedding, going over your list of special people or groupings you desire to be featured in your wedding album. When you put together your list, don't include the obvious: bride alone, groom alone, bride and groom together, bride with her parents, groom with his parents, bride and groom with each set of parents, etc. Simply let the photographer know of particularly special people with whom you want to be photographed.

Finding the Right Videographer

Videographers have received the worst reputation in the industry and, in some instances, deservedly so. For many years, anyone with a camcorder figured he could make money videotaping weddings. Thankfully, most of these amateurs have been driven out of business, though not before they ruined many a bride's wedding.

There are truly professional videographers, but they are few and far between. Your best bet is to check with a professional association that has standards or requirements. Roy Chapman, chairman of the Wedding and Event Videographers' Association International, stands by the qualifications of its members.

While shooting style is very important, it is the editing style that can truly distinguish a videographer. Also, it goes without saying that some videographers may have all the latest equipment but none of the social graces that are vital when sticking a camera in someone's face. Asking the wedding couple such questions as "How many children do you expect to have?" is highly insensitive. Apply the same investigative strategies to interviewing your videographer as you did when interviewing your photographer. Be sure to ask about his style; does he stage scenes during the event, or is he unobtrusive and simply records the events as they unfold?

Your contract with the videographer should cover these points.

- The name of your videographer. The videographer's arrival and departure times as well as setup and breakdown times.

- The number of hours he or she will be shooting.

- The type of equipment and backup as well as how many cameras.

- The delivery date of the edited tape.

- The total charges as well as what you will receive in exchange for your money (overtime should be cost out or at least listed on the contract).

- Explanation of nonperformability and insurance policies as well as what happens if the wedding is canceled. (If your wedding is canceled, are you able to get your money back if the videographer books the day?)

Interviewing a Videographer

Make sure the personality fits. You don't want a wanna-be star—or, to put it more succinctly, a ham—behind the camera.

Check that the videographer has the same backup equipment as her other equipment. Moreover, two cameras are essential. During the ceremony, both cameras should be running at the same time, preferably from different angles. Otherwise, what would happen if one camera breaks down during the vows? And, this is a real tip: The guests will be unable to see your faces during the vows. Unless you have an enlightened officiant who is willing to trade positions with the bride and groom and situate himself in such a way that the bride and groom are facing the congregation, your unique facial expressions will only be seen by the officiant. Many ceremonial sites will not object to a camera being placed in the sanctuary or vestry as long as a person isn't operating the camera but running it by remote control.

Editing the Video

Editing expertise is mandatory. This can mean the difference between soft, gradual fades and transitions and abrupt shifts. A professional videographer will spend as much as thirty hours editing your video into a one- or two-hour segment.

The price range of videographers can vary incredibly. "Someone who has less than three years' experience, uses a camcorder, and edits the video as he shoots it in the camera is going to be priced differently than one who uses broadcast-quality cameras and digital editing," says Eagan.

Here's a tip: Have your videographer edit a twenty-minute segment that captures the highlights of your wedding. While few people may be interested in watching a lengthy video, they may enjoy viewing a brief highlights "clip."

Audio and Lighting

Ask your videographer about audio. All individuals you want to be heard on the video should be individually miked (by attaching a wireless microphone to their garments); this includes the officiant, any and all readers, and the cantor or soloist. It is not necessary for videographers to use any special lighting if they have broadcast-quality cameras.

Digital Video Disc

Your videotape can be transferred to a digital video disc, or DVD. The resolution and compactness are much higher than with an ordinary VHS tape. Ask your videographer if he has the capability of doing this transfer.

OTHER TIPS ON VIDEOGRAPHY

- There will come a time, in the not-too-distant future, when VHF players as we know them will be obsolete. Consider having your video copied onto a digital format.

- Videographers who use broadcast-quality cameras will usually hold on to the master for four months and then recycle the old tape.

- While viewing samples, look for quality of images (color and resolution); are the colors consistent?

- Smooth scene transitions will tell you a lot about your videographer's skill.

- Inquire about the videographer's reputation for being inconspicuous on the wedding day.

- Check his reputation for delivery.

- Be aware of situations where the videographer might interfere with the work of the photographer and discuss how she handles these.

CHAPTER 12

The Language of the Soul

❧ The Music

THERE ARE A NUMBER OF QUESTIONS TO CONSIDER WHEN BEGINNING TO plan the music for your wedding. Are the ceremony and reception being held at sites that have restrictions and regulations? Does the site manager have a list of musicians preferred or approved for the site? What kind of mood do you envision? What kind of music will most guests relate to?

Finding and Interviewing Musicians

Where do you begin collecting names of talented, reliable musicians? Wedding consultants, photographers/videographers, caterers, friends, sites' preferred or required vendors lists, bridal trade shows, the local college or university, and entertainment agencies are just a few places to start.

Wedding consultants and site managers have already narrowed the list to proven professionals, so begin with them. Remember, these people have had the actual experiences of hearing and watching many musicians perform. They know if certain musicians conform to the rules and regulations of the site, and more than likely they have worked with the other vendors you are considering. In other words, they are team players, and that's what you want for your wedding—a team player! Bridal shows can give you the opportunity to meet the musicians and possibly pick up their demo tapes. Be sure to inquire about credentials. Also, ask if there are clients you can call as references, especially corporate clients like hotels, keeping in mind that the musicians must meet the criteria of your site(s) and that there may be religious or ethnic restrictions. Restrictions on amplified music are a major concern, especially in densely populated areas. "We always check with the sites regarding proper procedure, any restrictions, loading information, etc.," says B. Blake Howard of Swing Fever (San Rafael, California).

Don't be hesitant to ask about rates. If it sounds like they're in your ballpark, request a promotion kit, including a rate sheet, photograph, and list of songs performed regularly. Have they played at your site(s) before? This information may not be in the packet, so remember to ask about it up front. Put all this information you gather into your resource binder.

Hear the Musicians Perform

Once you have narrowed down your list based on site restrictions, mood, ambience, style, and segments needing music, you're ready to go shopping. Since you may be hiring these people for your wedding, you want to hear them perform. Do not even think about hiring musicians you have not heard.

QUESTIONS FOR THE MUSICIANS ✍

- What are any space requirements you might have?

- Is special lighting required?

- Do you have a portable mike for the toasts? Will you assist those giving the toasts? Will you remain in the room in case there is difficulty?

- Will you announce important moments (entrance, toasts, dances)? Can you provide appropriate music before the announcements?

- How long have you played together?

- Do you need any specific furniture (for example, folding chairs) or do you bring your own?

- What is your schedule once the reception starts?

- Will you abide by any special requests?

- Do you have liability insurance? Can we have a copy of your policy?

- Do you have emergency backup equipment and personnel?

- How will you, your support staff, and technicians be attired?

- Will all equipment be attractively set up and wires tucked away for safety?

- Can I see a video and/or listen to a cassette/CD of the group?

- Can we hear/see the musical group that will be playing at my wedding perform?

- Do we need to provide food and beverages for the musicians?

- How long and how frequent are breaks? When will these be scheduled?

- What is the cost for overtime? How is that broken down?

- Will the names of the musicians be on the contract?

- Can we be assured that you will be in contact with our wedding consultant as well as other vendors who will be working at our wedding?

- What are the costs for musicians to learn new music? To perform at the rehearsal?

- Will the musicians work with a nonprofessional or friend/relative we may ask to perform at our wedding? How would a rehearsal be arranged?

- If you are having a theme wedding, have musicians dress appropriately.

- Did you know that when you are being toasted, you are not to drink from your own glass?

- If you are going to have your parents, wedding party, and yourself and the groom announced, for example, on your entry into the reception, write out the names phonetically and give a copy to the lead musician or DJ. (And bring an extra copy the day of the wedding, as this person has no doubt forgot his.)

- A DJ may be less expensive and more versatile than a band, depending on the geographical area.

- All musical groups are booked for a minimum number of hours.

- Don't start the dance music until the guests have finished the main course.

- Make an agreement with the head musician that if the wedding consultant or family member in charge of the reception asks that the volume be lowered, it be done without question.

- You are not required to tip the musicians.

- No "union tax" is expected.

How do you get to hear them? Believe it or not, some musical groups will invite you to a current client's wedding. Let's say they had the forethought to get the client's OK; dress appropriately, stay in the background, and don't stay very long. Actually, this method of "interviewing" a musical group has its drawbacks. First, you'll be listening to another client's selected music, not your own. Second, you aren't going to stay long enough to see if the musicians keep their energy and focus strong to the end.

An alternative is to go to a public place where they might be performing. You can also get demo tapes, audio and video. The difficulty with demos, though, is that they only give clips of songs or else only a couple of songs all the way through. Finally, these tapes may be "spiked"—that is, recorded in a studio with a controlled environment where the performance might have been enhanced. As a courtesy, you should return any tapes after you have made your decision, so keep the mailers they arrive in.

Entertainment agencies can be a good place to shop for a wide variety of musicians. There are also production companies. Be aware, however, that these companies are not restricted in their fee structure and can add as much as they want to the price of the musicians; some even pay musicians less and pocket the profit. Reputable agents can let you know where musicians are performing publicly. Luana Stoutmeyer of Encore Productions Entertainment (Highlands Village, Texas), besides having her own band, also provides over 500 entertainers, including jazz, dance, and party bands; disc jockeys; string ensembles; solo performers; and specialty acts.

 Entertainment agencies are bonded by the state and can only add 25 percent to the price of the band. The client has to put the payment into escrow, and it will be released only after the event.

—JOHANNA KAESTNER, COAUTHOR OF *BY RECOMMENDATION ONLY*

Once you have met and heard them perform, you'll want to have a formal meeting with the musicians to discuss their rates and required minimum; most musicians contract for a minimum of three hours for the ceremony and four hours for the reception. Anything over and beyond "overtime" is determined by half-hour or one-hour increments. If you need them for an hour-and-a-half ceremony, they may play longer or during breaks at the reception. Be prepared to pay a fee if the musicians must relocate from a ceremony to a reception site.

Selecting the Music

When considering the music for your wedding, "break the day down into segments needing music," advises our music expert, Julie Tew of Moulin D'Or Recordings (Arlington, Texas). "After you've determined these different segments, then choose the songs you want to use and simply 'plug in' the titles," Tew adds.

You'll want to get the performers' recommendations on music suited for your event. You'll also want to write down your favorite songs, especially any you may want sung at the ceremony or for the first wedding dance and the last. Are the musicians able to learn new music and work with a friend or relative who might want to perform a "special" song?

After you've completed your interviewing, narrow down your list and put these musicians' packets of information in your wedding day binder behind the appropriate tab.

Determine the Formality or Ambience

While it's true that it is *your* wedding, consider your guests and the types of music they enjoy. What is their age group and how do their tastes run? As with every element of your wedding, you are going to have to compromise here. Do select musicians who will be able to entertain while sustaining the mood you desire.

Ethnic Music and Family Traditions

Affirming your culture and tradition during your wedding speaks volumes about how much you value your ancestry. Don't overlook this heritage when planning the music for your wedding day.

Music for the Ceremony

What is commonly known as the ceremony can be broken down into five parts: prelude, processional, ceremony, vows, and recessional. Music has to be selected for each of these segments.

First, envision the ceremony as a whole. To what extent is the mood a solemn one? How formal is the ceremony? What ritual is involved?

You'll also need to consider your site's restrictions, if any. For instance, did you know that Richard Wagner's "Bridal Chorus" from *Lohengrin* and Felix Mendelssohn's "Wedding March" from *A Midsummer Night's Dream* are banned from the traditional Catholic wedding ceremony? Why? They are considered secular music—secular in the sense of "worldly."

I remember one of my clients who wanted to play the Texas A & M College (Aggie) "fight song" for her recessional. The priest had already refused to distribute communion without a nuptial mass. I coached her, "When you play the tape recording of the song at the rehearsal, if the priest says anything, just start bawling, and I don't mean weeping! Sob uncontrollably, and in between gasps, try to explain why it's so important to you and Tim." Sure enough, after the rehearsal, the priest and I were standing in the back of the church. All of a sudden, the Aggie fight song blared over the intercom. He looked at me and gruffly asked, "She's not playing that for the recessional?" I simply replied, "I don't know anything about it, Father." Just as he began marching up the aisle toward the pulpit where the bride was standing with her attendants, she started to wail. Tears rolled down her cheeks. I didn't overhear their conversation, but after the ceremony the next day, Becky and Tim proudly marched out of the church to the tune of the Aggie fight song. Another victory for her wedding consultant!

A house of worship will more than likely have an organist, pianist, or even a choir. Ask the secretary of your church or synagogue (remember, you want to become friends with her). Or call the officiant presiding over your vows. If you haven't already, go hear these musicians perform; if you like them, hire them. You will find they are generally very economical.

Prelude

The ceremony begins with the prelude. You may be in the cry room, or bride's dressing room (also called the holding room), and not be able to hear the music being played as the guests arrive and are seated. This music is for the guests to enjoy as they await your big moment.

Processional

The big moment has arrived. The musicians strike up a special song for the seating of the grandmother(s) of the groom and, next, his mother. She is escorted by a son, favorite nephew, or usher. Her husband, if they are still married, follows behind; if the mother and father of the groom are divorced, the father is seated separately. (Determine ahead of time how you are going to handle any delicate family situations.) The bride's mother is then proudly escorted down the aisle. She's the official hostess. She may be escorted by your brother or other relative. Consider having a song that has particular significance to her played or sung as she walks down the aisle.

In the processional for a Jewish ceremony, the sets of parents accompany their son and daughter and remain standing under the chuppah during the entire ceremony. They usually precede the attendants.

Donna Griffith of La Verda Strings (Las Vegas, Nevada) finds that it is best to change the music for the attendants' processional. They should walk slowly but naturally; the heel-and-toe maneuver is reserved for royal weddings.

The music should change again for your entrance with your father. I don't know a better way to get the attention of your guests than with trumpets. If you appreciate classical music, there are some great pieces written for a trumpet and organ (Beethoven's "Ode to Joy," for example) or, if you can afford two trumpets, Vivaldi's majestic Concerto for Two Trumpets and Organ.

Have your wedding consultant close the back doors while your guests are sneaking peeks (after all, everyone wants to be the first to see the bride). The doors open; you step into the doorway with your father (in Victorian times, the bride and groom entered together, to the same tune but preceding the attendants). Pause to bask in the moment while your train and veil are being properly fluffed; then take a deep breath, look around, give your father the nod, and begin that long walk down the aisle. With each step, be confident, proud. You have put together a wonderful wedding.

Ceremony

Two or three particular songs that are meaningful to the bride and groom should be played or sung during the ceremony. This not only gives the bride and groom a moment to reflect on the occasion but also to take a "breather" from the rush of the day.

Allow me to say here and now that having a friend or relative perform at your wedding is not always the wisest choice. What happens if the person is unable to perform? I urge that the wedding day be left to the professionals. If a friend or relative really wants to give you a gift of their music, then at least have a backup if something should go wrong.

Recessional

For Kim DeLibero of Desertwind (Las Vegas, Nevada), the recessional should be upbeat and joyous. Also, the pace is faster than any preceding music. Obviously, the newlyweds are the first to start up the aisle. You may want to pause to give your mom and dad a hug.

Don't forget, your work isn't over yet! You have to take all those group shots with your photographer and videographer. Recognize that it's not going to be possible for you to take a side trip to the restroom to refresh your makeup. You only have about twenty to thirty minutes for the photos. Wait for the makeup refresher afterward, before greeting your guests at the reception. For the entertainment of your guests, I suggest you book your ceremony musicians for enough time so they can be playing for the ten or fifteen minutes it will take your guests to depart.

Music for the Reception

The next segment of music you will have to think about is the reception, or the cocktail period. This music can be supplied by a DJ or the musicians you hired for your ceremony. While this latter option may require a transfer fee, you may actually end up saving money. That's because musicians are hired for a minimum number of hours; once you have paid the base fee, they simply charge by the hour. You may even choose to book your ceremony musicians for the dinner/dance segment of your wedding.

Whether you are having a reception only or a reception preceding dinner, the music should be background music. Your guests want to meet one another and chat while they stand around sipping their punch and sampling the hors d'oeuvres. If yours is a simple reception (with no dinner following), you certainly may dance. But again, the music should be low-key.

Dinner/Dance Music

Until the entrée is served and consumed, all music should be background music. Under no condition should people be getting up to dance until the entrée has been eaten by at least most of the guests—otherwise, there will be total chaos in the kitchen. Note for the bride and groom: While it is true that this is *your* party, remember that it is the party that you *planned*; save your urges to request the music be louder and faster until after the dancing begins. This is "quiet time,"  and all the vendors you have hired are doing the job you have entrusted to them. I always stress that the bandleader or DJ should take his cue from the banquet manager.

As with most rules, there is an exception. If yours are the kind of guests who enjoy a less-rigid atmosphere, as I've said elsewhere, a great idea is to have food stations, even at a formal sit-down dinner. That way, your guests can nibble on finger foods while they are dancing or otherwise visiting with other guests. Just be sure to plan everything with your caterer well in advance.

There are focal points to the dinner dance, and the lead musician as well as banquet manager need to be prepared for them; they need to alert not only the bride and groom but also the photographer and videographer *before* these special moments. (You will have made certain your bandleader or DJ is the personable type so that he or she can effectively introduce such moments as the toasts, the cake cutting ceremony, and the wedding dance.) As the dinner progresses, I urge the bandleader to check with the banquet manager several times to monitor cues and timing.

I also advise that your music leader discuss with the site manager any emergency procedures beforehand, as well as what to do in case of a power failure. The musicians will be in the best position to get your guests' attention and direct them to safety.

Will it be necessary for the music leader to meet with the sound/electrical engineer at the site before the wedding day? Is there a cost for this, to be incurred by you? Make certain you know the answers to these questions before hiring the group or DJ.

The First and Last Wedding Dance Songs

The songs for these special wedding dances should be ones you are comfortable dancing to. They should also have special meaning for the two of you. It's another one of those moments in the day when you are alone together in the midst of others, and your attention should be on each other. If they're truly significant songs for you, you will momentarily forget about being "on stage" and your possible awkwardness on the dance floor. (Have you thought any more about those dance lessons? You still have time to sign up!) If you have several special songs, consider distributing them throughout the evening, at times when each of you wants to dance with your parent. Make this a surprise!

The Music Is Too Loud

Garth Weaver of GW Sound & Video (Las Vegas, Nevada) advises talking to your musicians about their role during the reception and dinner. For much of the time you want them to be unobtrusive. There is nothing worse than a bandleader or DJ who sees a wedding reception and dinner as a chance to be the star. Certainly, performers are a focal point, but as observers, not participants, they should maintain a certain distance.

The bandleader should be "taking the pulse" of the guests frequently. A rise in the conversation level doesn't mean amplifiers should be turned up; quite the opposite. Dinnertime is conversation time, not a shouting contest among guests. Musicians should treat this segment of the day as they would any intimate dinner.

I am stunned at events when a bandleader has to be asked three, four, and five times to lower the volume level. Granted, it's not always the fault of the band. It could be the acoustics of the room or its configuration. A conscientious bandleader will have checked this out in advance and be prepared to make the necessary adjustments. All the more reason to hire musicians who have played at your site.

If you specify that a certain type of music *not* be played, the band should not override your decision, even if a guest comes up and makes a request of such. Direct the bandleader to simply and politely inform the guest of your wishes.

Don't Let Band Breaks Kill Your Party Mood

I suggest having recorded music available when the band is taking a break. Otherwise, it makes for an awkward fifteen minutes of silence. This "filler" should be background music, giving your guests a chance to converse at a normal volume.

Alternatively, you can request that at least one of the musicians play during the breaks. If it is a four- or five-piece band, possibly two instruments can alternate. While you don't want to be overly demanding, the reality is the musicians are being paid to perform for the entirety of the reception, and there should be no additional costs for this service. Discuss how breaks are going to be handled before you sign your contract.

Let the musicians know ahead of time whether you or the facility is going to provide them with food and beverages during break time. This should be stated in the contract. Also, have the bandleader or DJ confirm with the caterer or banquet manager in advance. Under no conditions should the musicians be drinking alcoholic beverages at any time during the wedding!

Ending the Wedding

The evening shouldn't end abruptly with the musicians packing up. The music should start to wind down, providing a fitting background to the guests and wedding party and newlyweds bidding their fond wishes and adieus. Because the music sets the tone and mood, it should mellow to foster the intimate hugs and kisses. About fifteen minutes of this sort of mood helps guests make the transition from "party time" to "going home time."

Be conscious of the contracted agreements regarding overtime. It should have been determined in advance whether or not it will be possible for the band to go into overtime. The DJ or lead musician should be able to quote the contract accurately so you can make an informed decision about whether or not to request the band to play an extra thirty or sixty minutes.

- The names of the individual band members and especially the vocalist should be on the contract. If for some reason that person is unable to perform, the band must substitute someone of comparable quality, and you should be notified as much in advance as possible. Reserve the right to approve the substitute. If time allows, you will want to obtain a tape of the replacement or go see and hear him. The responsibility for this rests with the DJ/band.

- Any special needs (sound engineer, equipment) should be stated in the contract. If special services are required (amplifiers to be hooked up, wiring into the site's power source), it should be clear who is responsible for payment.

- Setup and breakdown times should be outside the total playing time contracted.

- You want it stated in the contract how not only the musicians but also any visible support staff or technicians will be dressed.

- Require that you and your husband be addressed by your names, instead of as "the bride and groom." Everyone knows you are the bride and groom!

- All payments and due dates should be clearly listed. A cancellation policy (if the wedding is called off) should be in force.

- A copy of the musicians' insurance policy should be provided.

- If you are providing food and beverage for the musicians, the contract should state what you are providing and when.

- If you are contracting musicians through an agent, your contract will be with the agency.

The Musicians' Contract

Again, musicians are usually hired for blocks of time, usually three or four hours. This is actual "playing time"; setup and breakdown time are not charged. Some church musicians may not have contracts, but we urge you to get an agreement in writing. Of course, when hiring professional musicians, a contract is a must.

If the musicians are represented by an agent (often a fellow musician), you will be paying an agent's fee. This is legitimate. Indeed, some musicians only work through agents. It saves them the hassle and administrative duties necessary to make a living.

Once you have signed the contract, put all the information in your wedding day binder, and give the original contract to your financial minister. Be sure to document the amounts and due dates for balance payments in the appropriate computer files.

Epilogue ❧

Sure, You're Having a Wedding, But It's the Marriage That's Important

When I told a friend that I had almost completed this manuscript, that all I needed to do was write the final few pages, he replied: "Just tell them, 'Write a big check to your wedding consultant, who will give you the name of a reliable travel agent, and elope!'" He was being serious. So, with these final words, I'll be serious too.

In this book, I have attempted to present a formula, that if followed will relieve some of the stress in planning a formal event. You have computer files, resource and wedding day binders, spreadsheets, and floor plans. You have learned what is necessary to find and hire competent vendors for your team (indeed, many of the best are listed in the back of this book). The necessary components of proposals and contracts have been spelled out for you so you can feel comfortable handling the business aspects of planning your wedding. You know how to prioritize and maintain a realistic budget and track your disbursements. You understand that you are to send your wedding day schedule and reception floor plans to all your vendors, the wedding party, and parents two to three weeks before the wedding. Ideas about trends and creating a mood or ambience have been presented. Now you can only wait and trust your team of experts to produce the wedding day of your dreams. Just check your contracts. Yours really will be the wedding you have planned.

If mishaps do occur on the day of the wedding, take them with a grain of salt. Don't let anything mar this special day. Ultimately, your wedding day is only one of many special events in your life, and it is your married life together that is most important.

A wedding is not just a party, though it is certainly that too! More importantly, a wedding is about getting married. The relationship between the two of you is ultimately the most important element, not the myriad details about planning the wedding. You are preparing for marriage; how you handle planning your wedding may be an indication of how you both are going to deal with being married. These months of interviewing vendors, shopping for clothes, tasting different menus and a variety of cakes, thinking about your vows, and meeting people who are going to be in control of your wedding day are going to be indicative of your relationship and how you communicate with each other.

It's important that you be sensitive to each other as major decisions are made about the ambience and mood of your wedding day. Although bridal magazines and books (including this one) primarily address the bride, the wedding day is a couple's day, not the bride's, not the groom's, not even the mothers'. Whether you choose to recite traditional vows or to write your own, the exchange of vows does not make you "one." What makes you one is living together in harmony, day in and day out. That doesn't mean you will live "happily ever after" like Cinderella and her Prince Charming, even if yours *is* a Cinderella wedding. Living in harmony doesn't mean you will never argue or disagree. Rather, it means that two separate personalities come together and walk a single path.

Sensitivity to each other and choosing to communicate make a marriage strong. You are committing yourselves to growing old together and together to accept whatever life brings you. Hopefully, the good times will balance out the difficult ones, and love will see you through the hardships that are inevitable, and sometimes too plentiful, in life. But just as you had a plan of attack to get you through the pre-wedding months, so you will have a plan to make you successful in your marriage. If during your marriage you could benefit from the help of experts in learning to communicate better, then seek their help as religiously as you sought professionals to see you through your wedding day. You may benefit greatly from marriage counseling. Don't feel that you have to handle things alone.

When it comes to counseling, you want someone who has experience, who knows what she is doing. Ask your friends or trusted professionals to refer you to someone. Then go together, as a couple. Learning to communicate better in a marriage is a couple's, not an individual, task. It doesn't necessarily take a crisis to benefit from counseling; you may simply want to grow deeper in your love and affection for each other. Or you may simply want to rejuvenate your "first love."

The best way to keep love alive is to do things together. Share each other's experiences and pleasures. Of course, this doesn't mean you have to be "glued at the hips." Believe me, you will need "time out" from each other, no matter how deep your love!

In marriage, you have the wonderful opportunity to continue your families' traditions *and* to create your own. Having left the security of your families, you have taken the leap into adulthood, together. Life is taking you through a rite of passage. Someday you may even help your son or daughter plan his or her wedding. Just don't forget what you learned in this book!

Marriage is the time to make real those values you learned (or perhaps didn't learn) as a child. The greatest value is love. That sounds mushy, but—after all—I am a wedding consultant. I'm an idealist. I entered into this profession because in the recesses of my soul, I'm a romantic.

Romance is to be taken seriously. Don't forget to take time simply to be with each other. Romance one another, as you did when you were dating.

Don't forget anniversaries. Do something particularly special on these milestones. Giving gifts such as a tie or a toaster doesn't cut it in the romance department. Go instead for flowers or a night on the town. Don't think the man has to take the lead all the time. We live in a liberated world—or at least, we should. Surprise your husband with dinner at a nice restaurant; buy *him* flowers. Give *him* a book of poetry, and see that he reads it!

Almost weekly one hears the statistic that 50 percent of marriages end in divorce. It's enough to scare any couple away from marriage. But let me remind you of the obverse, that 50 percent of marriages succeed. And since marriage involves two people, that means both of you—the husband and the wife—are responsible for its success. If you did not already know the necessity of teamwork before reading this book, then you have hopefully learned the important skills of adaptation and compromise. Apply them to your marriage so you can build a relationship that endures. Continue learning about each other; the more you know about each other, the more you can be a helpmate. That is a marvelous opportunity for both of you.

You know that fellow who for months has been saying, "Yes, dear. Anything you want, darling. Whatever you say!" Well, he's become the husband who's now saying, "Save the Last Dance For Me." Always save that one last dance for each other, and may your marriage be as happy as your wedding day!

Resources ❧

Consultants

Wedding Consultant Training and Certification Home Study Course

Robbi Ernst III
June Wedding, Inc.®
An Association for
Event Professionals
robbi@junewedding.com
www.junewedding.com

Other Associations

Richard Markel
Association for Wedding
Professionals International
2730 Arden Way, #218
Sacramento, CA 95825
1-800-242-4461
richard@afwpi.com
www.afwpi.com

Doris Nixon
National Bridal Service
(Weddings Beautiful)
3122 W. Cary Street
Richmond, VA 23221
(804) 355-0464

June Wedding, Inc.® Trained and Certified Wedding/Event Consultants

California

Patty Andersen, JWIC
24 Karat Gold
441 E. San Jose Avenue, #304
Burbank, CA 91501
(818) 843-2642
twenty4karat@earthlink.net

Josi Bartlett, JWIC
Savoir Faire Productions
70 Monte Vista
Novato, CA 94947
(415) 899-9434
jbartlet@george.com

Patricia Bruneau, JWIC
L'Affaire Du Temps
698 Ann Place
Milpitas, CA 95035
(408) 946-7758
laffaire@msn.com

Levan Earle, JWIC
Unique Celebrations
P.O. Box 79871
Sunnyvale, CA 94086
(650) 969-5696
uconly1@aol.com

Dolores Enos, JWIC
131 Magnolia Avenue
Larkspur, CA 94939
(415) 924-3563
russdee@earthlink.net

Marion Gizzi, JWIC
Bell'Amore Wedding Designs
39 Pillon Real
Pleasant Hill, CA 94523
(510) 944-9580

Marie Houson, JWIC
Just Married Productions
Creative Occasions
P.O. Box 534
Novato, CA 94948
(415) 897-9939
marie@creative-occasions.com

Paula Laskelle, JWIC
Champagne Taste
P.O. Box 3447
San Clemente, CA 92674
(949) 498-4806
champagnetaste@home.com

Marlies Lissack, JWIC
city celebrations
2969 Jackson Street, #604
San Francisco, CA 94115
(415) 776-4950
marlies@citycelebrations.com

Christy Lofton, JWIC
Hyatt San Jose Airport
1740 N. First Street
San Jose, CA 95112
(408) 793-3948
christyl@hyattsanjose.com

Helen Louie, JWIC
Mother of the Bride
P.O. Box 621568
Orangevale, CA 95662
(916) 989-1787
hlouieweddings@aol.com

Dee Merz, JWIC
Everlasting Memories
4619 Pepperwood Drive
Penngrove, CA 94951
(707) 795-7356
deemerz@conici.com

Suzanne Princiotta, JWIC
A Formal Engagement
150 Oak Shade Lane
Novato, CA 94945
(415) 898-5920
afeweds@slip.net

Annena Sorenson, JWIC
Tie The Knot
1276 Manet Drive
Sunnyvale, CA 94087
(408) 746-0881
ttknot@aol.com

Lora Ward, JWIC
A Day To Remember
2641 5th Avenue
Sacramento, CA 95818
(916) 452-4373

Colorado

Marcia Copp, JWIC
Weddings by Marcia
8148 W. Harvard Drive
Lakewood, CO 80227
(303) 987-9080
marciacopp@juno.com

Georgia

Gwen McCants-Allen, JWIC
Avant Garde Affairs
6349 Wedgeview Drive
Tucker, GA 30084
(770) 414-4477
agaffairs@aol.com

Illinois

Beverly Dembo, JWIC
Dembo Productions
2551 Windrush Lane
Northbrook, IL 60062
(847) 835-5000
demboprod@msn.com

Louisiana

Betty Downey Wise, JWIC
Great Expectations
124 Deville Place
Shreveport, LA 71115
(318) 797-0856
maean@aol.com

Maryland

Bonnie S. Aleshire, JWIC
P.O. Box 41
Smithsburg, MD 21783-0041
bales77822@aol.com

Michigan

Victoria M. Rohrer, JWIC
Weddings Unveiled
6146 Cottonwood
Whitmore Lake, MI 48189
(810) 231-4479
weddings@ismi.net

Montana

Lisa Michael, JWIC
Ever After Weddings
116 S. 9th Avenue
Bozeman, MT 59715
(406) 585-8104
lisa@everafterweddings.com

New York

Janet Graves Society Weddings
AKA Not Just Weddings
23 Eckerson Lane
Hillcrest, NY 10977
(914) 371-4517
njweddings@aol.com

Ohio

Packy Boukis, JWIC
Only You
8230 W. Ridge Drive
Broadview Heights, OH 44147
(440) 237-4257
awpacky@aol.com

Texas

Marsha Ballard, JWIC
Jenny Cline, JWIC
StarDust Celebrations Inc.
2728 Routh Street
Dallas, TX 75201
mb@stardustcelebrations.com
jc@stardustcelebrations.com
www.stardustcelebrations.com

Gaye Greenamyer, JWIC
Lyn Snyder, JWIC
Green Rose, LLC
P.O. Box 701133
Dallas, TX 75370
(972) 416-6464
greenrose@airmail.net

Julia Kappel, JWIC
Becky French, JWIC
Grand Occasions Consulting
710 Pearl Cove
Oak Point, TX 75068
(972) 294-1701
goc@iglobal.net

Kay Riley, JWIC
L.A. Celebrations
2406 W. Park Row
Arlington, TX 76013
(817) 498-3433

Tricia Thomas, JWIC
Thomas & Thomas Consultants
Houston, TX
(281) 861-9333
thomaswedd@aol.com

Jamaica

Myrtle Dwyer, JWIC
Executive Assistant Manager
Half Moon Golf, Tennis &
Beach Club
Half Moon P.O.
Rose Hall, Montego Bay
Jamaica, W.I.
1-800-626-0592
myrtle@halfmoonclub.com
www.halfmoon.com.jm

Destination Weddings and Honeymoons

Jamaica

Myrtle Dwyer, JWIC
Half Moon Club
Rose Hall, Montego Bay
Jamaica, W.I.
1-800-626-0592

Roy Anderson, JWIC
Glamour Tours
LOJ Commercial Centre
Montego Freeport, Unit N
P.O. Box 630
Montego Bay, Jamaica
(876) 979-8207

Florida

Marcia Bullock, JWIC
Manager, Groups &
Conventions
Jamaica Tourist Board
1320 S. Dixie Highway
Suite 1101
Coral Gables, FL 33146
(305) 665-0557
bullock@jamaicatravel-miami.com

Other Professional Consultants/Event Planners

JoAnn Gregoli
Elegant Occasions
16 Copeland Road
Denville, NJ 07834
(973) 361-9200
elegwed204@aol.com

Pat Kray
Affaire of Elegance
1858 Elkwood Drive
Concord, CA 94519
(925) 825-8552
afrelgance@aol.com

Freda McKenzie
To Have and To Hold
2058 Willowood
Grapevine, TX 76501
(817) 424-1559
fredam@iname.com

Mary Beth Menzies
Discount Bridal Service Inc.
Invitations, Etc.
600 S. Weatherred
Richardson, TX 75080
(972) 238-1754

Sheri Mosher
A Vision of Elegance
456 Clovis Avenue, #6
Clovis, CA 93612
(209) 297-7656
ms200@cvip.csufresno.edu

Linda Shafer
Veils & Vows in the Vail Valley
P.O. Box 1859
Edwards, CO 81632
1-888-W-BRIDE
shafer@vail.net

Lisa Stahl
Celestial Dreams
P.O. Box 814849
Dallas, TX 75381
(972) 247-8701
celesdream@aol.com

Rhona Streit
Rhona Streit Wedding
Consultant
P.O. Box 25012
Dallas, TX 75225
(972) 720-9771
rfstreit@aol.com

Bridal Mall

Ashley B. Tarver Jr.
Wedding Plaza
17618 Davenport, Suite 1
Dallas, TX 75252
(972) 447-0616
ashleytarv@aol.com

Cakes

Tsuki Caspary-Brooks
Dolci Wedding Cakes
4681 Fairfax Avenue
Dallas, TX 75209
(214) 526-1151
dolcicakes@aol.com

Cindy Cowan
Creations by C&M
4222 N. Losee, Suite J
Las Vegas, NV 89030
(702) 399-3588

Susan Morgan
Elegant Cheese Cakes
103-2 Harvard Avenue
Half Moon Bay, CA 94019
(650) 728-2248
susan@elegantcheesecakes.com

Catering

Sharon Graham
Fine Cuisine Inc.
505 Durham
Houston, TX 77007
(713) 784-1583
grahamfood@aol.com

Vernon Jacobs
Event of the Season
148 Stetson Avenue
Corte Madera, CA 94927
(415) 927-4721

Ann V. Lyons
Melons Catering & Events
100 Ebbtide
Sausalito, CA 94965
(415) 331-0888
melons@pacbell.net

Laurence Whiting/
Kathleen Kirkpatrick
Now We're Cooking! Inc.
2150 Third Street
San Francisco, CA 94107
(415) 255-6355

Dance Lessons

Kim Sakren
A Perfect Wedding Dance
P.O. Box 35291
Las Vegas, NV 89133
(702) 242-6400
firstdance@aol.com

Ethnic Weddings

The Balch Institute for Ethnic
Studies
18 S. 7th Street
Philadelphia, PA 19106
(215) 925-8090

Favors

Catherine M. Cavanagh
Nuptial Bliss: The Wedding
Phone Card
P.O. Box 682
Amawalk, NY 10501
1-800-391-2642
www.nuptialbliss.com

John Quist
The 3rd Millennium Time
Capsules
P.O. Box 41292
San Jose, CA 95160
(408) 927-9233
t3rdmil@ix.netcom.com

Edible Favors

Susan Morgan
Elegant Cheese Cakes
103-2 Harvard Avenue
Half Moon Bay, CA 94019
(650) 728-2248
susan@elegantcheesecakes.com

Terry Roark
Sweet Talk Promotions
22961 Triton Way, Suite B
Laguna Hills, CA 92653
1-800-50-FUDGE
www.sweettalkpromotions.com

Floral

Karen Axel, AIFD
Tapestry Bridal
& Special Event Flowers
842 Rhode Island Street
San Francisco, CA 94107
(415) 550-1015
karen@tapestryflowers.com

W. Donnie Brown
Five Star Floral Designs
& Events
2525 Turtle Creek Boulevard
#310
Dallas, TX 75219
(214) 522-2271
wdonnieb@airmail.net

Cathy Duncan
Earth Blooms
2101 Abrams Road
Dallas, TX 75214
(214) 823-6222
cdu382660@aol.com

Gloria Gasser
Floral Images
3595 E. Patrick Lane, #700
Las Vegas, NV 89120
(702) 597-0045

Susan Groves
In Full Bloom
100 Loyola Avenue
Menlo Park, CA 94025
(650) 364-1858

Karen Higginbotham
I Love Flowers
4347 W. Northwest Highway
#180
Dallas, TX 75220
(214) 357-9577

Laura Little
Floramor Studios
569 Seventh Street
San Francisco, CA 94103
(415) 864-0145
ojo2020@aol.com

Domonie Mattson
Dom Unique Designs
9179 Louisiana Avenue North
Brooklyn Park, MN 55445
(612) 424-4243
domonie@integrityonline31.com

Joy Norton
Stanford Designs
19021 Midway, #700
Dallas, TX 75287
(972) 473-8680
standsgn@flash.net

Scott Patterson
California Arrangements
224 Moana Way
Pacifica, CA 94044
(650) 738-9580

Lois Robinson
Floral Fantasies
6805 Angelbluff Circle
Dallas, TX 75248
(972) 233-7770

Floral Bouquet Preservation

Linda Sue Abbott
Sentimental Reasons
101 S. Rainbow Boulevard, #18
Las Vegas, NV 89117
(702) 821-1166
1-800-896-5765
sentreas@anv.net

Jeffery Barrett
Aiko & Co.
2950 Bay Village Circle, #1071
Santa Rosa, CA 95403
(877) 245-6626
www.pressed-bouquet.com

Linda Lee Sirmen
Special Arrangements by LL
1422 Avenue K
Plano, TX 75074
(972) 578-5189

Gifts

Specialty/Designer

Karen Starr Germany
Starr and Company
1815 Cobblestone Street
Richmond, TX 77469
(281) 344-9483

Phone Cards

Catherine M. Cavanagh
Nuptial Bliss: The Wedding
Phone Card
P.O. Box 682
Amawalk, NY 10501
1-800-391-2642
www.nuptialbliss.com

Gowns and Formal Wear

Lily Dong
Lily Dong Couture Bridal
22080 San Fernando Court
Cupertino, CA 95014
(408) 255-8850
lily@lilydongcouture.com

Karen Hicks
Gingiss Formal Wear
1117 Joshua Tree
Plano, TX 75023
(214) 638-4300

The International Formalwear
Association
401 N. Michigan Avenue
Chicago, IL 60611

Gown Preservation and Restoration/Cleaners

Christine Morrissey
National Gown Cleaners &
Archival Products
4100 Moorpark Avenue
San Jose, CA 95117
1-800-200-4696
(408) 241-3490
www.nationalgown.com

Norville R. Weiss
Wedding Gown Specialists
164 E. 2nd Avenue
Chico, CA 95926
(530) 342-4358
noret@worldnet.att.net

Internet Resources

E-mail

eileeninSD@aol.com
weddlist@aol.com

Web Sites

www.altarnet.com
www.asiasignworld.com
www.bridalclicks.com
www.bridalfaire.com
www.bridal-links.com
www.junewedding.com
www.smartbrides.com
www.tiffany.com
www.weddingideas.com
www.weddingnetwork.com
www.weddings-online.com

Internet Webmaster and Wedding Announcement Services

Jeffrey Brown
Eventus/Cybermedia Lane
1-888-373-1191
(561) 333-1191
jbrown@bridalclicks.com

Helen Lee, CEO
SmartBride Inc.
P.O. Box 57014
Bason Park, MA 02457
(781) 239-4491
hlee@smartbride.com
www.smartbride.com

Legal

"Love, Marriage, and The Law"
American Bar Association
Forder Fulfillment
1155 E. 60th Street
Chicago, IL 60637
Cost: $3.50

Limousines/ Transportation

Francis Cresci
Western Limousines Service
801 S. Main
Las Vegas, NV 89101
(702) 382-7100

Makeup and Hair Design

Jennifer Kalman
Jennifer Kalman, Licensed
Makeup Artist
4916 Hollow Ridge Road
Dallas, TX 75227
(972) 545-1306

Jenni Tarver
Jenni Tarver Studios
17618 Davenport, Suite 1
Dallas, TX 75252
(972) 447-9686
jennitarv@aol.com

Carol L. Werthman
Sachet 'n' Lace
2155 San Rafael Avenue
Santa Clara, CA 95051
(408) 241-3105

Music

The American Guild of
Organists
475 Riverside Drive
New York, NY 10115
(212) 870-3210

Andy Austin
Sight and Sound DJ's
718 W. Arappaho, Suite 90
Richardson, TX 75080
(972) 742-3869
www.andyaustin.com

Kim DeLibero (Instrumentalist)
Desertwind
Las Vegas, NV
(702) 240-9899

Donna Griffith (Instrumentalist)
La Verda Strings
Las Vegas, NV
(702) 438-0653

Jodi Harris (DJ)
Sight and Sound
Las Vegas, NV
(702) 365-9526

B. Blake Howard
Swing Fever
70 Pleasant Lane
San Rafael, CA 94901
(415) 459-2428
swingfever@sirius.com

Patrick Labbate (DJ)
The Music Solution
10025 Skipper Court
Las Vegas, NV 89117
(702) 256-1269

Carol Marks
Carol Marks Music
615 Business Parkway
Richardson, TX 75081
(972) 231-4091
carol@carolmarksmusic.com

National Association
of Pastoral Musicians
Pastoral Press
225 Sheridan Street NW
Washington, DC 20011
(202) 723-1254

The Orchestra Leaders
Association
1-800-359-0859

Luana Stoutmeyer
Encore Productions
Entertainment
785 Oak Leaf Court
Highlands Village, TX 75077
(972) 317-2336

Teri Wagner (Vocalist)
Las Vegas, NV
(702) 436-3824

Garth Weaver (DJ)
GW Sound & Video
4750 W. University Avenue
Las Vegas, NV 89103
(702) 248-0404

CDs

Here Comes the Bride:
The Complete Wedding Song
Collection
MBC Video, Inc.
(206) 885-7934

New Wedding Traditions
1-800-44-SONGS

Our First Dance
1-800-447-6647

The Ultimate Wedding Collection
Danny Wright
Moulin D'Or
(817) 793-3177

With This Song I Thee Wed
Paul Hampton
Romantic Expressions
1-800-444-6112

Name Change Kit

Katharine Weissmann
Official New Bride Name
Change Kit
One Greenview Drive
Carlsbad, CA 92009
1-800-439-0334
www.kitbiz.com

Officiants

The Most Reverend Robert M.
Dittler, OSB
The White Robed Monks
of St. Benedict
P.O. Box 27536
San Francisco, CA 94127
(415) 292-3228
rmdosb@sirius.com

Rabbis who perform interfaith
ceremonies
Rabbinic Center for Research
and Counseling
(908) 233-2288

The Reverend Ed Holt
A Wedding Ministry
1327 Pebble Drive
San Carlos, CA 94070
(650) 595-4225
revholt@batnet.com

The Reverend Heron
Freed Toor
Beautiful Weddings
2285 Bay Street
San Francisco, CA 94123
(415) 563-0469

Photography

Sue Altenburg
Sue Altenburg Photography
3017 S. Decature Blvd.
Las Vegas, NV 89107
(702) 252-7557

Ron Barbosa
Barbosa Studios
3840 Beltline Road
Dallas, TX 75244
(972) 620-1443
bsphotog@mindspring.com

Keith Clark
Jay Young
Clark & Young Photography
7670 W. Sahara, Suite 2
Las Vegas, NV 89117
(702) 360-0300

Ami Davenport
A Day To Remember
Photography
4011 W. Cheyenne
Las Vegas, NV 89032
(702) 396-4905

Jim and Barbara Eagan
Eagan Photography & Video
1082 Stockton Avenue
San Jose, CA 95110
(408) 295-6585
jimeagan@aol.com

Rusty and Dolores Enos
Photography by Rusty and
Dolores Enos, JWIC
131 Magnolia Avenue
Larkspur, CA 94939
(415) 924-3563
russdee@earthlink.net

Susan Gomez
Light Images by Susan
2912 S. Highland Avenue
Suite 1
Las Vegas, NV
(702) 735-4333

Jim Grant
Belinda Brooks
Avec Brisance Photographie Inc.
4202 Harvest Hill Court
Carrollton, TX 75010
(972) 395-3088
photos@avecbrisance.com

Heather Holman
Video & Photographic
Images Inc.
6269 Addington Court
Eden Prairie, MN 55346
(612) 934-7499
holman@videophoto.com

Anne Pantelick
Anne Pantelick Photography
4528 Lorraine Avenue
Dallas, TX 75205
(214) 219-0743
pantelick@aol.com

Professional Photographers
of America
57 Forsyth Street NW
Suite 1600
Atlanta, GA 30303
(404) 522-8600

Mike Schultz
Wind Dancer Studios Inc.
12915 Raven Street NW
Coon Rapids, MN 55448
(612) 755-0603
wndancr@citilink.com

Fred and Linda Smith
Reflections of Love
Photography
615 N. O'Connor, Suite 11
Irving, TX 75061
(972) 754-8849
fredsphoto@hotmail.com

M. Christine Torrington
M. Christine Torrington
Photography
210 Post Street, Suite 902
San Francisco, CA 94108
(415) 921-6333
christine@sfphotopro.com

Myra Zelikovics
A Story Album Weddings
Las Vegas, NV
(702) 361-1085

Publications

Bride's
Millie Martini Bratten
4 Times Square, 6th Floor
New York, NY 10036
(212) 880-8525

By Recommendation Only
Johanna Kaestner and
Tosca J. Clark
24439 NE 19th Street
Redmond, WA 98053
(425) 836-3763
johanna@byreconly.com
www.byreconly.com

DFW Wedding Guide
Jessica Francyzk
P.O. Box 671292
Dallas, TX 75367
(214) 891-9648
dava@txwedding.com

San Francisco Wedding Guide
Marianne Johnson
P.O. Box 10459
San Jose, CA 95157
(408) 343-1153
info@sfweddingguide

Story Book Weddings
(Themed Weddings)
Robin A. Kring
Clear Creek Publishing
P.O. Box 102324
Denver, CO 80250
(303) 671-8253
raksparkle@aol.com

The Wedding Guide
Darlene Thorne
P.O. Box 1990
Cupertino, CA 95015
(408) 996-7778
darlene@wed-guide.com

Weddingbells
Carolyn Carver
2812 Daybreak
Dallas, TX 75287
(972) 307-7236
ccarver@weddingbells.com

Wedding Pages
Cindy Martin
17194 Preston Road, #123-270
Dallas, TX 75248
(972) 557-2388
www.weddingpages.com

Registry

Crate and Barrel
1-800-967-6696

Farberware
(212) 683-9660

The Home Depot
(404) 433-8211

JC Penney
1-800-JCP-GIFT
catalog
1-800-527-4438

KitchenAid
1-800-541-6390

Krups
1-800-526-5377

Lenox
1-800-63-LENOX

Macy's
1-800-459-2743

Marshall Field's
1-800-243-6436

Mikasa
1-800-833-4681

Pfaltzgraf
1-800-499-1976

Royal Doulton
1-800-68-CHINA

Service Merchandise
1-800-251-1212

Target Stores
1-800-888-WEDD

Waterford Crystal
1-800-523-0009

Wedgewood
1-800-622-8345

Williams-Sonoma
1-800-541-2233

Stationery

Linda Sue Abbott
Casey Castagna
Sentimental Reasons
101 S. Rainbow Boulevard, #8
Las Vegas, NV 89145
(702) 821-1166
1-800-896-5765
sentreas@anv.net

Calligraphy

Adrienne D. Keats
Adrienne D. Keats Calligraphy
980 Ashbury Street
San Francisco, CA 94117
(415) 759-5678

Designer Guest Registry and Memory Books

Sherry M. Richert
Mad Moon Creations
695 Castro Street
San Francisco, CA 94114
(415) 552-0919
www.madmooncreations.com

Wholesale Manufacturers

Micah Chase
Checkerboard, Ltd.
99 Hartwell Street
West Boylston, MA 01583
(508) 835-2475
www.checkernet.com

Linda Hiniker
Carlson Craft
1750 Tower Boulevard
P.O. Box 8700
North Mankato, MN 56002
1-800-292-9207

Dolores Milam
NuArt
6247 W. 74th Street
Bedford Park, IL 60499
(708) 496-4900
nuart@dealernow.com

Videography

Jim and Barbara Eagan
Eagan Photography & Video
1082 Stockton Avenue
San Jose, CA 95110
(408) 295-6585
jimeagan@aol.com

Jodi Harris
Sight and Sound
4720 Cameron Street
Suite 6A
Las Vegas, NV 89103
(702) 365-9526

Joann Swanson
Swanson's Audio Video
Connection
101-A Hickey Boulevard, #402
South San Francisco, CA 94080
(415) 952-3277

Garth Weaver
GW Sound & Video
4750 W. University Avenue
Las Vegas, NV 80103
(702) 365-9526

Wedding and Event
Videographers' Association
International
1319 Carlsbad Drive
Gaithersburg, MD 20879
(301) 330-8984

Wedding Insurance

Jewelers Mutual
1-800-558-6411

Weddingsurance
R. V. Nuccio & Associates
P.O. Box 307
Fawnskin, CA 92333
1-800-ENGAGED or
1-800-364-2433

Suggested Reading ❧

Altman, Don. *151 Ways to Make Your Wedding Special*. Los Angeles: Moon Lake Media, 1994.

Anastasio, Janet. *The Wedding Shower Book*. Holbrook, Mass.: Bob Adams, 1995.

Anastasio, Janet, and Michelle Bevilacqua. *The Everything Wedding Vows Book*. Holbrook, Mass.: Bob Adams, 1994.

Barillo, Madeline. *The Wedding Sourcebook*. Los Angeles: Lowell House, 1996.

———. *The Wedding Sourcebook Planner*. Los Angeles: Lowell House, 2000.

Blayney, Molly Dolan. *Wedded Bliss: A Victorian Bride's Handbook*. New York: Abbeville Press, 1992.

Clark, Beverly. *Showers*. Carpinteria, Calif.: Wilshire Publications, 1989.

———. *Weddings: A Celebration*. Carpinteria, Calif.: Wilshire Publications, 1996.

Claro, Danielle. *How to Have the Wedding You Want*. New York: Berkeley, 1995.

Cole, Harriette. *Jumping the Broom: The African-American Wedding Planner*. New York: Henry Holt, 1993.

Dahl, Stephanie H. *Modern Bride Just Married*. New York: John Wiley, 1994.

Davis, Nancy. *Bridal Style*. Southport, Conn.: Hugh Lauter Levin Associates, 1994.

Editors of *Bride's*. *Bride's Book of Etiquette*. New York: Condé Nast Publications, 1993.

Eklof, Barbara. *With These Words . . . I Thee Wed: Contemporary Wedding Vows for Today's Couples*. Holbrook, Mass.: Bob Adams, 1989.

Emanuel, David, and Elizabeth Emanuel. *Emanuel Style for All Seasons*. Great Britain, 1983.

Fields, Alan, and Denise Fields. *Bridal Bargains: Secrets to Throwing a Fantastic Wedding on a Realistic Budget*. 4th ed. Boulder, Colo.: Windsor Peak Press, 1999.

Goldman, Larry. *Dressing the Bride*. New York: Crown Publishers, 1993.

Gray, Winifred. *You and Your Wedding*. New York: Bantam Books, 1985.

Hahn, Hannelore, and Tatiana Stoumen. *Places: A Directory of Public Places for Private Events and Private Places for Public Functions*. New York: Tenth House Enterprises.

Handler, Len. *The Perfect Wedding Song Book*. Port Chester, N.Y.: Cherry Lane Music Co., 1991.

Harvey, Lawrence D. *A Plaza Wedding*. New York: Villard Books, 1996.

Kaestner, Johanna, and Tosca J. Clark. *By Recommendation Only: Party and Wedding Resource Guide for the Greater San Francisco Bay Area*. Redmond, Wash.: Adobe Creek Publishing, 1999.

Kring, Robin. *Storybook Weddings: A Guide to Fun and Romantic Theme Weddings*. New York: Meadowbrook Press, 1999.

Lalli, Cele Goldsmith. *Modern Bride Guide to Etiquette*. New York: John Wiley & Sons, 1993.

Lalli, Cele Goldsmith, and Stephanie H. Dahl. *Modern Bride Complete Wedding Planner*. New York: John Wiley, 1997.

Lenderman, Teddy. *The Complete Idiot's Guide to the Perfect Wedding*. Indianapolis: Alpha Books, 1995.

Livers, Eileen. *The Unofficial Guide to Planning Your Wedding*. New York: Macmillan, 1999.

Lockwood, Georgene Muller. *Your Victorian Wedding: A Modern Guide for the Romantic Bride*. New York: Prentice Hall, 1992.

Loring, John. *The Tiffany Wedding*. New York: Doubleday, 1988.

McCoy, Deborah. *The Elegant Wedding and Budget-Savvy Bride*. New York: Plume, 1999.

Martin, Judith. *Miss Manners on (Painfully Proper) Weddings*. New York: Crown Publishers, 1995.

Medrich, Alice. *Cocolat: Extraordinary Chocolate Desserts*. New York: Warner Books, 1990.

Mellinger, Maria McBride. *The Wedding Dress*. New York: Random House, 1993.

Metrick, Sydney Barbara. *I Do: A Guide to Creating Your Own Unique Ceremony*. Berkeley, Calif.: Celestial Arts Publishing, 1992.

Monckton, Shirley. *The Complete Book of Wedding Flowers*. London: Casell Books, 1993.

Moulton, Bruce. *Bridal Shower Journal*. Wayzata, Minn.: Lakeland Color Press, 1995.

Naylor, Sharon. *1001 Ways to Save Money and Still Have a Dazzling Wedding*. Chicago: Contemporary Books, 1994.

Packer, Jane. *Flowers for All Seasons*. New York: Fawcett Columbine, 1989.

Packham, Jo. *Wedding Flowers: Choosing and Making Beautiful Bouquets and Arrangements*. New York: Sterling Publishing, 1993.

———. *Wedding Gowns and Other Bridal Apparel*. New York: Sterling Publishing, 1994.

———. *Wedding Receptions: Arranging a Joyous Celebration*. New York: Sterling Publishing, 1993.

Perry, Michael R. *The Groom's Survival Manual*. Old Tappan, N.J.: Pocket Books, 1991.

Peters, Colette. *Colette's Wedding Cakes*. Boston: Little, Brown and Co., 1995.

Post, Elizabeth L. *Emily Post's Complete Book of Wedding Etiquette*. New York: HarperCollins, 1991.

Post, Peggy. *Emily Post's Weddings*. New York: Harpers Perennial, 1999.

Pritchard, Tom, and Billy Jarecki. *Madderlake's Trade Secrets: Straight Talk about Finding and Arranging Flowers Naturally*. New York: Clarkson N. Potter, 1992.

Roberts, Jan. *The Beverly Hills International Party Planner*. Beverly Hills, Calif.: Jan Roberts Publications, 1994.

Rogers, Jennifer. *Tried and Trousseau: The Bride Guide*. New York: Simon & Schuster, 1992.

Roney, Carley. *The Knot's Complete Guide to Weddings in the Real World*. New York: Broadway Books, 1999.

St. Marie, Satenig, and Carolyn Flaherty. *Romantic Victorian Weddings Then & Now*. New York: Dutton Studio Books, 1991.

Sowden, Cynthia Lueck. *Wedding Occasions: 101 Party Themes for Wedding Showers, Rehearsal Dinners, Engagement Parties, and More!* Brighton, Minn.: Brighton Publications, 1990.

Stewart, Arlene Hamilton. *The Bride's Book of Wedding Traditions*. New York: Hearst Books, 1995.

Stewart, Martha. *The Wedding Planner*. New York: Clarkson N. Potter, 1988.

Swartz, Oretha D. *Service Etiquette*. Annapolis, Md.: Naval Institute Press, 1988.

Tuckerman, Nancy. *In the Tiffany Style: Gift-Giving for All Occasions*. New York: Doubleday, 1990.

Warner, Diane. *Beautiful Wedding Decorations and Gifts on a Small Budget*. Cincinnati: Betterways Books, 1995.

Warner, Penny. *The Best Party Book: 1,001 Creative Ideas for Fun Parties*. New York: Simon & Schuster, 1992.

Zimmerman, Catherine S. *The Bride's Book: A Pictorial History of American Bridal Dress*. New York: Arbor House, 1985.

Index ❧

Meetings, term, 78
Mendelssohn, Felix, 275
Menopause, 156
Menstrual cycle, wedding date, 38, 39
Menus, 178
Merz, Dee, JWIC, 19, 63
"Method of payment," disbursement
    spreadsheet, 22-23
Milam, Delores, 168
Mineral water bars, beverage service, 191
Miniskirt, gown style, 131
Miscellaneous
  resource binder, 43
  wedding day binder, 44
"Modeled effect," photography, 250
Modern Bride Complete Wedding Planner,
    6-7, 10, 36, 96, 162, 163
Modern Bride magazine, 6, 29, 32, 129
Moiré, gown fabric, 149
Money order, payment method, 25
Morgam, Susan, 214
Morrissey, Christine, 142, 152-153, 154
Mother of the Bride Consultancy Firm, 64
Mothers
  dresses for, 155
  gown selection, 124
  seating of, 88-89
Moulin D'Or Recordings, 274
Music
  financial responsibility for, 30, 32
  resource binder, 43
  selection of, 274-282
  volume of, 281
  wedding day binder, 44
  wedding day schedule, 87-88
Music leader
  caterer selection, 194, 196, 197
  at reception, 280
  reception planning, 184, 190
  site selection, 112
Musicians, 5, 28, 269-270
  contract of, 283-284
  food/drink provision, 224

photographer/videographer, 246
questions for, 271
at reception, 281-282

N

Name change kit, 54
National Gown Cleaners, 152, 153, 154
Natural color, photographic term, 255
Negative, processed film, 252
Newspapers, engagement notice, 97-98,
    256
Nonperformability, photographer/
    videographer, 263, 265
Norton, Joy, 232, 238-239
Now We're Cooking! Inc., 195, 196, 197,
    201, 202
NuArt, 168
Nuptial Bliss: The Wedding Phone Card,
    106

O

Official New Bride Name Change Kit, 54
Officiants
  resource binder, 43
  selecting, 114-117
  site selection, 112
  wedding day binder, 44
  wedding day schedule, 89-90
Ordering
  gown salon consultant, 136
  of stationary, 160-161
  wedding gown, 144-145
Organza, gown fabric, 149
Originals, printed film, 253
Overall Wedding Budget, budget spread-
    sheet, 14-15, 16
Overtime, musicians, 271, 273, 282

P

Packages, photograph prices, 258

Panoramic images, 254

Paper showers, 107

Parties
   resource binder, 43
   wedding day binder, 44

Pastry chef
   floral design, 228
   questions for, 208
   reception planning, 184
   selecting, 207-209

Patterson, Scott, 220, 234

Percentage basis payment, wedding
   consultant, 76

Perchloroethylene, 152

Performance, musician selection, 270,
   272-273

Perry, Michael R., 108

Petite sizes, wedding gown, 143

Petticoats, 151

Pew cards, 167, 168

Photo album
   cost of, 250-251
   wedding story, 258-259

Photographer
   bouquet/garter toss, 221
   cake cutting ceremony, 218-219
   contract for, 263
   "last wedding dance," 222
   portrait display, 223
   questions for, 262
   "receiving guests," 225
   reception planning, 184, 188
   seating provision 224
   selection of, 259-261
   site selection, 112
   tips for selecting, 260
   wedding day binder, 44

Photographers, 245-246
   caterer selection, 194, 196, 197
   changes in technology, 4

pricing packages, 18

resource binder, 43, 260

Photographs
   color terminology, 250, 255-256
   financial responsibility for, 30, 32
   formal, 250, 257
   wedding day schedule, 90, 278

Photography
   current trends, 250
   digital imaging, 251
   formats, 247, 251-252
   panoramic image, 254

Photography by Rusty and Dolores Enos,
   248-249

Photojournalism, photography style,
   247-248, 252

Physical exams, financial responsibility
   for, 29, 30

Picture hat, veil style, 140

Pill box, veil style, 140

Place cards, 168-170, 178

Planning process
   duration of, 7-8
   tools for, 42, 45

Plated or sit down service, food service,
   193

Point d'Esprit lace, 128, 132

Polyester gown, 134

Portfolios, wedding story, 258-259

Portrait, 132, 332

Portraiture photography, 246-247

Posed photographs, 248, 257

Pouf, sleeve style, 132

Pregnancy, and gown fitting, 142

Prelude
   selection of music for, 276
   wedding day schedule file, 87-88

Premarital counseling, 115-116

Preparation planning, wedding consultant,
   68-70

Preserved flowers, 235-236, 241

Pressing, bridal gown, 137

Price list, vendor information, 18
Prices
　　for musicians, 270, 273
　　photo album, 250-251
　　photographs, 258
　　videography, 266
"Price shop," 233
Princess, gown style, 131
Princiotta, Suzanne, JWIC, 28
Print, finished photographs, 253
Printing, types of, 161
Problem solving, wedding consultants, 75
Processional
　　selection of music for, 276-277
　　wedding day schedule file, 89
Professional associations, wedding planners,
　　48-49
Professional Photographers of America, 262
Professional wedding consultants, value
　　of, 27-28, 47, 59-61
Progressive photography, 250
Promotional material, vendor information,
　　18
Proofs, printed film, 173, 253
Props, floral designer, 239
Punch and cake, food service, 192
Punch and coffee, beverage service, 187

Q

Queen Anne, collar/shoulder style, 132
Queen Elizabeth, collar/shoulder style, 132
Questions
　　for caterer, 199
　　for determining budget priorities, 19
　　for floral designers, 235
　　for florists, 234
　　for gown salon consultant, 136
　　for musicians, 271
　　for pastry chef, 208

for photographers, 262
for reception site manager, 120
for secular ceremonial site manager, 119
for videographers, 266
for wedding consultant, 67

R

Rain card, 167
"Realistic budget," budget spreadsheet,
　　14-17, 18-19, 22, 144
Realistic costs, determining, 18-19
Receiving line, 224, 225-226
Reception
　　belated, 109
　　budget priorities, 26
　　card, 164, 187
　　with dinner, 186, 188-190
　　enjoying your, 215-218
　　financial responsibility for, 30, 32
　　flow of events, 218-223
　　with lunch, 186, 189-190
　　selection of music for, 278-282
　　wedding day schedule file, 91-92
Receptions
　　tips for, 224-225
　　types of, 186-191, 193
Reception site manager
　　floral design, 228
　　questions for, 120
　　site selection, 112
Reception sites, 39-40, 118-119.
　　　See also Sites/venues
　　selecting, 183-186
　　resource binder, 43
　　wedding day binder, 44
Recessional
　　selection of music for, 278
　　wedding day schedule file, 90
Referral fees
　　floral designers, 230